BAKE AND FREEZE

Chocolate Desserts

BAKE AND FREEZE
Chocolate Desserts

ELINOR KLIVANS

BROADWAY BOOKS NEW YORK

BROADWAY

Broadway Books titles may be purchased for business or promotional use or for special sales. For information, please write to: Special Markets Department, Bantam Doubleday Dell Publishing Group, Inc., 1540 Broadway, New York, NY 10036.

BROADWAY BOOKS and its logo, a letter B bisected on the diagonal, are trademarks of Broadway Books, a division of Bantam Doubleday Dell Publishing Group, Inc.

Klivans, Elinor.
    Bake and freeze chocolate desserts / Elinor Klivans. — 1st ed.
        p.   cm.
    Includes bibliographical references and index.
    ISBN 0-7679-0013-8
    1. Desserts.   2. Make-ahead cookery.   3. Cookery (Chocolate)   I. Title.
    TX773.K573   1997
    641.8′6—dc21   96-46742
                                                                        CIP

Peanut Butter Cup Cheesecake, Frozen Milky Way Mousse with Bittersweet Chocolate Sauce, Raspberry-Filled Chocolate Mousse, Chocolate Ganache Cake, Garden Party Strawberry and White Chocolate Cake, Sorbet Bouquet Terrine with Grand Marnier Chocolate Sauce, Chunky Banana Frozen Yogurt Pie with Chocolate Sauce, Toffee-Oatmeal-Cookie Frozen Yogurt Sandwiches, Nutella Ice Cream Torte, Chocolate-Covered Raisin Brownies, Mocha Marble Mousse, Lemon and Pistachio Praline Meringue Cake, Choco-Colada Cheesecake, Cinnamon Chocolate Ribbon Cake, Chocolate Plus Chocolate Mousse Sandwiches, Striped Strawberry and White Chocolate Terrine with Dark Chocolate Sauce: BON APPÉTIT is a registered trademark of Advance Magazine Publishers Inc., published through its division, the Condé Nast Publications Inc. Copyright 1995 by the Condé Nast Publications Inc. Reprinted with permission.

FIRST EDITION

Designed by Bonni Leon-Berman
Photographs © 1997 by Melanie Acevedo

97 98 99 00 01 10 9 8 7 6 5 4 3 2 1

TO JEFFREY, LAURA, AND PETER

my best friends who give me my wings

CONTENTS

Contents

ACKNOWLEDGMENTS

Judith Weber, my agent, who always steers me on the right path.

Harriet Bell, my editor, who took such good care of every part of this book.

Susan Derecskey, my copyeditor, who makes the words fall easily into the right place.

My husband and partner, Jeff, who never gets tired of tasting my desserts and helping me figure out the best solutions.

My daughter, Laura, who proofread every recipe, sometimes far into the night, and wrote her encouraging words in the margins.

My son, Peter, who checked every headnote, then baked my desserts in his tiny oven and froze them in his even tinier freezer while living on the other side of the world.

My mother, Selma Wishnatzki, who brought me up in a house filled with homemade chocolate desserts; and my father, Lester, who taught me to appreciate good chocolate bars and chocolate ice cream.

Helen Hall, who is always there at the end of a telephone line to share my triumphs and help me fix my disasters; and Reg Hall, who conscientiously checks my food chemistry.

A special thank you to the caring doctors and their support teams who got me through a bad patch and cheered this book through every stage: Doctors Robert Laurence, Bonnie Mayer, Gordon Paine, Stephen Ross, Gail Venuto, and Jeffrey Young; and their special support people Valerie Baker, Diane Batley, Fay Carr, Sandi Carslick, Paula Collins, Ray Fredrick, Donna Green, Joyce Hills, Jane Littlefield, Becky Sawyer, Karen Veit, and Beth Young.

I want to thank the companies who supplied information and the businesspeople who offered their expertise: Bruce Stillings and The Chocolate Manufacturers and Confectionery Association, John Park of Park Appliance, the helpful experts answering the Saran Wrap consumer line, Amana Refrigeration Inc., Frigidaire Company, Sub-Zero Freezer Co., Inc., and everyone at the General Electric Company consumer answer phone.

A big thank you to my circle of supporters and encouragers: Melanie Barnard, Flo Braker, Sue Chase, Lisa Ekus, Lou Ekus, Carole and Woody Emanuel, Barbara Fairchild, Betty and Joe Fleming, Mutzi Frankel, Karen and Michael Good, Kat and Howard Grossman, Heather Harland, Carolyn and Ted Hoffman, Kristine Kidd, Mom and Dad Klivans, Susan Lasky, Rosie and Larry Levitan, Dale Mudge, Julia Schultz, Louise and Erv Shames, Elaine and Wil Wolfson, and the family and friends who shared their baking heritage and knowledge with me.

INTRODUCTION

After reading a chapter of recipes from this book, my daughter, Laura, commented that my entire childhood must have revolved around chocolate. I laughed, but then I thought about what she said. It was true. Whenever I recall my childhood summers spent in Brooklyn, all I remember are dark chocolate cakes from Ebingers' bakeries, Swiss chocolate penny candy from subway station vending machines, and the neighborhood candy store—newsstand that served chocolate egg creams and ice cream cones covered with chocolate sprinkles. At the end of each summer, when my family took the train from New York back to our home in Florida, I always carried a bag full of chocolate-covered marzipan bars and several tiers of cake boxes tied together that I would stash in the freezer and try to make last all winter. I thought all ten-year-olds and their families traveled this way. You would have thought there was no chocolate in the entire state of Florida. Not so; my mom kept our house filled with chocolate desserts. She baked a chocolate chiffon pie for every one of my birthdays, not to mention the weekly batches of chocolate chip cookies. My dad did his part keeping us supplied with large, half pound milk chocolate candy bars to munch on in front of our first television set. Every family occasion included at least one chocolate dessert.

Once I was married and had my own kitchen, I continued the tradition. There was always a new chocolate cake or another chocolate mousse variation to try. I tasted different brands and kinds of chocolate to find my favorites. I practiced various techniques to better understand the special requirements of baking with chocolate. I tried chocolate recipes from every cookbook and magazine I owned, and checked cookbooks out of the library to increase my repertoire of chocolate recipes. The more chocolate desserts I baked, the easier techniques such as melting chocolate smoothly and combining warm chocolate with cold ingredients became.

After mastering these techniques, I put my own spin on chocolate desserts. The more I baked, the more ideas came to me. Why not make butter cookies into chocolate butter cookies? How much chocolate could a brownie hold? How many chocolate chips could possibly stay afloat in a cake? Should there be chocolate chips between the layers of a mocha brownie?

I had always frozen desserts ahead for parties and kept an assortment of cookies in the freezer, but now I began to freeze frosted cakes, tarts, pies, even chocolate mousse desserts and cheesecakes. I discovered that most desserts freeze beautifully if handled carefully and chocolate desserts, in particular, lend themselves to do-ahead preparation and freezing.

After we moved to Maine, I worked as a pastry chef in a restaurant for twelve years and continued to develop my baking skills. Each week, I prepared a large number of desserts, tried many new recipes, and utilized the same techniques so often that they became habit. As the only dessert chef in the restaurant, I soon realized I could make the freezer my "assistant." I could bake in large quantities, make two or more desserts in almost the same time as one, bake at my own convenience, and take time off when I needed. I froze hundreds of desserts. Each year the list of chocolate desserts that tasted as good when they came out of the freezer as the day they were baked grew longer.

When my agent, Judith Weber, and I first discussed my writing a chocolate cookbook, I said it would be a dream job. I would get to write about my favorite food, have a good excuse to eat a lot of chocolate, and be able to try all of the new ideas that had been rolling around in my head. During the several years of testing recipes, I usually had two or three chocolate desserts sitting on the kitchen counter waiting to be tasted. Even the flops weren't all that bad. The freezer was filled with chocolate cakes, tarts, pies, and cheesecakes. I was an easy touch when it came to volunteering to bring desserts anywhere, anytime. When we had several chocolate dessert parties, all I had to do was go to my freezer and choose what I wanted for a chocolate buffet. See what I mean about a dream job?

I was lucky as a child, because I could watch my mom bake. She baked often, and I learned that baking was fun and no recipe was scary. When someone prepares cake after cake as part of her everyday cooking, baking seems natural. If you didn't grow up with a baker in your house, I hope you'll find my book to be your someone-to-watch, and use it to bake lots of chocolate desserts.

When I was a child, I thought all desserts were made from chocolate. *Bake and Freeze Chocolate Desserts* will make you wonder why that isn't so.

All About Chocolate

Bold explorers, powerful emperors, brilliant inventors, and pioneer industrialists—the story of chocolate reads like a Hollywood adventure movie script. It's a fitting plot for this extraordinary food that brings us so much pleasure.

If the Aztec civilization of Mexico had not been so sophisticated, who knows when we would have discovered the chocolate treasure concealed in the odd-looking cocoa pods found growing wild in tropical jungles. Christopher Columbus brought cocoa beans back to Spain in 1502, but no one knew what to do with the bitter beans, so they were looked upon as a curiosity and ignored as food. The Aztecs, however, had unlocked the secret of the cocoa pod. They dried, roasted, and ground the cocoa beans, and the coarse mixture was combined with spices and cornmeal. After whipping the mixture into a frothy drink, they served this "food of the gods" in golden goblets to their emperor Montezuma. In 1519, Montezuma welcomed the Spanish explorer Hernando Cortés to his Aztec empire with a lavish feast and the bitter, spicy drink called *xocolatl,* or bitter water. Cortés was the first European to taste this early chocolate drink. When he took the precious cocoa beans and the Aztec brewing techniques back to Spain, the Spaniards added sugar and sweet spices such as cinnamon to the chocolate drink and launched Europe's passion for chocolate.

For a long time the Spaniards kept their chocolate discovery a secret. It wasn't until 1606 that Antonio Carletti, a Florentine merchant, discovered Spain's chocolate treasure and brought it to Italy, and from there chocolate's popularity quickly spread to France, England, and the rest of Europe.

Until the Dutchman Conrad van Houton developed a press in 1828 to remove much of the cocoa fat from chocolate, chocolate was served only as a drink. Chocolate was a grainy paste that was dissolved in water, wine, or beer and was a far cry from the hot chocolate beverage we drink today. With his new process van Houton succeeded in extracting cocoa powder and cocoa butter. The extracted cocoa butter was added to chocolate to produce the first smooth, creamy chocolate. Van Houton also invented the dutching process, which treats cocoa powder with alkali to mellow its flavor and darken its color. In 1847, the English company of Fry and Sons, now a part of the Cadbury Company, introduced the first solid chocolate bars. The bars were an instant success and manufacturers competed to produce the most velvety textured chocolate.

James Baker and John Hannon rented a gristmill in Milton Lower Mills, Massachusetts, in 1765, and established the first chocolate factory in the United States. New England traders and fishermen often returned from their trips to the West Indies carrying cocoa beans, which they had accepted as payment for their cargoes. This assured a fairly steady supply of cocoa beans for Baker's factory.

Milton Hershey, another American chocolate pioneer, developed the beloved Hershey Bar. In 1904, he established a factory in rural Pennsylvania, now the town of Hershey, Pennsylvania, and the headquarters of the Hershey Foods Corporation. Hershey's goal was to provide a quality milk chocolate candy bar at an affordable price. He began with the Hershey Bar and soon followed it with Hershey's Kisses, two American classics available at every candy counter.

The Swiss came rather late to the chocolate industry, but after taking up the manufacture of chocolate in 1819, they became masters of the process and developed many of the techniques still used today for making fine chocolate taste better. Names of pioneer Swiss chocolate manufacturers sound like a hall of fame of chocolatiers. Daniel Peter and Henri Nestlé added milk in the form of condensed milk to chocolate and created milk chocolate. Rodolphe Lindt developed a machine for conching or kneading chocolate, which made a true melt-in-your-mouth chocolate. Many of these early Swiss companies still exist today.

Cocoa Trees: Harvesting Their Treasure

The Swedish botanist, Linnaeus, chose a fitting name for chocolate when he named the genus *Theobroma,* food of the gods. Cocoa trees require a hot tropical climate with abundant rainfall. The trees thrive within 10° latitude of the equator, but can grow up to 20° latitude from the equator. West Africa and Central and South America produce most of the world's cocoa crop, but some islands of the West Indies and Southeast Asia also produce cocoa beans.

The two classifications of cocoa beans found in the wild are Forastero and Criollo. Forastero is the more plentiful bean, has a neutral flavor, and is considered the base bean for chocolate. Criollo beans are the flavor beans and supply the subtle taste nuances found in different chocolates. A third classification, Trinitario, is a hybrid bean that is gaining popularity among planters and is considered a quality blending bean. Chocolate manufacturers blend the different beans to achieve their own unique chocolate flavor.

Cocoa pods look rather unusual, since they grow right out of the trunk or branch of the cocoa tree. When ripe, they look like small oval pumpkins hanging from the tree. At this stage there is no odor of chocolate. The pods contain the cocoa beans encased in a sticky white pulp. After the pods are harvested, they go through a fermentation and drying process to ready them for shipment to chocolate factories. The beans, along with the sticky pulp that adheres to them, are removed from the pod. The sweet, sticky mass is heaped in piles or boxes, covered with a layer of banana leaves, and left to ferment. After fermenting for several days, the beans are released from the sticky pulp. They turn from white to their characteristic brown color, and chemical changes take place that begin to develop the flavor and aroma of the bean. The almond-size beans are then dried to reduce their weight before shipping; after drying, the beans have a moisture content of only 5 to 7 percent. They are shipped to chocolate manufacturers around the world to be processed into chocolate.

The Voyage from Cocoa Beans to Chocolate Bars

At last the chocolate beans arrive at the chocolate factory to be processed into chocolate. As soon as the beans arrive, they are cleaned to remove dirt and any inferior beans are discarded. Next the beans are roasted, and the aroma of chocolate fills the air. Roasting cocoa beans is a carefully controlled process, with many chemical changes taking place that determine the final flavor of the chocolate. The shells are now easy to crack and the nibs, or kernels, are removed. The shells are sent off to be used for fertilizer, garden mulch, or animal food; the nibs are processed into chocolate.

Manufacturers blend nibs from many varieties of cocoa beans to produce a particular chocolate taste. These nibs are just over half cocoa butter and just under half dry cocoa mass (cocoa solids). When the nibs are finely ground between large rollers, chocolate liquor, made up of the cocoa butter and cocoa mass, is produced. The liquor is a dark brown paste that cools and hardens into unsweetened chocolate; it is the chocolate base from which all kinds of chocolate can be manufactured. When some of the cocoa butter is pressed out of chocolate liquor, cocoa powder is left. When additional cocoa butter and sugar are added to chocolate liquor, eating chocolate is produced. The amount of added sugar and cocoa butter controls the sweetness and texture of the chocolate, from semisweet to bittersweet. Milk chocolate contains powdered or condensed milk in addition to the cocoa butter and sugar, while white chocolate contains only cocoa butter, milk solids, sugar, and flavorings.

To achieve its smooth, melting texture the chocolate is further refined between giant steel rollers. Refining grinds the chocolate and sugar into tiny particles and produces a silken-textured chocolate. Fine chocolate then goes through a conching process in which it is kneaded and stirred. Conching, by further reducing the size of the particles and rounding off their edges, gives the chocolate an ultra-smooth texture. Finally the chocolate is molded into its many forms: large blocks for commercial use, small blocks for candy bars, or specialized bars and squares for baking all kinds of chocolate desserts.

Baking with Chocolate

Baking with chocolate is easy, but once you understand its idiosyncrasies, such as melting it properly and storing it to preserve its flavor, you will be comfortable with using all kinds of chocolate in your desserts.

Types of Chocolate

In the United States, the Food and Drug Administration sets the requirements for each type of chocolate and requires that each type contains certain amounts of chocolate liquor. Unsweetened chocolate is chocolate liquor and is required to contain 50 to 58 percent cocoa butter. Unsweetened cocoa powder is chocolate liquor with some of the cocoa butter pressed out, and it must contain from 10 to 22 percent cocoa butter.

European standards differ from ours and comparisons are difficult to make. The United States requirements for sweet chocolate are based on the amount of chocolate liquor as follows:

- Semisweet chocolate, 15 to 35 percent chocolate liquor
- Bittersweet chocolate, at least 35 percent chocolate liquor
- Milk chocolate, at least 10 percent chocolate liquor with added milk solids
- White chocolate contains cocoa butter, sugar, milk solids, and flavorings. The Food and Drug Administration is currently working on a standard of identity for white chocolate and has issued temporary permits that allow some white chocolate products containing cocoa butter to be labeled as white chocolate rather than as white confectionery coating.

European companies usually list the cocoa butter (cocoa fat) content of their chocolate, and you can use this content to judge if the type of chocolate is suitable for the dessert you plan to bake. For instance, if a European chocolate has 40 percent cocoa butter, it is at the low end of United States bittersweet chocolate requirements and could be used for a recipe that calls for semisweet or bittersweet chocolate.

Choosing the Best Chocolate for Your Baking

Follow two simple guidelines when you choose chocolate. Taste the chocolate and use a good quality brand. My reliable method for selecting good chocolate (except unsweetened) is to taste it—not a bad job in itself. Taste two or three different brands of chocolate in sequence, and keep to the same type of chocolate for each tasting—all semisweet or all milk. Place a small bit on your tongue, let it melt in your mouth, and decide which one you prefer. You're looking for a pleasant chocolate flavor with no sugary or chemical aftertaste. Chocolate that tastes good by itself will taste good in your desserts. Any money spent on buying a good quality chocolate is a good investment in a great dessert.

Unsweetened chocolate, lacking sugar, does not make for pleasant tasting, so I rely on quality national brands. When buying white chocolate, choose a brand that contains cocoa butter as one of the ingredients.

I taste unsweetened cocoa powder by putting a dab on my finger and tasting it. If the cocoa powder is fresh and of a good quality, it will have a true chocolate taste. Cocoa powder that has been stored too long will taste flat and have no chocolate taste at all.

My neighborhood supermarket sells many brands and types of chocolate. Add these to the varieties available at specialty shops and the choices become confusing. After tasting hundreds of chocolates and testing desserts made with various brands, I have my definite favorites. All of the chocolates I use are available in my small-town Maine area, and they should be easy to find in yours. A list of mail order sources for chocolate can be found on page 295 if your local stores do not stock a particular brand. In addition to the supermarket, all-purpose drug stores often carry a good selection of chocolate. The following chocolates are the ones I use most frequently, and were used to test the recipes in this book.

- Unsweetened chocolate: Baker's, Nestlé, and Guittard
- Semisweet chocolate: Baker's, Guittard, Dove Bar, Hershey's Special Dark, and Callebaut
- Bittersweet chocolate: Guittard, Perugina, Lindt, and Callebaut
- Semisweet chocolate chips: Nestlé and Guittard
- Milk chocolate: Dove Bar and Callebaut
- White chocolate: Callebaut, Baker's Premium, and Lindt
- White chocolate chips: Ghirardelli Classic White Chips and Guittard Vanilla Milk Chips
- Unsweetened cocoa powder: Droste or Hershey's European Style (both Dutch process, see page 1)

When chocolate is used for baking, it is usually melted and combined with other ingredients, or chopped or grated into small pieces and folded into a dessert. Chocolate chips, available in several sizes and many flavors, are processed to retain their shape when baked, making them a good choice when uniform pieces of chocolate are desired. Softened or melted chocolate can be formed into chocolate curls or chocolate bands to be wrapped around cakes. Cocoa powder is either used in its dry form, often sifted with flour, or it is dissolved in a warm liquid.

The flat side of a meat pounder is useful for breaking large chocolate pieces into small pieces suitable for melting. For chopping chocolate a large chef's type knife is ideal. Milk and white chocolates, containing butter fat, are softer at room temperature and chop more easily than the firmer unsweetened, bittersweet, and semisweet chocolates. Chocolate chips can sometimes offer a quick alternative to chopped chocolate.

Melting Chocolate

Say to yourself "slow and gentle" when melting chocolate, and there will be no problems. The goal is to melt the cocoa butter but not the sugar in the chocolate. Cocoa butter is one of the few fats that is solid at room temperature and will not soften, as butter will, if left at room temperature. At 92°F. cocoa butter and, in turn, chocolate begin to melt. When it reaches body temperature (98.6°F.), the chocolate melts; it should be completely melted by the time the temperature of the chocolate reaches 113°F. At higher temperatures the sugar in chocolate begins to melt and burn, which ruins the chocolate, turning it grainy and lumpy. This window between the melting temperature and the scorching temperature is small, making gentle heating important. Avoid subjecting the chocolate to sudden bursts of high heat from steam or boiling water which can shock and scorch the chocolate. Stirring the chocolate and removing it from the heat as soon as it melts will assure smoothly melted chocolate.

Following a few simple guidelines will ensure that your chocolate melts properly. Chop large pieces of chocolate into approximately ½-inch pieces for even melting. When melting chocolate with other ingredients such as butter, put everything in a heatproof container, a small saucepan, or the top of a double boiler. Place the container with the chocolate and other ingredients over very hot or barely simmering water and stir until the mixture is smooth. Keep the heat about low medium and decrease the heat if steam forms. Remove the chocolate mixture from over the hot water as soon as it is melted. White chocolate should be melted in a nonreactive container. Pyrex glass or stainless steel containers are nonreactive; aluminum is not.

When melting chocolate by itself, I melt it in the oven, which requires no stirring. I preheat the oven to 175°F., cut the chocolate into ½- to ¾-inch pieces, and put it in an ovenproof container. Remove the chocolate from the oven as soon as it is melted. You are not heating the chocolate to 175°F. since you remove the chocolate from the oven as soon as it melts, long before it reaches 175°F. The familiar one-ounce squares of baking chocolate do not need to be cut, but will take longer to melt than smaller pieces. This method of melting chocolate usually takes about ten minutes, depending on the amount of chocolate to be melted and the size of the pieces. I don't own a microwave oven, but they can be used to melt chocolate. Follow the manufacturer's directions for melting chocolate.

Storing Chocolate

If stored properly, unsweetened and dark chocolates can be stored up to one year. I wrap chocolate tightly in plastic wrap, then in aluminum foil, and store it in a cool dark place. Ideally the storage temperature should range between 60° and 70°F. Milk and white chocolates contain milk solids and are more perishable than dark chocolate. Since white chocolate contains no cocoa solids, only cocoa butter, it is even more perishable than milk chocolate. I store milk chocolate, tightly wrapped, in a cool dry place up to one month or freeze it for up to six months. If I am going to store white chocolate more than three weeks, I keep it in the freezer. To freeze chocolate, break any large blocks into one-pound pieces and wrap them tightly in plastic wrap and heavy aluminum foil. Defrost the wrapped chocolate in a cool dry place at room temperature to prevent moisture from forming as the chocolate defrosts. If moisture condenses on chocolate, some of the sugar can dissolve and produce what is called sugar bloom, that undesirable crusty, grainy surface on the outside of the chocolate. Sugar bloom is different from fat bloom, which occurs when chocolate is exposed to warm temperatures. Here the cocoa butter melts slightly, then firms again, and a whitish film forms on the outside of the chocolate. Aside from appearance, fat bloom doesn't harm the chocolate, but it does indicate the chocolate has been shipped or stored under less than ideal conditions. I often see fat bloom on chocolate chips in the summer, and if you shopped in my grocery store you might see me hunting through the display of chocolate chips looking for a perfect bag. During warm weather taste chocolate before using it, especially milk chocolate, to make sure that it still has a good, fresh chocolate taste.

Tightly sealed unsweetened cocoa powder that is stored at room temperature will keep in good condition for up to two years.

Understanding Terms and Techniques

Knowing why a technique is done in a specific way and what the desired results are guarantees successful results when baking and preparing desserts. If you understand that the reason for whipping egg whites is to beat air into them so they can lighten mixtures, and that well beaten egg whites will look smooth and shiny and form soft pointed peaks when a spoon is dipped into them, then beating egg whites to the correct stage becomes comfortably routine. Knowing that chocolate burns if subjected to too high a temperature makes you aware of the guidelines for melting chocolate. In the following sections are described the desired results of some familiar baking techniques so you can "see" and understand what their outcomes should be.

Creaming Fats and Sugar

Creaming fat and sugar together beats air into the fat-sugar mixture and forms a smooth mixture that combines easily with other ingredients in a recipe. The fluffy, light-colored mixture that results from thoroughly creaming ingredients together is full of air cells that help expand a cake or cookies during baking. Most of the sugar crystals do not dissolve during creaming, and their rough texture helps hold the air in the creamed mixture. To achieve a smooth, fluffy mixture, the butter, margarine, or vegetable shortening should be at room temperature, 65° to 75°F. Cakes, which achieve much of their light texture from thorough creaming, usually require a longer creaming time than cookies, which have a denser texture. Sugar and fat are creamed when making cookies to form a smooth mixture rather than to aerate the batter.

Beating Eggs

When eggs are beaten, they form a foam that is filled with air cells. These foams lighten baked and unbaked mixtures. If the mixture is baked, the heat expands the air cells and helps leaven and lighten it. Mixtures that are not baked, like mousses, acquire much of their light texture from the air cells in beaten eggs.

Whole eggs and egg yolks are beaten until their color lightens and they thicken. Sometimes, the eggs or yolks are warmed before they are beaten so that they whip faster and achieve greater volume. When eggs are beaten with sugar, the mixture becomes more dense and the foam more stable. Usually this sugar and egg mixture is beaten to what is called the ribbon stage, that is, if you lift up some of the thickened mixture and let it fall back in the bowl, a thin, flat ribbon pattern will form.

When egg whites are beaten, they form a delicate foam. Because acid helps to stabilize egg white foams, a small amount of cream of tartar, an acid, is usually beaten in. Egg whites will not whip properly if they come in contact with fat. As long as the egg whites do not contain any egg yolk, and the mixing bowl and utensils are clean and absolutely free of fat, there should be no problem.

Properly beaten egg whites are shiny and will form a soft point or peak if you dip a spoon in the egg white and lift it out. At the soft peak stage, the moving beaters form smooth curving lines in the egg whites. Egg whites at the soft peak stage look creamy; they combine smoothly and easily with other mixtures. It is preferable to underbeat egg whites slightly than to overbeat them. Overbeaten egg whites look lumpy and dull and form big, white clumps if you try to fold them into another mixture.

I beat egg whites with a standing electric mixer on low speed just until the cream of tartar is dissolved, then increase the speed to medium and beat the egg whites until the soft peaks form. I find it's easier to check the egg whites and control the results on medium rather than high speed.

Adding sugar to beaten egg whites stabilizes the foam just as it stabilizes an egg yolk foam, and the mixture can sit for a while before being used. After sugar is added to egg whites, the mixture thickens and can even be baked into a crisp meringue. When adding sugar, begin adding it just as the egg whites reach the soft peak stage. Add it slowly so the egg whites have time to absorb it. Adding one tablespoon of sugar every thirty seconds is a good interval. Egg whites beaten with sugar form firm peaks if you dip a spoon in the egg whites and lift it out.

Adding a hot sugar syrup to the beaten egg whites stabilizes the egg whites even more than granulated sugar. The hot sugar syrup heats the egg whites, causing some of the protein in the egg whites to coagulate, so that the air cells that were beaten into the egg whites are less likely to burst. The resulting mixture is called an Italian meringue (see page 10).

Cooking Sugar

Hot sugar syrups are used for some of the desserts in this book. Italian meringue, which is the base for several frostings and some of the mousse recipes in this book, requires a hot sugar syrup cooked to a specific temperature. Cooking sugar syrups properly so that crystals do not form requires some patience and an understanding of a few standard procedures. Let the sugar dissolve in the water over low heat before allowing the mixture to boil. Before the mixture boils it can be stirred gently to help the sugar dissolve, but after the mixture boils it should not be stirred. The mixture can be covered until it boils, but when boiling begins the mixture should be uncovered. As soon as the sugar dissolves, clip a candy thermometer to the inside of the pan so that you will know when the sugar reaches the correct temperature. The boiling mixture sometimes throws some sugar crystals on to the side of the pan; these should be wiped off with a brush dipped in water. Corn syrup interferes with and helps prevent this crystallization, so I usually cook sugar syrups with a small amount of corn syrup.

I use caramelized sugar for nut pralines, caramel syrups, caramel fillings, and caramel sauces. Caramelizing sugar is simply a process of melting the sugar and heating it to an amber (dark golden brown) color. A good thing about cooking caramel is that the sugar is heated to such a high temperature, over 310°F., that the sugar actually breaks down and crystals will not form. It doesn't matter if you stir the sugar at any stage or dissolve it after it boils, the final caramelized sugar will still be smooth. Just remember to melt and caramelize all of the sugar so there are no hard lumps of sugar and to be careful that the hot caramel does not splash on you. Use a wooden spoon to stir the mixture. Melt and caramelize the sugar slowly and evenly so that spots of sugar do not blacken and burn. The only time I ruin caramel is when I burn it by trying to do other things at the same time. When the caramel becomes an amber color or if wisps of smoke form, remove it from the heat immediately.

Italian Meringue

Italian meringue is prepared by beating a hot sugar syrup into egg whites that have been whipped to soft peaks. It is a fluffy, stable mixture often used as the base for buttercream frostings and mousse desserts. After the sugar syrup is cooked to the soft ball stage of 240°F., it is poured slowly over the beaten egg whites and whipped until the mixture cools to about room temperature. Sugar syrup at the soft ball stage combines smoothly with the egg whites, whereas a sugar syrup cooked to a higher temperature (hard ball stage) would form small hard pieces if added to the egg whites. I've tried to get away with this when my sugar syrup had become too hot but it doesn't work—you can't fool egg whites!

Italian meringue is easy to work with, but it requires careful attention while the sugar syrup boils and when the hot syrup is beaten into the egg whites. Cook the sugar syrup carefully so that the sugar does not crystallize; adding some corn syrup also inhibits crystallization. All bowls, pots, and utensils used for the meringue should be clean and greasefree. The beating time varies with the number of egg whites used and the kitchen temperature. Smaller quantities of egg whites and sugar syrup in a cool kitchen require a shorter beating time than larger quantities beaten in a warm kitchen.

To prepare an Italian meringue, beat egg whites to the soft peak stage. Beat a small amount of sugar into the egg whites to stabilize them if they must wait for the sugar syrup to reach the proper temperature. When the sugar for the syrup dissolves, clip a candy thermometer to the inside of the pan. As soon as the hot sugar syrup reaches 240°F. and with the mixer on low speed, slowly pour the hot syrup in a thin stream onto the softly beaten egg whites. The two mixtures seldom reach these stages at the same time. If the syrup reaches 240°F. before the egg whites reach the soft peak stage, remove the syrup from the heat for a few seconds and finish beating the egg whites. If the egg whites are ready first, they can hold for a few minutes. Continue beating the meringue at medium-low speed for about 5 minutes. The outside of the bowl will be lukewarm and the meringue will be stiff and have a temperature of 72° to 78°F. if measured with a food thermometer.

Buttercream prepared with an Italian meringue has a light silky texture. When the butter is added, it must be very soft, about the same temperature as the beaten meringue. If checked with a food thermometer, both the beaten meringue and the softened butter should be about 72° to 78°F. If the butter is too cold, it will form small lumps in the buttercream. If this happens, whisk the bowl of buttercream over a pan of hot water until the butter lumps disappear and the buttercream becomes smooth, then continue with the recipe.

Whipping Cream

The bowl, beaters, and whipping cream should be cold. Add any flavorings such as powdered sugar, vanilla extract, or coffee to the cream in the mixing bowl, then begin beating the cream. Powdered sugar, which contains cornstarch, stabilizes the cream slightly so that it can be held for about two hours before it is served. If the cream is beaten with a standing mixer, beat the cream at medium speed, but if it is beaten with a handheld mixer, beat at high speed. Slowly move a handheld mixer around the mixing bowl as you beat the cream so that it all beats evenly.

Beat the cream either to the soft peak stage or the firm peak stage. At the soft peak stage, the movement of the beaters will form smooth lines in the cream, and if you dip a spoon in the cream and lift it out, the cream will form a point that falls over at its tip. The texture of the whipped cream is like a thick, fluffy sauce. At the firm peak stage, the movement of the beaters will form a teardrop shape in the cream, and if you dip a spoon in the cream and lift it out, the cream will form a point that stands straight up and remains that way. To check the stage of the whipped cream, I watch the pattern that the movement of the beaters makes in the cream. When you beat cream, watch the patterns form, and it will soon be easy to judge the stages. If the whipped cream is not used immediately, cover and refrigerate it up to two hours, then give the whipped cream a quick stir with a whisk just before serving.

Folding

When a light mixture is combined with a heavy mixture, the two are usually folded together gently so as not to push the air out of the lighter mixture and break up the air cells. I whisk a little of the lighter mixture into the heavier one to lighten the heavier mixture, then I use a large rubber spatula to fold in the rest. Use the spatula to dig down to the bottom of the mixture and bring the two mixtures up and over each other. Use a large bowl and turn the bowl as you fold so that the mixtures blend quickly.

Peeling, Toasting, Chopping, and Grinding Nuts

Toasting nuts improves their flavor. Prove this to yourself by toasting a few nuts, then tasting a toasted nut and an untoasted one. When almonds, pine nuts, and hazelnuts are toasted, the flavor of the nut actually changes. To toast nuts, spread them out in a single layer on a baking sheet and bake them in an oven preheated to 325° F. Walnuts and pecans should bake about eight to ten minutes; pine nuts about eight minutes until golden; blanched, sliced, or slivered almonds about twelve minutes until golden; and blanched whole almonds and hazelnuts about fifteen minutes until golden. Just before the nuts are ready, you should smell a pleasant aroma of toasting nuts. Pistachio and macadamia nuts are normally sold roasted.

Since hazelnuts must have their skins removed before they are used for baking, try to buy blanched (peeled) hazelnuts. If the hazelnuts need to be blanched, fill a saucepan with enough water to cover the hazelnuts and bring the water to a boil. Add the hazelnuts and boil for five minutes. Drain the hazelnuts, immerse them in cold water for several minutes to cool, drain again, and peel the nuts with a small sharp knife. The skin will come off easily, and the nuts will dry out as they toast. If the hazelnuts are not toasted immediately, dry them with a clean dish towel and refrigerate or freeze them.

I chop nuts by hand with a large sharp knife which gives me control over the size of the chopped nut. Finely chopped nuts should be $1/8$ inch in size and coarsely chopped nuts between $1/4$ inch and $3/8$ inch in size. When I need ground nuts, I grind them in a food processor fitted with the steel blade. Processing the nuts with some of the sugar or flour from the recipe allows the nuts to become finely ground without forming a paste.

Preparing Baking Pans

When pans need to be greased, I use the same shortening to grease the pan that I use in the recipe. I grease pie crust pans with vegetable shortening, cake pans with butter, and the pan for an oil-based cake like Chocolate-glazed Rum Chocolate Chip Cake (page 212) with oil. Any flavor that might be added to the dessert from the fat used to grease the pan will match the taste of the fat used in the dessert. Butter burns at a lower temperature than vegetable shortening or oil, but I have never had any problem.

Baking Times

Baking times given for desserts are only approximate. Ovens vary in their performance and temperature accuracy, batters may be at different temperatures when they go into the oven, or baking pan measurements and the weight of the pan may be slightly different than the one called for in a recipe. Where you place the baking pan—on the front or rear of the oven shelf, in the upper or lower part of the oven—will also affect the baking time. Take the time to check that a dessert is properly baked before removing it from the oven.

To avoid overbaking a cake, begin checking it when about three quarters of the stated baking time has passed. To test a cake, gently press your fingers on the middle of the cake. It should feel firm and slightly springy. If it does, insert a toothpick into the center. When the toothpick comes out clean, the cake is done. Remember an overbaked cake will also yield a clean toothpick, so don't wait too long to test a cake. Moist dense cakes may have a few crumbs clinging to the toothpick when it is removed. If the cake has a crisp crumb topping, just check it with a toothpick.

Cookies are usually done when they reach a certain color, golden or light brown, or when their edges turn light brown. A moist pie is baked if you give it a gentle shake and the center remains firm. Insert a toothpick into a fruit pie or crisp to see if the fruit is cooked. Apples, pears, and other chunky fruits will be soft. When you think a cheesecake is ready, give it a gentle shake and check that the top looks firm. And don't forget your nose—if you smell something burning, check it fast.

Kitchen Temperatures

Kitchen temperatures affect recipes, so keep this in mind when you bake. On a hot summer day, when the temperature in my kitchen can climb above 80°F., preparing a pie crust, filling ice cream sandwiches, or handling chocolate decorations can be a challenge. When making pie crust or sweet pastry for tarts on a hot day, chill the shortening and the flour mixture in the freezer for thirty minutes and take care not to overwork the dough. On a warm day the chocolate for making chocolate curls may need little or no softening and ingredients will come to room temperature quickly. A cold winter morning, when my kitchen can be as cool as 60°F., is ideal for making pie crust and glazes will thicken quickly, but butter and cream cheese will take longer to soften, and yeast doughs longer to rise.

Equipment

When choosing equipment for my kitchen, I think of myself as a kitchen carpenter. Just as a carpenter needs the right tools that will hold up under heavy use for his building, tools for baking—and building desserts—are just as important. My list is small and basic, and I steer away from gadgets, but I spend a few extra dollars to buy the best quality equipment I can find. I save money in the end because it seldom needs replacing. My KitchenAid mixer and Cuisinart food processor are the two major pieces of equipment that I wouldn't want to do without, and they sit out on my kitchen counter so they're always ready to go to work. Often there is more than one good choice when it comes to picking a baking pan or other piece of equipment. What follows is my personal view on what is necessary and what is nice to own.

Baking Pans

The baking pan measurements given are the inside measurements of the pan. Take care to use the size baking pan called for in a recipe. Using a different size baking pan can cause overbaked or underbaked desserts, not to mention the mess of batter overflowing out of a too-small baking pan.

BAKING SHEETS Heavy aluminum is a good choice for baking sheets since it conducts heat evenly and will not warp or bend after repeated use. Precise measurements are not crucial, but baking sheets should not be so large that they touch the oven walls. This would prevent proper air circulation, and the oven would not heat evenly. Allow at least an inch of air space between the sides of the baking sheet and the oven walls. I recently tested some cookies using a nonstick heavy aluminum Calphalon baking sheet and was pleased with the results. I use the general term, baking sheet, for cookie sheets and jelly-roll pans.

Cookie sheets usually have open sides so that cookies slide easily off the pan. These sheets have a rim at one or both ends to grasp when removing the hot cookie sheets from the oven. Standard measurements suitable for home ovens range from about 15×12 inches to about 17×14 inches.

Jelly-roll pans are baking sheets with a one-inch rim around all sides; they are used for baking cookies, thin sheet cakes, cake for cake rolls, and bars. Their measurements range from about $15\frac{1}{2} \times 10\frac{1}{2}$ inches to about 17×12 inches.

CAKE PANS When I got married, someone gave me several lightweight, round cake pans with 1¼-inch high sides. I felt obliged to use them, and for years I baked cakes with humped, overbrowned tops. Finally, after a batter overflowed out of the pan and all over my oven, I went out and purchased several heavy aluminum 9- and 10-inch diameter layer pans with 2-inch-high sides. What a difference the correct pan made in my cakes. I wish I had done it sooner.

Rectangular and square pans should be heavyweight aluminum, preferably with a nonstick coating and with 2-inch-high sides.

Whenever springform pans are appropriate for a dessert, I use them. Cheesecakes, charlottes, and ice cream pies are easily removed from the springform and hold their shape perfectly. I prefer no-rust Hillside brand aluminum or Kaiser La Forme heavy-gauge steel and nonstick-coated springform pans with 3-inch-high sides and a sturdy clip mechanism. The sides of a springform should be at least 2¾ inches high. La Cuisine (see page 295) sells spare springform bottoms.

I use an aluminum nonstick tube pan that is 10 × 4½ inches with a 16-cup capacity and a permanently fixed bottom, but a smaller tube pan with as little as a 14-cup capacity will work fine for the recipes in this book. Even if a pan has a nonstick coating, I line the bottom with parchment or wax paper. The nonstick coating helps release the cake sides smoothly from the pan, but the paper liner ensures that even a sticky cake will release smoothly from the bottom of the pan.

Bundt pans have a ridged bottom so they can't be lined with paper, and it is critical to use a heavyweight pan. For years I searched for a bundt pan from which cakes would remove easily. I recently purchased a La Forme heavy-gauge steel bundt pan with a nonstick surface manufactured by the Kaiser company and every bundt cake I have baked in it turned out of the pan perfectly. It has a 9-inch diameter and a 12-cup capacity.

I used to struggle with steamed puddings when I baked them in ovenproof bowls. They were slippery to lift out of the kettle and gave me steam burns when I tried to untie the seal and check the pudding. A steamed pudding mold with a snap-on lid is far better. Mine is an inexpensive aluminum mold with a 2-quart capacity.

LOAF PANS Loaf pans come in two standard shapes with numerous small measurement differences. The standard loaf pan has about a 7-cup capacity and measures about 9 × 5 × 3 inches, and the long narrow loaf pan, sometimes called a terrine pan or terrine mold, has a capacity of 7 to 8 cups and ranges in size from 12 × 4 × 2¾ inches to the slightly larger 12¾ × 4¼ × 2½ inches. I prefer the long, narrow loaf pan for my desserts. I use metal loaf pans with sharp corners to produce cakes and frozen terrines with attractive even edges.

PIE AND TART PANS I use 10-inch diameter heavy aluminum pie pans for baking pies. These pans allow for a liberal amount of filling, and the pies are large enough to be cut into eight generous slices. I have four pie pans so I can store several pans in the freezer filled with unbaked pie crusts. Eleven-inch diameter black steel tart pans with a removable bottom are my choice for baking tarts. Since tarts usually have a thinner layer of filling and bake for a shorter time than pies, black steel pans retain the heat efficiently and help the crust brown even more quickly than aluminum. Black steel pans must be thoroughly dried after washing or they will rust.

PAN SIZES

Here is a quick reference list of the baking pans used in this book:

PAN	SIZES
Cookie sheet	15×12 to 17×14 inches
Jelly-roll pan with 1-inch rim	$15^{1}/_{2} \times 10^{1}/_{2}$ to 17×12 inches
Bundt pan	9-inch diameter
Long, narrow loaf pan	$12 \times 4 \times 2^{3}/_{4}$, $12^{3}/_{4} \times 4^{1}/_{4} \times 2^{1}/_{2}$ inches, or $10 \times 4 \times 2^{3}/_{4}$ inches (7- to 8-cup capacity)
Loaf pan	$9 \times 5 \times 3$ inches or $8^{1}/_{2} \times 4^{1}/_{2} \times 2$ inches ($6^{1}/_{2}$- to 8-cup capacity)
Round cake pan	9×2 and 10×2 inches
Pie pan	10-inch diameter
Steamed pudding mold	2-quart capacity
Tart pan	11-inch diameter
Rectangular pan	$13 \times 9 \times 2$, $15 \times 10 \times 2$, and $11 \times 7 \times 1^{3}/_{4}$ inches
Square pan	$8 \times 8 \times 2$ inches
Springform pan	8×3, 9×3, and 10×3 inches
Tube pan	$8 \times 2^{3}/_{4}$ inches, $9^{1}/_{2} \times 4^{1}/_{2}$ or up to $10 \times 4^{1}/_{2}$ inches

Electric Mixers

My heavy-duty KitchenAid mixer with its 5-quart bowl performs every mixing job I require. It's my best friend in the kitchen. This mixer comes with a flat beater for beating, a wire whip for whipping, and a dough hook for kneading yeast dough. Other standing countertop mixers will work fine in any of my recipes. Handheld mixers are especially good for whipping small amounts and can perform most beating jobs. With less powerful electric mixers, plan on slightly longer beating times and on increasing the mixing speed a notch. Most double recipes of batters are too large to mix with handheld mixers; they should be mixed in separate batches.

Food Processors

It makes sense to buy a machine with a large capacity and a powerful motor, which can handle both small and large jobs.

Freezers

It is not all that long ago that I bought my first upright freezer. For many years I used a side-by-side refrigerator/freezer combination, but there is no question that a freestanding freezer, which is opened infrequently and has its own temperature control, maintains a more constant, colder temperature than a refrigerator/freezer combination and is preferable for storing frozen foods. Lacking space for a full freezer, a compact under-the-counter freezer is often a good solution. If freezer space is limited, try setting aside one small shelf or section of the freezer for desserts. You'll be amazed at how many desserts can be frozen in a small amount of space.

Ovens

Oven temperatures vary about ten degrees within the oven, with the upper third and rear of the oven usually being the warmest. If your oven thermometer and oven thermostat register more than a ten-degree difference, or if your baked goods suddenly begin burning or underbaking during their normal baking period, the oven should be recalibrated. Even when calibrated to the correct temperature, different ovens bake desserts faster or slower, so baking times are approximate and visual tests for doneness should be applied.

When baking in a standard oven, if desserts are not browning evenly, reverse desserts front to back and from the lower rack to the upper rack during the baking to ensure even browning. Be careful to avoid overloading the oven. Air has to circulate properly.

My oven bakes with either convection or standard heat. Since most household ovens are standard ovens, I tested all of these recipes using my oven as a standard oven. With the exception of cheesecakes, which I prefer to bake in a standard oven, I recommend baking with convection heat if you have it. Convection ovens have a fan that circulates the air in the oven to produce even heat throughout the oven. Desserts seldom need to be rearranged in the oven for even browning. For convection baking, follow the baking instructions for a recipe but lower the oven temperature by 50°F., that is, if a cake normally bakes at 350°F., bake it at 300°F. Some manufacturers claim baking times will be shortened, but I find baking times to be the same as standard oven baking.

Saucepans and Double Boilers

I use stainless steel saucepans, which will not react with acidic foods. The saucepans have either a copper- or aluminum-clad bottom to help the pans conduct heat evenly. The small saucepan holds one quart, the medium saucepan holds two quarts, and two large saucepans hold three and four quarts.

My two-quart saucepan has an insert to convert it into a double boiler. If you don't have a double boiler, heat a small amount of water in a 4-quart saucepan and place a 2-quart nonreactive saucepan filled with whatever needs to be melted over the 4-quart saucepan. The rim of the smaller saucepan must rest on the rim of the larger saucepan. A copper- or aluminum-clad bottom on the saucepan diffuses the heat evenly and reduces the chance of overheating the ingredients. It is easy to see the water in the saucepan below and prevent it from boiling or producing steam, which could burn a delicate ingredient like chocolate.

Scales

A scale with a removable bin on the top rather than a flat top is practical for kitchen use. The bin holds whatever food must be weighed without the food rolling off the top of the scale.

Thermometers

I use four kinds of thermometers—oven, freezer, food, and candy. I use a mercury oven thermometer to check my oven accuracy about once a week. I leave a freezer thermometer in my freezer and adjust the freezer control to maintain a freezer temperature between 0° and 8°F. To measure temperatures of custards or melted chocolate, I use an instant-read food thermometer that measures from 0° to 220°F. Since this thermometer does not have to be clipped to the side of the pan, there is no worry about knocking the thermometer off the pan as you stir. Instant-read food thermometers are also useful for checking the temperature of ingredients such as soft butter or hot milk. These thermometers actually register a temperature within ten to fifteen seconds which is fast but not instantaneous, so wear an oven mitt on the hand holding the thermometer for protection from heat or steam. Finally, I use a mercury candy thermometer to measure the high temperatures needed for testing sugar syrups. It has a stainless steel back, clips to the side of the pan, is easy to read, and gives a slightly more accurate reading than an instant-read thermometer. It will register a temperature within twenty to thirty seconds.

This candy thermometer can also double as an oven thermometer for temperatures up to 400°F. Do not leave it in the oven for a long period of time or in an oven set for a higher temperature than the thermometer is set to measure since the glass tube can break if the thermometer overheats. I use Taylor thermometers; they are high quality and readily available.

Utensils

The following utensils and small tools are the ones I find useful to have on hand.

CARDBOARD CAKE CIRCLES Cookshops sell these corrugated paper circles in several sizes. They provide a good flat surface for holding a cake and are useful for freezing a cake so that a favorite platter doesn't have to sit in the freezer for several months. If a dessert has a high butter content that might be absorbed by the cake circle, use a coated, moisture resistant cardboard cake circle or wrap a cardboard circle with aluminum foil. Moisture resistant and other cardboard cake circles can be ordered from Sweet Celebrations division of Maid of Scandinavia (see page 295).

COOLING RACKS I cool many desserts in their pans, but for the few that require cooling racks, like the sticky Chocolate Cinnamon Twists (page 259), which must be removed from their pan while still warm, or crisp cookies, I use a rectangular cooling rack with thin cross-woven wires, which support a cake without digging into it. Unlike round racks, rectangular racks hold almost any size cake or a large number of cookies. When I cool a cake in its pan, I still place it on a cooling rack so that air circulates around the pan and the cake cools evenly.

GRATERS AND PEELERS I use a four-sided box grater for grating citrus zest and chocolate. This type of grater rests securely on the counter. The tiny teardrop holes are the best hole for grating zest.
   A stainless steel vegetable peeler with a 2½-inch vertical blade that is an extension of the handle is a good tool for grating chocolate curls and removing large strips of rind from citrus fruit.

KNIVES I use a small sharp paring knife with a 4½-inch blade to loosen desserts from their pans. A large chef's knife with an 8-inch blade is good for cutting large cakes and firm desserts like ice cream pies. A serrated bread knife with an 8-inch blade splits cake layers evenly.

MEASURING SPOONS AND CUPS Have two sets of measuring spoons available, one for dry ingredients and one for wet ingredients. For accurate measuring, use dry measuring cups to measure dry ingredients and liquid measuring cups to measure liquid ingredients. This may sound obvious, but it does make a difference. Measure dry ingredients by filling the cup and leveling the top with a thin metal spatula. For liquids, use cups with clear markings and place the measuring cup on a flat surface when measuring. Liquid measuring cups in 1-, 2-, and 4-cup sizes make a good assortment to have on hand. Dry measuring cups are sold in sets of four gradations.

MIXING BOWLS Small mixing bowls should have a 2- to 3-cup capacity; medium, 6-cup capacity; and large, 2- to 5-quart capacity. When choosing a mixing bowl, it is preferable to use one that is too large rather than one that is too small. Pyrex bowls are heatproof and chip resistant, and I have been using the same set for over twenty years. Stainless steel bowls are easy to clean, will not react with ingredients, and are virtually unbreakable. I do not recommend plastic mixing bowls because they can absorb odors and fat.

MIXING SPOONS Have at least one wooden spoon to use when cooking sugar to a high temperature. Since wood is a poor conductor of heat, a wooden spoon will not draw heat from a mixture, nor will the mixture melt the spoon. For general mixing, use heatproof plastic mixing spoons, which do not absorb odors as wooden spoons might.

PAPER LINERS Parchment paper, which usually comes in rolls, is the most practical liner for baking pans and for lining baking sheets for meringues. Wax paper can be used to line cake pans since the paper is covered by the cake batter, but it is not suitable for lining cookie sheets since it will smoke and burn where it is not covered by the cookies. Heavy aluminum foil makes a good liner for cookie sheets and prevents cookie bottoms from burning.

PASTRY BAGS AND PASTRY TIPS I use Ateco cloth pastry bags with a plastic-coated lining that makes them easy to clean. Dry the pastry bags on a sunny windowsill to prevent them from developing a musty odor. A sixteen-inch pastry bag is a good all-purpose size. Ateco also makes good quality pastry tips that do not rust easily. A large star tip like the Ateco #5 and round tips with $^3/_8$- and $^1/_2$-inch openings are the pastry tips I use most often. I prefer 2-inch-long pastry tips to the 1-inch-long size.

PASTRY BRUSH Buy a good quality pastry brush that will not drop its bristles into your desserts. A 1-inch wide brush with 2-inch long bristles is a useful size.

ROLLING PINS AND ROLLING SURFACES I prefer a fixed rolling pin, without ball bearings but with handles. For a rolling surface, I use a freestanding white ceramic Corning Counter Saver with hard rubber feet. The surface remains cool; it measures a substantial 18 × 16 inches; it is lightweight; and it can be washed in the kitchen sink. When I'm not using it for rolling, it doubles as an extra cutting surface.

SPATULAS Use rubber spatulas with wooden handles to scrape bowls clean and fold mixtures together. I have a long narrow metal spatula with a 9 × 1-inch blade for frosting cakes, smoothing glazes, and smoothing the top of batters before they are baked. An offset spatula, which looks like a pancake turner with a long blade, is useful for sliding desserts onto a platter or cookies off a baking sheet. My offset spatula has a 9-inch-long blade and is 2½ inches wide. Its long length allows me to slide it under the entire bottom of many desserts, such as an ice cream pie, to loosen them from their pan. I use a rigid pastry scraper to loosen dough from a rolling surface and scraping chocolate tubes. The stainless steel blade is 5 × 3½ inches and does not have sharp edges.

STRAINERS AND SIFTERS I use a fine mesh strainer to strain food and sift dry ingredients. Mine has a 7-inch top diameter and will hold about four cups of dry ingredients. It is easy to clean and does a fine job of straining lumps from dry ingredients, removing overcooked bits from custards, and removing small seeds from fruit. To remove every small seed from a fruit, I clean the strainer and strain the fruit a second time. You can use the strainer to sift dry ingredients on to a large piece of wax paper and save cleaning an additional bowl. I have a flour sifter with a rotary handle, but if I use it to sift cocoa, it must be cleaned, which is difficult.

TURNTABLES When I frost or decorate a cake, I place the cake on the kind of plastic turntable normally used for storing spices. It's much less expensive than a professional cake-decorating turntable.

WHISKS Stainless steel sauce whisks are invaluable for whisking out a few lumps, and for adding melted chocolate to cold cream or smoothing out thick mixtures like chilled sauces. Since I prefer to beat egg whites and whipped cream with an electric mixer, I seldom use a balloon whisk, which has a round bottom and more wires than a sauce whisk.

Ingredients

Since I prefer to spend my time baking rather than searching for ingredients, I give all my recipes the "Easy to Find Ingredient Test." With the exception of a few items, these recipes use ingredients that I can buy in my small town. I thought that if I can buy something in Camden, Maine (population 5,000), it should be easy to find almost anywhere, although I discovered this does not always hold true. I once did a demonstration in New York City—where I assumed you could buy just about anything—and I wasn't able to get peppermint ice cream because it wasn't the holiday season. I was secretly pleased that something was easier to buy in Camden than New York City, but I learned not to take availability for granted. Peeled hazelnuts and shelled pistachios are about the only items that I find it necessary to mail order, but if I felt like peeling hazelnuts or shelling pistachios, I could buy those nuts in Camden too. There is a list of mail order sources at the end of the book in case you find it necessary to order an ingredient or some equipment.

Butter, Shortening, and Oils

Unsalted butter is used in all of the recipes requiring butter, and corn oil margarine with salt in any recipe that calls for margarine; I store both in my freezer to keep them fresh. Crisco vegetable shortening is used in pie crusts and corn or canola oil in recipes requiring oil. Room temperature butter or margarine should measure between 65° and 75°F.; check it with a food thermometer to see exactly how it looks and feels at this temperature.

Chocolate

Chocolate is discussed on pages 4–7.

Citrus and Citrus Zest

Use fresh citrus juice for all of the recipes. Citrus zest is the rind of the fruit without any of the bitter white pith. Before grating zest from citrus fruit, wash the fruit with hot water and dry it.

Cream and Milk

Heavy whipping cream contains from 36 to 40 percent butterfat. Cartons may be labeled heavy whipping cream, whipping cream, or heavy cream. I use the term heavy whipping cream. I use heavy whipping cream for whipped cream toppings and fillings. For other recipes light whipping cream, called simply whipping cream, which has slightly less fat (30 to 36 percent), works fine.

I have noted on the recipes if a particular type of milk is required or if any fat content milk is suitable.

Eggs

Large eggs are used in the recipes in this book. I use room temperature eggs in cheesecakes and cold eggs in most other desserts. Cold eggs are easier to separate, and bacteria are less likely to multiply in an egg that is kept cold. I haven't noticed a significant difference between whipping egg whites cold or at room temperature.

If you have egg whites left over from a recipe, freeze them for up to three months. Put them in a clean, greasefree plastic freezer container leaving at least an inch of air space, press plastic wrap onto the surface of the egg whites, and cover tightly. Label the container with the date and the number of egg whites in the container. I defrost the covered egg whites overnight in the refrigerator. I do not freeze or store leftover egg yolks. Either use them immediately or discard them. Fortunately, eggs are one of the less expensive baking ingredients.

Although salmonella have been found in only a small percentage of the millions of eggs sold in the United States, I still take precautions with eggs. Salmonella is killed at 160°F. I cook all custards, including those for ice cream, at least to this temperature, and I use an instant-read food thermometer to check. Before adding egg yolks to uncooked mousse desserts, I heat the yolks with other ingredients from the recipe just to 160°F. Egg whites, which contain little protein, provide an unfriendly environment for salmonella, and I use cold, raw egg whites in some of my recipes. There is much debate about this issue; the final decision will have to be up to you whether or not to prepare a specific dessert.

Flavorings and Spices

Always use pure vanilla extract. It would be better to omit vanilla than to use an artificial substitute. I tested the recipes with McCormick pure vanilla extract, which is readily available. When flavoring desserts with almond extract, be stingy. Adding too much almond extract will give the dessert a chemical taste. Recently I have found pure almond extract in my supermarket. Choose the pure almond extract rather than imitation almond extract if you have a choice.

When flavoring desserts with liqueurs, use a good quality one and add it sparingly. Too much liqueur can cause a bitter taste. Grand Marnier, Crème de Cacao, brandy, and amaretto are flavors I use often. I use decaffeinated, freeze-dried instant coffee granules to add coffee flavoring to desserts. To dissolve the coffee, mix equal parts of hot liquid and instant coffee.

Use fresh spices and store them tightly covered. Storage times and conditions for different spices vary; a simple way to check to see if a spice is fresh is to taste it. If the spice is stale, it will add little or no taste to a dessert. Recently, I began substituting mace for nutmeg in recipes. Mace is the outer covering of the nutmeg seed and is usually sold ground. It has a subtle and sweet flavor that I prefer to nutmeg. Although I used supermarket cinnamon to test the recipes, extra fancy China Tunghing cinnamon, an exceptionally strong sweet cinnamon, and extra fancy Vietnamese cassia cinnamon, a strong spicy cinnamon, are worth trying. Both are available from Penzey's Spice House Ltd. (see page 295).

Flour

I tested the recipes using either unbleached all-purpose flour or cake flour. Cake flour contains less gluten than all-purpose flour; it is usually packaged in two-pound boxes. Supermarkets stock cake flour in the same section as all-purpose flour. If you could see gluten strands under a microscope, they would look like a bunch of tangled, stretchy rubber bands. A higher gluten flour adds a tougher structure to baked goods, which is desirable in a bread dough, but not in a tender cake. Some of the recipes, like pie crust, use a combination of all-purpose flour and cake flour to balance the gluten content and achieve a tender pastry. If the pie pastry was prepared completely with cake flour, it would have a structure too tender to form flaky layers and would crumble and fall apart. Store flour, tightly covered, and keep it dry.

Leavening Agents

Air, steam, yeast, baking soda, and baking powder leaven baked goods. Air is beaten into batters, and the liquid in batters produces steam during baking. Yeast, baking soda, and baking powder are ingredients that when activated in some way, produce carbon dioxide gas cells in a batter or dough. The gas cells are like tiny bubbles or air pockets that form during baking and lighten the batter or dough.

YEAST The slowpoke leavening, yeast is activated by moisture and warmth; it produces the carbon dioxide gas cells slowly. Yeast doughs have rising periods which give the carbon dioxide gas cells time to form. If yeast is fresh when purchased, it will stay active for three to six months. Yeast in packets is marked with an expiration date. I use granulated yeast and store it, tightly covered, in the refrigerator.

BAKING SODA OR SODIUM BICARBONATE This alkaline leavening is activated when it is combined with an acid ingredient like sour cream, molasses, or buttermilk. Carbon dioxide gas cells are produced quickly and results are fast. If kept dry, baking soda can be stored indefinitely.

BAKING POWDER Baking powder contains baking soda (alkaline) plus an acid ingredient and is activated when combined with a liquid. Double acting baking powders contain two acid ingredients, one activated by liquid and one activated by heat. I use double acting baking powder. Store baking powder, tightly covered, and do not use it past the expiration date on the can.

Nuts

I use blanched almonds (without skins), unblanched almonds (with skins), pecans, walnuts, hazelnuts, macadamia nuts (preferably unsalted), unsalted roasted cashew nuts, unsalted roasted pistachio nuts, pine nuts, and chestnuts in the recipes. Generally, the new crop of nuts appears in supermarkets from September to December; this is a good time to buy a year's supply. Store the nuts in the freezer in a tightly sealed heavy-duty freezer bag or plastic freezer container. Fresh nuts can be stored for a month in the refrigerator, but the freezer is best for longer storage. Nuts may be stored in the freezer for up to one year. For details on peeling, toasting, chopping, and grinding nuts, see page 12.

Sugar

Three types of sugar are used in the recipes: granulated sugar, brown sugar, and powdered sugar. Brown sugar contains molasses, and light brown sugar has less molasses than dark brown sugar. Powdered sugar, or confectioners' sugar, is granulated sugar that has been ground to a powder. Cornstarch is added to powdered sugar to prevent caking, but it's still a good idea to sift powdered sugar before using it to remove any lumps. Store all sugar tightly covered and in a dry place; brown sugar should be stored in a tightly sealed plastic bag to preserve its moisture.

Freezing Chocolate Desserts

After freezing a chocolate dessert, I want it to be just as good when I defrost and serve it as the day it was baked. By following a few simple guidelines when freezing desserts and by choosing ones that adapt well to freezing, I have found desserts that live up to these high expectations every time. Much of the following information was previously published in my first book, *Bake and Freeze Desserts*, and is repeated here for your convenience.

Understanding How Desserts Freeze

Having an understanding of what happens to food when it freezes ensures that your desserts remain in prime condition while they are frozen and after they defrost.

When food freezes, the water (moisture) in it freezes in the form of ice crystals. Small ice crystals preserve the fine texture and quality of a dessert while large ice crystals cause a coarse texture to form. A grainy texture in ice cream or an unpleasant mushy texture in a baked dessert after it defrosts is the result of large ice crystals. If you look at a piece of frozen cake you can see the ice crystals. When the cake defrosts, small ice crystals will dissolve and help retain the good quality of the cake, but large ice crystals form soggy spots. Large ice crystals can rupture the cell walls of food and cause moisture to flow out of the food as it defrosts. When fruit collapses and softens as it defrosts, it is caused by large ice crystals breaking the cell walls of the fruit.

Cool or chill desserts thoroughly before wrapping and freezing them. Cold desserts will freeze quickly and have less condensation (little or no frost will form) and will taste good when they defrost. We've all seen the layer of frost that forms if a warm cake is put in the freezer, but cooling a cake thoroughly prevents frost from forming. Cold desserts freeze quickly, and the faster a dessert freezes, the smaller the ice crystals that form.

Maintain a freezer temperature as close as possible to 0°F. Temperature fluctuations during frozen storage affect desserts. Each time a dessert defrosts slightly and freezes again, the small ice crystals melt and refreeze on larger ice crystals, which then become larger still, and the dessert loses some of its quality. Inevitably, temperatures fluctuate in a home freezer, especially during a defrost cycle, but a cold freezer keeps any slight defrosting to a minimum. Store desserts inside the freezer, not on the door shelves where the greatest temperature fluctuations occur. Put desserts in the coldest part of your freezer, usually the bottom rear shelf, to freeze. Leave the dessert overnight to freeze solid. After it is frozen, the dessert can be moved to another place inside the freezer. Since some temperature fluctuation is unavoidable, desserts have a limited frozen shelf life. Recommended storage times are listed later in this chapter.

Deciding If a Dessert Is Suitable for Freezing

The water (moisture) content of the dessert is the prime factor to consider when deciding if a dessert will freeze successfully. Lower moisture content means fewer ice crystals form, so there are fewer ice crystals to interfere with creamy texture or to rupture cell walls. Cakes and cookies have a low moisture content, so they freeze more easily and for a longer time than an ice cream dessert or mousse with a high moisture content. If a dessert is a good keeper, it will usually freeze well. A chocolate fudge cake that remains in good condition unfrozen for at least three days is a good choice for freezing, while a fragile seven-minute frosting and a lemon meringue pie that must be served the same day they are prepared are not good choices for freezing. Custards and custard sauces made without cornstarch or flour thickening are also fragile; their delicate structure can be damaged by freezing. A high water content and light texture in a dessert usually indicate that it should be left frozen for a shorter time than a dessert with less moisture and a dense texture. For example, a frozen chocolate terrine stores best for a shorter period than a thick chocolate fudge sauce, which can be stored for longer.

Fat is an important component in any dessert that will be frozen. Since fat helps keep ice crystals separated in frozen food, small ice crystals find it difficult to join with other ice crystals and undesirable large ice crystals do not form easily. Adding chocolate to a dessert improves a dessert's freezing capabilities since chocolate contains fat in the form of cocoa butter.

Picking the Best Desserts to Freeze

Many more desserts than are included in this book are appropriate for freezing. Desserts that freeze well fall into certain categories. With an understanding of how to identify the types of desserts suitable for freezing, you can determine which of your own favorite recipes can be frozen successfully.

BROWNIES, BARS, AND CHOCOLATE CHIP COOKIES Brownies, bars, and cookies are among the easiest desserts to freeze. Put them in the freezer as soon as they cool, leaving out a few for munching, of course. Then you can remove as many cookies as you want at a time and know they will always taste fresh-baked. Since even a large batch of cookies or brownies doesn't take up much room in the freezer, they make a good choice if your freezer space is limited.

CAKES After they bake, cakes have a low moisture content and freeze well. You probably have already successfully frozen loaf cakes, layer cakes, tube cakes, coffee cakes, steamed puddings, and yeast cakes, but frosted and filled cakes freeze just as successfully. Freeze cakes baked rather than trying to freeze unbaked batter.

Frostings and fillings for cakes that will be frozen should be of a dense-textured type such as buttercream or mousse. They need to contain fat, usually in the form of butter or heavy cream. Chocolate and white chocolate add density and fat to frostings and fillings and make them suitable for freezing. I find plain whipped cream has too much water content and too light a texture to freeze successfully, so I add whipped cream to cakes after I defrost them.

When I prepare a frosted cake, I often bake extra layers for the freezer. It takes about the same time to prepare four cake layers as two, but there is only one clean-up. Another advantage is that frozen cake layers are easy to split, handle, and frost.

Crisp meringue layers freeze as well as cake layers, but once they are filled with a buttercream or ice cream, their time in the freezer is limited. Meringues filled with a dense buttercream, as in the Pistachio Praline Meringue Cake with Lemon and White Chocolate Buttercream (page 189), will remain crisp for one month, but meringue combined with ice cream, as in the Mocha and Almond Praline Meringue Bombe (page 291), softens after one week.

CHEESECAKES With their high fat content and dense texture, cheesecakes freeze easily. Allow cheesecakes to cool thoroughly before freezing them, and defrost them slowly, usually overnight, in the refrigerator. Unbaked cheesecakes do not freeze well.

ICE CREAM DESSERTS Ice cream desserts certainly freeze well, but their time in the freezer is limited. The longer ice cream is stored in your freezer, the larger the ice crystals will become and these larger ice crystals reduce the creamy texture of ice cream. Any ingredients combined with ice cream, such as the cookies in an ice cream sandwich, crushed praline in a terrine, or meringue in a bombe, soften while frozen. Most ice cream desserts remain in good condition for no more than two weeks if frozen.

The homemade Cinnamon Ice Cream in Chocolate Cups with Dark Chocolate Sauce (page 264), lacking the preservatives and stabilizers of commercial ice cream, should be stored only up to ten days.

MOUSSE DESSERTS Mousse desserts can be served frozen or defrosted and served cold. Chocolate and white chocolate add to the density and fat content of mousse desserts and make them especially suited to freezing. Another major ingredient of mousse desserts, whipped cream, also increases the fat content and helps frozen mousse desserts retain a creamy, light texture. The addition of praline keeps a frozen mousse smooth by lowering its freezing point slightly. Since these desserts do have a high moisture content, their ideal storage time in the freezer is about three weeks.

PIES, TARTS, AND TRUFFLES Freeze pie and tart crusts unbaked, but roll them out and put them into the baking pan before freezing. They will taste better when freshly baked with the dessert. On the other hand, crumb crusts can be frozen after they are baked with no problem.

Pies and tarts filled with dense chocolate and cream truffle mixtures make good choices for freezing. These truffle mixtures can be formed into balls for candy truffles and frozen. For a cream filling to freeze in a pie crust, prepare a dense cream filling by combining some truffle mixture with whipped cream. Such a chocolate truffle mixture mixed with whipped cream makes a dense pie filling that adapts well to freezing.

For adding fruit to a pie, it is helpful to know what happens to fruit when it freezes. When the water in fruit freezes, it expands and can break the rigid cell walls of the fruit. If the cell walls are broken when fruit defrosts or bakes, it releases a large amount of juice and desserts become soggy. Raspberries, blackberries, and blueberries are fairly easy to deal with if a pie contains only a small amount of fruit. In the Razzle-Dazzle Raspberry Fudge Pie (page 108), raspberries are only one layer of a multilayered pie, so any moisture from the raspberries can be absorbed by the cream cheese and brownie layers. For a fruit crisp, freeze the crisp unbaked so that no juice is released until the crisp bakes and use a thickening agent such as flour to absorb and thicken some of the liquid that forms during baking. For the Pear and Dark Chocolate Crisp (page 102), the pears bake for twenty minutes before they are frozen in the unbaked crisp. Prebaking the pears before freezing them softens the rigid cell walls and prevents them from bursting and releasing excess liquid when baked. I have baked the frozen crisp with both prebaked and raw pears; the difference in the liquid released by the pears was astounding.

To defrost frozen fruit, defrost it slowly in the refrigerator. Slow gentle defrosting is less likely to break the cell walls, and the fruit gives up less liquid and holds its shape better than fruit defrosted at room temperature.

SAUCES Sauces based on caramel, brown sugar, chocolate, and white chocolate and cooked and uncooked fruit sauces freeze well. Some of these sauces may separate upon defrosting, but blending them with a whisk or a vigorous stirring will bring them back. Fragile custard sauces are not a good choice for freezing.

Freezer Temperatures

Try to keep your freezer temperature as close to 0°F. as possible. Most home freezers are designed to maintain a temperature between 0° and 8°F. Keep a freezer thermometer in the back of the freezer and adjust the thermostat as necessary. Keep temperature fluctuations to a minimum by opening the freezer door as little as possible and not adding a lot of unfrozen items to your freezer at the same time.

Protecting Desserts During Freezer Storage

It is imperative to wrap and seal desserts carefully before putting them in the freezer. The air in the freezer is dry and has a natural inclination to pull moisture from any food that it comes in contact with. This dry air will find any hole in the packaging or gap in a seal and draw the moisture out of your carefully prepared dessert. Frozen food with freezer burn is an example of food that has been exposed to dry freezer air and has had the moisture sucked right out of it. Since it is impractical to package desserts in a vacuum, some moisture will be lost, but good packaging holds this loss to a minimum and keeps desserts in good condition. Chocolate tends to absorb odors from anything nearby, but careful packaging protects desserts from absorbing odors during freezer storage.

Your carefully prepared desserts are worth spending a few extra pennies on the best supplies for wrapping them. I use heavy-duty freezer bags, heavy aluminum foil, plastic wrap, rigid plastic freezer containers, and metal tins. This supply list is short, but it offers maximum protection and will protect your desserts from air, moisture, and odors. Heavyweight aluminum foil is so easy to use that I prefer it to the coated freezer wrap that requires tape for sealing. Square or rectangular containers that can be stacked take up less room in your freezer than round containers. Saran Wrap, made from polyvinylidene chloride, is the plastic wrap rated as having the best barrier against water and odor transmission. Do not reuse bags from the produce department, which are too lightweight to offer protection.

Different categories of desserts lend themselves to certain kinds of packaging. Large desserts such as cakes, pies, tarts, cheesecakes, and terrines should be tightly wrapped with plastic wrap, then with a layer of heavy aluminum foil. The plastic wrap fits smoothly against the dessert and forms a tight seal, while the heavy aluminum foil provides a strong barrier against moisture and resists punctures.

Check your packages to see if there are any spots that are not covered completely. Cakes with frosting or other desserts with soft toppings should be put in the freezer to firm before they are wrapped. Plastic wrap alone is sufficient for two weeks of frozen storage, but I have changed my dessert plans too many times, so I always add the heavy foil.

Smaller desserts such as cookies, brownies, bars, truffles, small tarts, and individual cakes should be individually wrapped in plastic wrap, then placed in a metal or rigid plastic container and covered tightly. The difference between wrapping cookies or other small desserts in plastic wrap before putting them in a container rather than just stacking them in the container is enormous. Individual wrapping protects them from the air that is inevitably trapped in the container; this way, the desserts won't pick up off flavors or develop dreaded freezer burn. If cookies aren't sticky, you can wrap several together in plastic wrap. Clean and dry coffee or shortening tins work fine for containers.

Ice cream and sauces should be frozen in rigid plastic containers. Leave one inch of air space for expansion at the top and press a piece of plastic wrap onto the surface of the sauce or ice cream before you seal the container. This small piece of plastic wrap will prevent ice crystals from forming on the surface of the ice cream or sauce. Plastic containers should be clean and free of any odors.

Labeling Desserts

Whenever I open my freezer and see the labels on all of those aluminum foil packages, I'm reminded of how important it is to mark each package. It only takes a few extra seconds to label packages with the date and contents. Keep a roll of masking tape and a pen in a kitchen drawer, so you're never tempted to put off labeling a dessert. Plastic freezer bags usually have a white area to write information with a ballpoint pen or felt tip marker. Since a cold moist surface is hard to apply a label to or to write on, label packages before the dessert goes into the freezer.

Defrosting Desserts

Some of the desserts in this book are served frozen and require no defrosting at all, but defrosting desserts correctly is crucial. A general rule of thumb for defrosting desserts is that if the dessert will be served cold, defrost it in the refrigerator, and if it will be served at room temperature, defrost it at room temperature. Keep desserts wrapped or in covered containers while they defrost; then, the moisture that forms as the desserts defrost will form on the wrapping, and not on the dessert.

Once the dessert is defrosted, it is ready to serve. Each of the recipes gives specific storage and serving suggestions.

STORAGE TIMES

This chart lists the maximum storage times that desserts can be stored in the freezer without losing quality.

DESSERT ITEM	STORAGE TIME
Baked crumb crusts	1 month
Baked fruit desserts	1 month
Bombes and parfaits	2 weeks
Cakes with frosting	1 month
Cakes without frosting	3 months
Cheesecakes	1 month
Cookies and brownies	3 months
Frozen terrines	3 weeks
Fruit sauces, cooked or uncooked	1 month
Homemade ice cream	10 days
Ice cream pies	2 weeks
Ice cream sandwiches	1 week
Mousse desserts	3 weeks
Nonfruit sauces, cooked	2 months
Nuts	1 year
Pies or tarts without fruit	2 months
Praline	3 months
Steamed puddings	2 months
Unbaked fruit pies	1 month
Unbaked pie crusts and pastry	2 months

The Frozen Pantry

The basic recipes in this chapter give me a head start on many desserts; they certainly make my baking easier. I try to keep an assortment of these items in my freezer, but I don't find it necessary to have them all available at one time. There are always pie crust, praline, cake layers, chocolate curls, and a sauce or two. If I know I'm going to bake a specific dessert that requires a frozen pantry item, I try to have it frozen ahead of time. A Milk Chocolate and Caramel Pecan Tart (page 111) can be assembled in minutes if you have the crumb crust and caramel filling ready in the freezer. Chocolate Cream Pie (page 66) is ready in no time once the truffle sauce and crumb crust are prepared.

Some of these items even improve after being frozen. A frozen pie or tart crust holds its shape well during baking, cake layers are easy to handle and split into even layers, and chocolate decorations won't melt when you touch them. Storing nut praline in the freezer means you can spoon out exactly what you need and save the remainder for another use. Since frozen praline is not affected by a humid kitchen, it remains crunchy for several months.

The secret to my success is to bake several items at one time. It's the same amount of clean-up whether I prepare one or four recipes, and once you have the ingredients and utensils out, it makes sense to use them more than once. I make truffle sauce while the praline cools and chill pie crust dough while I mix cake layers. Soon I have an assortment of components basic to many desserts, and putting a dessert together is a breeze.

SWEET BUTTER PASTRY

Look no farther for a never-fail easy crust for tarts. This one is just like the rich butter pastry found in the best French bakeries. The dough, prepared in an electric mixer, holds its shape well even if mixed a few seconds more or a few seconds less. With its cookielike crust, it is strong enough to support any tart filling, but tender enough to melt in your mouth.

MAKES ONE 11-INCH TART CRUST

1 large cold egg
1 cup unbleached all-purpose flour
$^1/_4$ cup cake flour
$^2/_3$ cup powdered sugar
2 tablespoons ground blanched almonds
$^1/_2$ teaspoon baking powder
$^1/_8$ teaspoon salt
$^1/_4$ pound (1 stick) cold unsalted butter, cut into 8 pieces

1. Butter an 11-inch metal tart pan with a removable bottom.

2. Put the egg in a small bowl and mix with a fork just to break up the yolk. Put the flours, powdered sugar, almonds, baking powder, and salt in the large bowl of an electric mixer and mix on low speed just to blend the ingredients, about 10 seconds. Add the butter and mix until most of the butter pieces are the size of peas, about 1 minute and 30 seconds. The mixture will look crumbly and the crumbs will vary in size. With the mixer running, add the egg. Mix until the mixture clings together and pulls away from the sides of the bowl, about 30 seconds. The dough will look smooth and have a golden color. Form the dough into a round disk about 6 inches in diameter. Wrap in plastic wrap and refrigerate until firm, for at least 1 hour or overnight.

3. Remove the dough from the refrigerator and unwrap it. If the dough has become cold and hard, let it sit at room temperature until it is easy to roll, about 20 minutes. Lightly flour the rolling surface and rolling pin. Roll the dough from the center out into a circle 3 inches wider than the bottom of the tart pan;

· Using cake flour and ground almonds adds to the tenderness of the pastry, while the powdered sugar adds a fine texture. The only liquid added to the dough is an egg, which helps guarantee a tender dough.

· If you mix the dough with a hand mixer, rather than a countertop mixer, allow about 30 seconds longer for mixing.

· This is not a stretchy dough; it rolls out smoothly, like a cookie dough.

· I put the pastry in a black steel tart pan with 1-inch-high sides and a removable bottom. Check to see that there is no rust on the pan, as this can impart a metallic taste to the crust.

for an 11-inch tart pan you will have a 14-inch circle, $^3/_{16}$ inch thick. Lift and turn the dough several times as you roll it to prevent it from sticking to the rolling surface, but don't flip the dough over while rolling it. Dust the rolling surface and rolling pin with more flour as necessary. Use a rigid pastry scraper to loosen the dough from the rolling surface and carefully roll the dough circle over the rolling pin. Unroll it into the tart pan. Gently press the dough into the pan and trim the edges to leave a $^1/_2$-inch overhang. Fold the overhang into the pan and press it against the edge of the pan to form slightly thickened sides, about $^1/_4$ inch thick. Use dough scraps to patch any cracks in the dough.

Doubling the Recipe

Double the ingredients. For more than two crusts, make another batch of dough.

To Freeze

Wrap the unbaked butter pastry tightly with plastic wrap. Wrap any remaining dough scraps in plastic wrap for patching when the crust is baked and place them on the pastry. Wrap with heavy aluminum foil, gently pressing the aluminum foil against the dough. Label with date and contents. Freeze up to 2 months. Once the tart pastry is frozen, other items may be placed on top of it.

CHOCOLATE BUTTER PASTRY

Cocoa powder gives this buttery pastry crust a dark chocolate color and intense flavor. Using some cake flour tenderizes the pastry, yet it remains strong enough to support a tart filling. The finished pastry is not as flaky as a pie crust pastry but more like a bittersweet chocolate butter cookie. It makes a good contrast to sweet tart fillings.

MAKES ONE 11-INCH TART CRUST

1 large cold egg
$3/4$ cup plus 1 tablespoon unbleached all-purpose flour
$1/3$ cup cake flour
$1/2$ teaspoon baking powder
$1/8$ teaspoon salt
3 tablespoons unsweetened Dutch process cocoa powder, such as Droste or Hershey's European Style
$3/4$ cup powdered sugar
$1/4$ pound (1 stick) cold unsalted butter, cut into 8 pieces

1. Butter an 11-inch metal tart pan with a removable bottom.

2. Put the egg in a small bowl and mix with a fork just to break up the yolk. Put the flours, baking powder, and salt in the large bowl of an electric mixer. Sift the cocoa powder and powdered sugar into the mixing bowl. Mix on low speed just to blend the ingredients, about 10 seconds. Add the butter and mix until the butter pieces are the size of peas, about 1 minute and 30 seconds. The mixture will look crumbly. With the mixer running, add the egg. Mix until the mixture clings together and pulls away from the sides of the bowl, about 30 seconds. The mixture will look dry and floury at first, but will come together as you mix it. The dough will look smooth and you will see flecks of butter. Form the dough into a round disk about 6 inches in diameter. Wrap in plastic wrap and refrigerate until firm, for at least 1 hour or overnight.

3. Remove the dough from the refrigerator and unwrap it. If the dough has become cold and hard, let it sit at room temperature until it is easy to roll, 5 to 10

Good Advice

· The pastry will hold its shape better if baked while frozen. This pastry does not form bubbles when it bakes, so pricking is unnecessary.

· The egg, water, and butter must be cold. You will see small yellow flakes of butter in the crust before it bakes. These flakes of butter will melt and disappear as the pastry bakes.

· Save the extra dough scraps for patching the pastry. It seldom happens, but sometimes cracks form when the tart crust is baked before it is filled. When the crust is baked, check it during the last 10 minutes of baking and patch any cracks with raw dough at that time.

minutes. Lightly flour the rolling surface and rolling pin. Roll the dough from the center out into a circle 3 inches wider than the bottom of the tart pan; for an 11-inch tart pan roll a 14-inch circle. Lift and turn the dough several times as you roll it to prevent it from sticking to the rolling surface, but don't flip the dough over while rolling it. Dust the rolling surface and rolling pin with more flour as necessary. Use a rigid pastry scraper to loosen the dough from the rolling surface and carefully roll the dough circle over the rolling pin. Unroll it into the tart pan. Gently press the dough into the pan and trim the edges to leave a $1/2$-inch overhang. Fold the overhang into the pan and press it against the edge of the pan to form slightly thickened sides.

Doubling the Recipe

Double the ingredients. For more than two crusts, make another batch of dough.

To Freeze

Wrap the unbaked pastry tightly with plastic wrap. Wrap any dough scraps in plastic wrap and place on the pastry. Wrap with heavy aluminum foil, gently pressing the aluminum foil against the dough. Label with date and contents. Freeze up to 2 months. Once the pastry is frozen, other items can be placed on top of it.

EASY AS PIE CRUST

The world is divided into two types of pie crust people—those who make pie crust all the time and think nothing of it and those who are afraid to make pie crust. My theory is that if you had someone to watch making pie crust when you were growing up, then the preparation comes easy. My mom is a great baker but seldom makes pies, so I never saw a pie crust being made until I was more than thirty years old. I had a fear-of-pie-crust syndrome for a long time. Finally, I cornered an experienced pie crust maker, watched the crust-making process, and practiced until I got it right. Now I spread the word that there's nothing to fear. Just "watch" by reading this recipe carefully and join the fearless group.

Most of the pie recipes in this book call for crumb crusts, but the Walnut Chocolate Chip Pie (page 110) requires a flaky pie crust. It will give you a good opportunity to practice the technique. Spend a rainy afternoon making several pie crusts, and before long you will feel comfortable preparing them.

To Bake a Pie Crust Blind (Without Filling)

Position a rack in the middle of the oven. Preheat the oven to 400°F. Butter a piece of aluminum foil or parchment paper and place it, buttered side down, on the frozen pie crust. Fill with metal pie weights, raw rice, or dried beans (about 3½ cups rice or beans). Push some of the weights against the edges of the pan to ensure the sides are supported. Bake for 15 minutes. Reduce the oven heat to 350°F. Carefully remove the paper and weights and prick the crust in several places with a fork. Bake for 10 to 15 minutes more, or until the crust is golden brown. Cool the crust. It is now ready to fill.

MAKES ONE 10-INCH PIE CRUST

1 cup unbleached all-purpose flour
⅓ cup cake flour
½ teaspoon salt
1 tablespoon sugar
6 tablespoons (¾ stick) cold unsalted butter, cut into 4 pieces
2 tablespoons plus 2 teaspoons cold vegetable shortening
3½ to 4 tablespoons ice water
Sifted cake flour, for rolling pie crust

Good Advice

· A combination of all-purpose and cake flour lowers the gluten content of the total flour, making the crust tender.

· This recipe uses butter for flavor and vegetable shortening for flakiness. The butter and shortening must be cold so they form little fat pockets in the crust; these will form the flaky layers of the crust. Use ice water for the liquid so the cold shortening doesn't soften.

· If you use a hand mixer, use a large bowl to mix the ingredients and allow more time for mixing than with a countertop mixer.

· Baking pie crusts frozen helps the crust hold its shape during baking. If you don't have time to freeze a crust, put it in the freezer for 15 minutes so it is cold when you bake it. Use aluminum pie tins rather than glass or ceramic to prevent the possibility of a cold glass pie plate breaking when placed in a hot oven.

1. Lightly grease a 10-inch pie pan with vegetable shortening. Or spray the pie pan with a vegetable oil spray.

2. Put the flours, salt, and sugar in the large bowl of an electric mixer and mix on low speed just to blend the ingredients, about 10 seconds. Stop the mixer, add the butter and shortening, and mix just until the butter and shortening pieces are the size of small lima beans, about 20 seconds. They will not all be the same size, and you will still see loose flour. Slowly add the water, 1 tablespoon at a time. Stop mixing as soon as the mixture begins to hold together, about 20 seconds. You may not need all of the water. The dough will form large clumps and pull away from the sides of the bowl but will not form a ball. Stop the mixer at any time and squeeze a small piece of dough to check if it holds together. Mixing the crust with a hand mixer will take about 30 seconds longer.

3. Turn the dough mixture out onto a lightly floured rolling surface. With the heel of your hand push the dough down and forward against the rolling surface. Fold the dough in half and repeat 6 times. The dough will look smooth. Form the dough into a round disk about 4 inches in diameter. It will be easier to roll into a circle if it is round and the edges are smooth, but don't handle it a lot just to get smooth edges or a perfect circle. Wrap the dough in plastic wrap and chill it in the refrigerator for at least 20 minutes or as long as overnight.

4. Remove the dough from the refrigerator and unwrap it. If the dough has become cold and hard, let it sit at room temperature until it is easy to roll, 5 to 10 minutes. Lightly flour the rolling surface and rolling pin. Roll the dough from the center out into a circle about 4 inches wider than the bottom of the pie pan. Lift and turn the dough several times as you roll it to prevent it from sticking to the rolling surface, but don't flip the dough over while rolling. Dust the rolling surface and rolling pin with more flour as necessary. Use a rigid pastry scraper to loosen the dough from the rolling surface and roll the dough circle over the rolling pin. Unroll it onto the pie pan. Press the dough into the pie pan. Trim the edges evenly to a ¾-inch overhang. Press ½ inch of the overhang under itself to form an even edge. Form a crimped edge around the top of the pie pan by pressing the dough between your thumb and forefinger.

· Double this recipe and keep a well-wrapped unbaked pie crust in the freezer, ready to fill.

· Sprinkle leftover dough scraps with sugar or cinnamon sugar and bake them in a 400°F. oven until golden brown for snacks.

Doubling the Recipe

Double the ingredients. For more than two pie crusts, make another batch of dough.

To Freeze

Wrap the unbaked pie crust tightly with plastic wrap. Wrap any scraps in plastic wrap and place on the pastry. The pie crust scraps can be used to patch the crust or can be sprinkled with sugar and baked when you bake the pie crust. Cover with heavy aluminum foil, gently pressing the foil against the dough. Label with date and contents. Freeze up to 2 months. Once the pie crust is frozen, it can be stacked inside other pie crusts in the freezer.

$\mathcal{P}$ie crusts made from cookie crumbs are fast and foolproof. I use graham crackers, chocolate wafers, and chocolate sandwich cookies for them. Simply mix the crushed cookie crumbs with melted butter and the appropriate spices, nuts, or chocolate chips and press into a pie pan or springform pan. Bake, cool, and add the filling. If you're looking for a crust that will taste good served frozen in an ice cream pie or other frozen dessert, a crumb crust is a good choice.

Good Advice

· After trying many brands, my favorite cookies are Sunshine Graham Crackers or crumbs, Nabisco Famous Chocolate Wafers, and Nabisco Oreos. Sandwich cookies with their filling make a sweeter crust and require less butter. I buy ready-to-use graham cracker crumbs, but I grind chocolate wafers or Oreos in a food processor or put about eight cookies at a time between two pieces of wax paper and crush them with a rolling pin.

· Using your fingers is the easiest way to press crumb crusts into a pan. When pressing the crumbs into the pan, check to see that the crust doesn't become too thick where the sides and bottom of the pan meet.

Doubling the Recipe

Multiply the ingredients for as many crusts as you need.

GRAHAM CRACKER CRUMB CRUST
Makes one 10-inch pie crust

1½ cups graham cracker crumbs
¾ teaspoon ground cinnamon
5 tablespoons unsalted butter, melted

Makes one 9-inch springform crust

1¾ cups graham cracker crumbs
1 teaspoon ground cinnamon
6 tablespoons (¾ stick) unsalted butter, melted

GRAHAM CRACKER CRUMB CRUST WITH NUTS
Makes one 10-inch pie crust or 9-inch springform crust

1 cup finely chopped nuts (walnuts, pecans, or toasted almonds)
1 cup plus 1 tablespoon graham cracker crumbs
½ teaspoon ground cinnamon
5 tablespoons unsalted butter, melted

GRAHAM CRACKER OR CHOCOLATE WAFER CRUMB CRUST WITH CHOCOLATE CHIPS
Makes one 9-inch springform crust

1½ cups graham cracker or chocolate wafer cookie crumbs
¼ teaspoon ground cinnamon
5 tablespoons unsalted butter, melted
½ cup miniature semisweet chocolate chips

CHOCOLATE WAFER COOKIE CRUMB CRUST
Makes one 10-inch pie crust

1½ cups chocolate wafer crumbs
4 tablespoons unsalted butter, melted

Makes one 9-inch springform crust

2 cups chocolate wafer crumbs (9-ounce package)
6 tablespoons (¾ stick) unsalted butter, melted

OREO COOKIE CRUMB CRUST
Makes one 10-inch pie crust

2 cups Oreo cookie crumbs with filling (about 3 cups Oreos)
2 tablespoons unsalted butter, melted

Makes one 9-inch springform crust

2¼ cups Oreo cookie crumbs with filling (about 3⅓ cups Oreos)
2 tablespoons unsalted butter, melted

1. Position a rack in the middle of the oven. Preheat the oven to 325°F. Butter the baking pan of your choice. Springform pans should have sides at least 2¾ inches high.

2. Put the cookie crumbs and cinnamon, chocolate chips, or nuts, if using, in a large bowl and mix together. Add the melted butter and stir the mixture until the crumbs are evenly moistened with the butter. Transfer the crumbs to the buttered baking pan. Using your fingers, press the crumbs evenly over the bottom and sides of the pan. If using a springform pan, press the crumbs 1 inch up the sides of the pan. Check to see that the crust isn't too thick where the sides and the edges of the pan meet. Bake the crust for 6 minutes.

3. Cool the crust thoroughly before filling or freezing it. Crumb crusts can be baked a day ahead, covered, and stored overnight at room temperature.

To Freeze
Press plastic wrap tightly onto the cooled crumb crust. Cover the pan with heavy aluminum foil and press the aluminum foil tightly around the edges of the pan. Freeze up to 1 month.

DEVILISH CHOCOLATE CAKE

After reading about twenty-five recipes for devil's food cake, I realized that there was no agreement on the ingredients of this truly American chocolate cake. So I created my own version. I decided it should have a light texture, fine crumb, and a dark chocolate color— just like these dark, moist, devilish cake layers.

Makes two 9-inch round layers

2 ounces unsweetened chocolate, in 1-ounce pieces
2 cups cake flour
$^2/_3$ cup unsweetened Dutch process cocoa powder, such as Droste or
    Hershey's European Style
1 teaspoon baking soda
$^1/_2$ teaspoon salt
$^1/_4$ pound (1 stick) soft unsalted butter
2 cups sugar
3 large eggs
$1^1/_2$ teaspoons vanilla extract
$1^1/_4$ cups buttermilk

Makes one 10-inch round layer or one 9-inch square cake

$1^1/_2$ ounces unsweetened chocolate, in $^1/_2$-ounce pieces
$1^1/_2$ cups cake flour
$^1/_2$ cup unsweetened Dutch process cocoa powder, such as Droste or
    Hershey's European Style
$^3/_4$ teaspoon baking soda
$^1/_2$ teaspoon salt
6 tablespoons ($^3/_4$ stick) soft unsalted butter
$1^1/_2$ cups sugar
2 large eggs
1 teaspoon vanilla extract
$^3/_4$ cup plus 3 tablespoons buttermilk

Makes two 10-inch round layers or two 9-inch square cakes

3 ounces unsweetened chocolate, in 1-ounce pieces
3 cups cake flour
1 cup unsweetened Dutch process cocoa powder, such as Droste or
    Hershey's European Style
$1^1/_2$ teaspoons baking soda
$^3/_4$ teaspoon salt
6 ounces ($1^1/_2$ sticks) soft unsalted butter

Good Advice

· Take the time to beat the butter and sugar well and to beat the eggs into the batter for the time directed. These two thorough beatings develop the cake's structure.

· Adding the dry ingredients alternately with the buttermilk is only a matter of combining them thoroughly into the batter and does not require long beating.

· Use sturdy pans with $1^3/_4$- to 2-inch-high sides. A 9-inch square pan should have 2-inch-high sides.

· Cold cake layers are easy to cut and handle, so when filling and frosting frozen cake layers, defrost them just enough to cut easily. Then fill and frost the layers and return them to the freezer. If I am filling and frosting a cake layer and returning it to the freezer, I freeze it only for up to 2 months since it can remain frozen for a third month after the frosting is added.

Doubling the Recipe

For more than two 9- or 10-inch layers, prepare separate batches. Use a 5-quart mixing bowl when preparing two 10-inch layers.

3 cups sugar
4 large eggs
2 teaspoons vanilla extract
1³/₄ cups plus 2 tablespoons buttermilk

1. Position an oven rack in the middle of the oven. Preheat the oven to 175°F. Butter the bottom and sides of the baking pan or pans. Line the bottom of each pan with parchment or wax paper and butter the paper.

2. Place the unsweetened chocolate in a heatproof container and melt it in the oven, about 6 to 8 minutes. As soon as the chocolate is melted, remove it from the oven and stir it smooth. Increase the oven temperature to 350°F. Set the chocolate aside to cool slightly while you mix the batter.

3. Sift the flour, cocoa powder, baking soda, and salt together and set aside. Put the butter in the large bowl of an electric mixer and mix on low speed for 15 seconds. (Use a 5-quart bowl for two 10-inch layers.) Add the sugar and beat on medium speed for 2 minutes, or until the mixture is fluffy and lightens from yellow to cream color. The mixture will look sugary. Beat in the eggs, one at a time. Stop the mixer and scrape the sides of the bowl during this mixing. Beat for 2 more minutes. Decrease the speed to low and mix in the vanilla extract and melted chocolate. Stop the mixer and scrape the sides of the bowl during this mixing. Add the flour mixture and the buttermilk alternately, beginning and ending with the flour mixture (3 flour, 2 buttermilk). Let the mixture absorb the flour before adding more buttermilk. Stop the mixer and scrape the sides of the bowl after the last addition of flour. The batter is ready when the final addition of flour is mixed completely into the batter. If any flour is clinging to the sides of the bowl, stir it into the batter. Pour the batter into the prepared pan or pans and smooth the top of the batter.

4. Bake for about 40 minutes for 9-inch round layers and about 50 minutes for 10-inch round layers or 9-inch square layers. To test for doneness, gently press your fingers on the middle of the cake. It should feel firm. If it does, insert a toothpick into the center of the cake. When the toothpick comes out clean, the cake is done.

5. Cool the cake in the baking pan on a wire rack.

To Freeze

Use a small sharp knife to loosen the sides of the cake from the pan. Invert each layer onto a piece of plastic wrap. Carefully remove and discard the paper liner. Wrap the cooled cake tightly with plastic wrap and then with heavy aluminum foil. Label with date and contents. Freeze up to 3 months. After the layers are frozen, they may be stacked in the freezer.

To Defrost

Remove the cake layers from the freezer and defrost the wrapped cake at room temperature. Fill or frost the layers as soon as they are thawed enough to cut into thinner layers.

To Serve Plain Cake Layers

Defrost the wrapped cake at room temperature at least 4 hours or overnight. Cut the cake into wedges and serve with ice cream or whipped cream and/or Slightly Thinner Chocolate Truffle Sauce (page 50). Leftover plain cake can be covered with plastic wrap and stored at room temperature up to 4 days.

· Since this cake is somewhat fragile until it bakes firm, don't move it around in the oven during the baking.

· Use a serrated knife and a sawing motion to slice the cake into layers for filling or to cut the cake into servings.

Doubling the Recipe
For more than two layers, prepare separate batches.

To Freeze
Wrap each layer tightly with plastic wrap then heavy aluminum foil. Label with date and contents. Freeze up to 3 months.

To Cool, Roll, and Freeze a Baked Sponge Sheet
After cooling the cake in the baking sheet for 5 minutes, use a strainer to sift 1 tablespoon powdered sugar evenly over the top. The top of the cake should be evenly covered with a thin layer of powdered sugar. Invert the baked sponge sheet onto a clean dish towel. The long side of the cake should be parallel to the edge of the counter. Carefully peel off

HOT MILK SPONGE CAKE

This sponge cake is light and moist and exceptionally simple to mix. It's not even necessary to separate the eggs, so you need only one mixing bowl. Whenever I want light cake layers for, say, a Summertime Peach and White Chocolate Buttercream Cake (page 186) or a loaf cake to slice into thin layers for a fast Magnificent Five-Layer Chocolate Buttercream Cake (page 202), I choose this recipe.

Makes one 9-inch round layer, one 9 × 5-inch loaf, 1 long, narrow loaf, or one 17 × 12-inch sheet

3/4 cup plus 2 tablespoons cake flour
3/4 teaspoon baking powder
1/4 teaspoon salt
1/2 cup skim, low fat, or whole milk
3 large eggs
1 cup sugar
1 teaspoon vanilla extract

Makes two 9-inch round layers, 2 loaves, or two 17 × 12-inch sheets

1 3/4 cups cake flour
1 1/4 teaspoons baking powder
1/2 teaspoon salt
1 cup skim, low fat, or whole milk
6 large eggs
2 cups sugar
2 teaspoons vanilla extract

1. Position an oven rack in the middle of the oven. Preheat the oven to 350°F. Butter the bottom and sides of the baking pan or pans you are using. Line the bottom of each pan with parchment or wax paper and butter the paper.

2. Sift the flour, baking powder, and salt together and set aside. Heat the milk in a small saucepan over medium heat until it is hot, about 150°F. on a food thermometer. Do not let the milk boil. Set aside.

3. Put the eggs in the large bowl of an electric mixer and mix on medium

speed just to combine the yolks and whites. Add the sugar and beat for about 2 minutes, or until the mixture is fluffy, thick, and lightened in color. Mix in the vanilla. Decrease the speed to low and mix in the flour mixture just until it is incorporated. Slowly add the hot milk and mix for about 30 seconds, or until the mixture is smooth. Stop the mixer and scrape the sides of the bowl once during this mixing. The batter will be thin. Pour the batter into the prepared pan or pans. If baking a sponge sheet, spread the batter evenly on the baking sheet.

4. Bake cake layers for 20 to 25 minutes, a loaf cake for about 40 minutes, and a sponge sheet for about 10 minutes. To check for doneness, insert a toothpick in the center of the cake. When the toothpick comes out clean, the cake is done.

5. Cool the cake in the pan on a wire rack for 15 minutes. Use a small sharp knife to loosen the sides of the cake from the pan. Place the cake rack on top of the cake and invert the cake onto the rack. Carefully remove and discard the paper liner. Turn the cake right side up and cool thoroughly, about 1 hour.

the paper and place it back on the cake. Roll up the cake in the dish towel. Let the cake cool in the towel for 1 to 2 hours. Unroll the cake sheet. Discard the paper and place a piece of plastic wrap over the cake. Using the towel to help, roll up the cake with the plastic wrap, but not the towel. Carefully wrap plastic wrap then heavy aluminum foil around the cake roll and freeze up to 3 months.

To Defrost

Remove the cake layer from the freezer and defrost the wrapped cake at room temperature. Fill or frost the layers or loaf as soon as they are defrosted enough to split. The cake is easy to split and handle when it is still cold. Defrost the wrapped cake sheet in the refrigerator. A cold cake sheet is easier to handle than a warm one.

To Serve

To use the cake layer plain, defrost the wrapped cake at room temperature 3 hours or overnight. Leftover cake can be covered with plastic wrap and stored at room temperature up to 2 days.

CHOCOLATE SOUFFLÉ CAKE

Although always light and airy, sponge cake can sometimes be dry and have about as much flavor as a cardboard cake circle. Not this one. Even though these layers contain no shortening, they are moist and have a rich chocolate flavor. The soufflélike batter will rise as the cake bakes and fall slightly as it cools, leaving the cake with a tender texture similar to that of a cooled soufflé. Cocoa powder plus unsweetened chocolate give the cake its appealing dark chocolate color and taste.

Makes one 9-inch round layer or one 17 × 12-inch sheet

1 ounce unsweetened chocolate
2 tablespoons cake flour
1 tablespoon cornstarch
2 tablespoons unsweetened Dutch process cocoa powder, such as Droste or Hershey's European Style
5 large egg whites
1/4 teaspoon cream of tartar
6 tablespoons plus 1/4 cup sugar
3 egg yolks
1 teaspoon vanilla extract
1/4 teaspoon almond extract

1 tablespoon unsweetened Dutch process cocoa powder, for dusting over baked soufflé sheet

Makes two 9-inch round layers or two 17 × 12-inch sheets

2 ounces unsweetened chocolate
1/4 cup cake flour
2 tablespoons cornstarch
1/4 cup unsweetened Dutch process cocoa powder, such as Droste or Hershey's European Style
10 large egg whites
1/2 teaspoon cream of tartar
3/4 cup plus 1/2 cup sugar
6 egg yolks
2 teaspoons vanilla extract
1/2 teaspoon almond extract

2 tablespoons unsweetened Dutch process cocoa powder, for dusting over baked soufflé sheets

1. Position an oven rack in the middle of the oven. Preheat the oven to 175°F. Butter the bottom and sides of a 9-inch layer pan (or 2 pans) with 2-inch-high sides or a 17 × 12-inch baking sheet (or 2 sheets) with 1-inch-high sides. Line the bottom of each pan with parchment paper, butter the paper carefully, and dust lightly with flour.

2. Put the unsweetened chocolate in a small ovenproof container and melt it in the oven, about 6 to 8 minutes. Remove the chocolate from the oven as soon as it is melted and stir it smooth. Set aside to cool slightly. Sift the flour, cornstarch, and cocoa together and set aside. Increase the oven temperature to 350°F.

3. Put the egg whites and cream of tartar in the clean, large bowl of an electric mixer and with clean, dry beaters beat on low speed until the egg whites are foamy and the cream of tartar is dissolved. Increase the speed to medium-high and beat the egg whites to soft peaks. Slowly beat in 6 tablespoons of sugar if preparing 1 cake or ¾ cup of sugar if preparing 2 cakes, 1 tablespoon at a time. Set the egg white mixture aside while you prepare the egg yolk mixture.

4. Put the egg yolks in the large bowl of an electric mixer and mix on medium speed just to break up the yolks. It is not necessary to wash the beaters that were used for the egg whites. Add the remaining ¼ cup of sugar if preparing 1 cake and remaining ½ cup of sugar if preparing 2 cakes. Beat until the mixture thickens, the color lightens to pale yellow, and the mixture looks like soft mayonnaise, about 2 minutes. Stop the mixer and add the melted chocolate, vanilla, and almond extract, then beat on low speed to blend in the chocolate. Stop the mixer and scrape any chocolate from the sides of the bowl. With the mixer running, slowly add the flour mixture, mixing just until the flour is incorporated. Stop the mixer and scrape the sides of the bowl once during this mixing. Use a large rubber spatula to stir in any loose flour.

5. Gently stir one fourth of the egg white mixture into the chocolate mixture until smooth. Fold the remaining egg whites into the chocolate mixture. Continue folding just until no white streaks of egg white remain. Spread evenly in the prepared pan or pans. Use a thin metal spatula to gently spread the batter for a soufflé sheet evenly over the baking sheet.

· Sprinkle the top of a baked cake roll with cocoa powder to prevent the roll from sticking to itself when you unroll it. The cake will shrink about an inch as it cools; a cooled cake layer baked in a 9-inch round pan will shrink to about 8 inches and a rolled cake sheet will be about 16 inches long.

· This thin cake is delicate, so remove the paper liner and roll up the cake carefully. If the cake should break, any cracks will not show when it is rolled with the filling.

Doubling the Recipe

For more than two layers, prepare separate batches.

To Freeze Cake Layers and Sheets

Wrap cake layers tightly with plastic wrap then heavy aluminum foil. Label with date and contents. Freeze up to 3 months. Once the cake freezes, it may be stacked in the freezer.

To Cool, Roll, and Freeze a Baked Soufflé Sheet

After cooling the cake in the baking sheet for 5 minutes, use a strainer to sift 1 tablespoon cocoa powder evenly over the top. The cake will be evenly covered with a thin layer of cocoa powder. Invert the cake onto a clean dish towel. The long side of the cake should be parallel to the edge of the counter. Carefully peel off the paper and place it back on the cake. Roll up the cake in the dish towel. Let the cake cool in the towel for 1 to 2 hours. Unroll the cake sheet. Discard the paper and place a piece of plastic wrap over the cake. Using the towel to help, roll up the cake with the plastic wrap, but not the towel. Carefully wrap plastic wrap then heavy aluminum foil around the cake roll. Freeze up to 3 months.

To Defrost

Defrost the wrapped cake in the refrigerator. A cold cake sheet is easier to handle than a warm one.

6. Bake until a toothpick inserted in the center of a layer cake comes out clean, about 18 minutes. If using a baking sheet, bake the cake for exactly 10 minutes; the center may look slightly moist. Remove the cake from the oven. Immediately use a small sharp knife to loosen the cake from the edges of the pan.

7. Cool a cake layer in the pan for 5 minutes. Invert the cake layer onto a cake rack. Carefully peel off the paper and discard. Invert the cake right side up and cool thoroughly.

DARK
CHOCOLATE SAUCE

*C*hocolate sauce made with unsweetened cocoa powder rather than chocolate produces a dark, smooth sauce that I use to surround a slice of Frozen Milky Way Mousse (page 288) or Iced Fresh Ginger Mousse (page 284). Even when chilled, the sauce has a syrupy rather than a fudgelike consistency.

MAKES ABOUT 1 1/2 CUPS

1 cup half-and-half
3 tablespoons unsalted butter, cut into 3 pieces
1/3 cup unsweetened Dutch process cocoa, such as Droste or Hershey's
  European Style, sifted
1/2 cup sugar
1/2 teaspoon instant decaffeinated coffee granules
1 teaspoon vanilla extract

Put the half-and-half, butter, cocoa, sugar, and coffee granules in a medium saucepan. Whisk over medium-low heat until the butter melts and the sugar, cocoa, and coffee dissolve. Bring the mixture to a simmer. Simmer 1 minute, whisking constantly; the mixture will form small bubbles but should not boil. Remove the saucepan from the heat and add the vanilla. Pour the sauce into a storage container and refrigerate, loosely covered with plastic wrap, until the sauce is cold. Cover tightly and store the sauce up to 2 weeks in the refrigerator or freeze.

VARIATION Stir 1 tablespoon Grand Marnier or dark rum into the cooked chocolate sauce.

Good Advice
· Sift the cocoa powder and use a whisk rather than a mixing spoon to stir the sauce so the cocoa powder dissolves easily.

Doubling the Recipe
Double the ingredients.

To Freeze
Divide the sauce between two plastic freezer containers. Leave at least 1 inch of space in the top of each freezer container. Press a piece of plastic wrap onto the top of the chilled chocolate sauce and cover the container tightly. Label with date and contents. Freeze up to 2 months.

To Serve
Defrost the sauce in the covered container overnight in the refrigerator. Stir the sauce until smooth and serve cold. Or heat the sauce in a small saucepan over low heat. Cook until the sauce is warm to the touch, about 110°F. if measured with a food thermometer.

CHOCOLATE TRUFFLE SAUCE

Good Advice
· Stir the chocolate gently into the hot cream so that it does not splash out of the pan.

· Stir the sifted cocoa powder into the hot half-and-half with a whisk, and it will dissolve easily.

Doubling the Recipe
Double or triple the ingredients.

To Freeze
Pour the sauce into a plastic freezer container leaving 1 inch of space at the top of the container. Loosely cover and cool for an hour at room temperature. Press a piece of plastic wrap onto the top of the sauce and cover the container tightly. Or divide each batch of sauce between two plastic containers. Label with date and contents. Freeze up to 2 months.

I probably make Chocolate Truffle Sauce more often than any other recipe in this book. It can be used as a fudge sauce drizzled over a dish of ice cream or an ice cream pie, as a glaze to cover a cake, or even as a filling for a pie. When lightly whipped, the sauce becomes a creamy filling for a cake or tart. Now I, as much as anybody, like easy recipes, and preparing this truffle sauce, which is simply a matter of melting chopped chocolate in hot cream and butter, is about as easy as it gets.

I offer two truffle sauces. One is Thick Chocolate Truffle Sauce, my super thick, fudgy version made from whipping cream and plenty of chocolate. It forms a firm chocolate glaze for the Peanut Butter Pie with Fudge Topping (page 68) and adds a rich chocolate flavor to a Vanilla and Chocolate Truffle Cheesecake (page 150) or Chocolate Cream Pie (page 66). The other one, my Slightly Thinner Chocolate Truffle Sauce, uses half-and-half instead of cream and less chocolate, and it forms softer chunks when it freezes—as in the Dark Chocolate and Chunky Banana Ice Cream Pie (page 272). It combines smoothly with whipped cream for the frosting in Lisa's Chocolate Chip Birthday Cake (page 184) and flavors the Ribbon of Fudge Chocolate Cake (page 214). Cocoa powder darkens the thinner sauce and gives it a bittersweet flavor. Either sauce can be whipped to a creamy consistency or warmed to serve over ice cream.

THICK CHOCOLATE TRUFFLE SAUCE
Makes about 2 cups

3/4 cup whipping cream
2 tablespoons (1/4 stick) unsalted butter, cut into 2 pieces
12 ounces (2 cups) semisweet chocolate chips or semisweet chocolate, chopped
1 teaspoon vanilla extract

SLIGHTLY THINNER CHOCOLATE TRUFFLE SAUCE
Makes about 1 1/2 cups

3/4 cup half-and-half
1 tablespoon unsalted butter
2 tablespoons unsweetened Dutch process cocoa powder, such as Droste
   or Hershey's European Style, sifted
8 ounces (1 1/3 cups) semisweet chocolate chips or semisweet chocolate,
   chopped
1 teaspoon vanilla extract

Put the cream and butter or half-and-half and butter in a medium saucepan and heat over medium-low heat until the cream is hot and the butter is melted. The hot cream mixture will form tiny bubbles and measure about 175°F. on a food thermometer. Do not let the mixture boil. Remove the pan from the heat. Add the chopped chocolate and cocoa powder, if using, and let it melt in the hot cream mixture for about 30 seconds to soften. Add the vanilla and whisk the sauce until it is smooth and all of the chocolate is melted and any cocoa powder is incorporated.

To Serve
Remove as many containers of sauce from the freezer as needed. Defrost the sauce in the covered container overnight in the refrigerator. Warm the sauce in a medium saucepan over low heat, stirring frequently. Use the sauce warm as hot fudge sauce or as directed in the recipes in this book. If you need the sauce in a hurry and don't have time to defrost it, run hot water over the covered container and remove the frozen sauce from the container. Warm the sauce in a heatproof container placed over (not touching) barely simmering water, stirring often. Leftover sauce can be stored up to 2 weeks in the refrigerator.

CARAMEL FILLING AND CARAMEL SAUCE

Good Advice

· As the sugar cooks, it may crystallize and harden. Keep cooking it, and the crystals will melt; the mixture will become smooth when the sugar caramelizes. Since the sugar is cooked to above 320°F., any sugar crystals will melt. When the sugar starts to turn golden, watch it carefully, as it will caramelize quickly. The cooking method is the same for Caramel Filling and Caramel Sauce; only the amount of cream varies.

· Caramel is very hot, so be careful not to splash any on yourself. When you add the hot cream to the hot sugar, the mixture will bubble vigorously. Cook caramel in a large saucepan so that the mixture doesn't bubble up out of the pot.

Doubling the Recipe

Double the ingredients. Use a large saucepan, about 8-quart size, for a double recipe.

Cooking sugar to the caramel stage is one of the easiest cooking techniques I know, yet it always impresses people when you serve homemade caramel. It's simply a matter of melting sugar, cooking it to a dark golden or caramel color, and adding hot cream, which turns the caramelized sugar into a creamy caramel mixture. The amount of cream added to the caramelized sugar determines the consistency of the caramel: Use less cream for a thicker mixture ideal for filling a pie or tart, more cream for a sauce for serving with desserts or pouring over ice cream.

CARAMEL FILLING
Makes 2 cups

1½ cups whipping cream
½ cup water
2 cups sugar

CARAMEL SAUCE
Makes 1⅓ cups

1 cup whipping cream
¼ cup water
1 cup sugar

I. Heat the cream in a small saucepan and keep it hot, about 150°F. when measured with a food thermometer, without boiling it.

2. Put the water and sugar in a 4-quart heavy-bottom saucepan. Cover and cook over low heat until the sugar dissolves, about 5 minutes. Stir the mixture occasionally to help the sugar dissolve. Remove the cover, increase the heat to medium-high, and bring to a boil. Boil the mixture until the sugar melts, caramelizes, and turns a dark golden color, about 5 minutes. Watch the sugar carefully and stir it with a wooden spoon occasionally to ensure the sugar cooks evenly and all of the sugar caramelizes. Remove the caramel from the heat.

3. Slowly and carefully add the hot cream to the hot sugar. The mixture will bubble up, so be careful. Return the saucepan to medium heat and cook, stirring with the wooden spoon, until the caramel is completely dissolved and the mixture is smooth. The caramel mixture is ready to use. Or it can be covered and refrigerated up to 2 weeks or frozen up to 2 months.

VARIATION For a coffee-flavored caramel sauce, dissolve 2 teaspoons instant decaffeinated coffee granules in the whipping cream. Heat the dissolved coffee with the cream in the small saucepan.

To Freeze

Pour the warm sauce into a plastic freezer container or divide it between two plastic freezer containers, leaving at least 1 inch of space in the top of the container. You will need $1\frac{1}{2}$ cups caramel filling for the Milk Chocolate and Caramel Pecan Tart (page 111), so you might want to divide the caramel filling with this in mind. Loosely cover and cool for 1 hour at room temperature. Press plastic wrap onto the surface of the caramel sauce and chill thoroughly. Cover the container tightly. Label with date and contents. Freeze up to 2 months.

To Use Filling or Serve Sauce

Defrost the filling or sauce at room temperature for about 5 hours. Put the filling or sauce in a medium saucepan and warm it over low heat just until it pours easily.

NUTTY PRALINES

Cook sugar to the caramel stage, then add nuts to the hot caramel, and you have praline, a brittle that can be ground to a powder or crushed into small pieces. It's a multipurpose dessert ingredient that you can use to flavor meringues or garnish a cake. Hazelnuts and almonds are the nuts traditionally used for praline, but you can use all kinds of nuts. Every time you change the nut, you have a new flavor of praline.

MAKES 2 CUPS

¾ cup sugar
1 cup unsalted nuts, such as slivered blanched almonds, cashew nuts, skinned toasted hazelnuts, macadamia nuts (unsalted macadamia nuts are hard to find; use salted ones and brush away as much salt as possible), roasted pistachios, pecans, or walnuts

1. Lightly oil a metal baking sheet.

2. Put the sugar in a medium saucepan and cook over low heat. Stir occasionally with a long-handled wooden spoon to ensure the sugar melts evenly. When the sugar begins to melt, increase the heat to medium and cook the melted sugar to a light golden color. Add the nuts, stirring with the wooden spoon to coat them completely with the caramelized sugar, about 1 minute. The mixture will turn a slightly darker golden color. Immediately pour the praline onto the baking sheet and spread it with the wooden spoon. Be careful as the mixture is very hot. Cool the praline until it hardens and is cool to the touch.

3. Break the praline into 1- to 2-inch pieces. Wrap several pieces at a time in heavy aluminum foil. Crush the praline with a rolling pin, or into ¼- to ⅜-inch pieces. To prepare praline powder, transfer the crushed praline to a food processor fitted with a metal blade and process just until the praline forms a powder. Overprocessing can turn the praline into a paste. Use the same day or freeze.

Good Advice

· Caramelized sugar is very hot, so be careful not to touch it or to splash any on yourself. Since the sugar is cooked to over 320°F., if any sugar crystals form, the high heat will melt them. There is no worry about sugar crystallizing and becoming grainy. When the sugar starts to turn golden, watch it carefully as it will darken and caramelize quickly.

· Stir smaller nuts or chopped nuts constantly since they burn easily. The larger the nut the less the praline will spread when you pour it onto the baking sheet to cool.

· Brush away loose skins from pistachio nuts before adding the nuts to the sugar.

Doubling the Recipe
Double the ingredients.

To Freeze
Put crushed or ground praline in a plastic freezer container. Press plastic wrap onto the praline and cover tightly. Freeze up to 3 months. Praline can be used directly from the freezer. Spoon out the amount needed and return the remaining praline to the freezer.

CHOCOLATE CURLS, TUBES, STRIPES, LACE, FANCIFUL SHAPES, AND CUPS

I keep several containers of these chocolate finishing touches in my freezer ready to dress up desserts at a moment's notice. Delicate chocolate decorations are easy to handle and less likely to break when they are cold. With these decorations, I can quickly cover an 80th Birthday Strawberry and White Chocolate Cake (page 192) with white chocolate curls, add stripes of chocolate bark to a Winter White Yule Log (page 205), top an ice cream sundae with long chocolate tubes, or serve scoops of Cinnamon Ice Cream in Chocolate Cups (page 264).

When preparing chocolate decorations, I use several techniques to achieve the different results. After years of experimentation, I finally found an easy way to make smooth-sided, graceful chocolate cups. I spread a circle of melted chocolate over a parchment paper square and form cups over the bottom of a small glass. The chocolate-covered paper falls in graceful folds around the glass and the parchment paper peels easily from the finished chocolate cup. For chocolate stripes, lace, and various shapes, I spread melted chocolate over parchment paper and peel off the paper after the chocolate hardens. Chocolate curls require just a vegetable peeler and a large block of chocolate; long chocolate tubes can be scraped easily from a sheet of melted chocolate applied to the back of a baking sheet.

CHOCOLATE CURLS
Makes about 4 cups

8 ounces semisweet, bittersweet, milk, or white chocolate, in 1 piece about 1 to 1¼ inches thick and about 3 inches square, Callebaut or Guittard preferred

· Since the heat of your hands can melt fragile chocolate decorations, use a spoon or pastry scraper when handling them.

· The only challenge involved in making chocolate curls is getting the block of chocolate to the correct temperature. Too cold and the chocolate forms grated shreds; too warm and it sticks to the vegetable peeler. When the chocolate is just the right temperature, it rolls off the peeler in smooth curls. I have several ways to bring the chocolate to the proper point—where it looks as if it's starting to melt but isn't actually melted. One is to put the chocolate in a sunny window or in a barely heated oven. My most dependable method is to hold the chocolate between the palms of my hands until it warms slightly. When you do this, it's easy to feel the chocolate begin to soften, and there's no danger of it melting. The process, however, can take several minutes and requires some patience. Scrape chocolate curls from a large block of chocolate rather than a thin chocolate bar, which will easily break. Once the chocolate becomes too small to scrape comfortably, set it aside to melt in another recipe and switch to a large piece of chocolate.

· When preparing chocolate tubes, warm the baking sheet before spreading melted chocolate over it. The melted chocolate will spread smoothly and evenly on the warm baking sheet.

Doubling the Recipe

Increase the amount of chocolate to make a larger quantity of decorations.

To Freeze Chocolate Decorations

Spoon or lift cold chocolate curls, tubes, stripes, lace, and shapes into a plastic freezer container. Gently press plastic wrap onto the

1. Have ready a baking sheet lined with wax paper and a stainless-steel vegetable peeler with a 2$\frac{1}{2}$-inch swivel blade.

2. Hold the chocolate between the palms of your hands and warm it with your hands for about 2 minutes. White and milk chocolate may take less time to soften and any chocolate will take longer to warm in a cold room. On a hot day Callebaut white chocolate may not need any hand warming. If your hands are cold, run them under warm water to warm them slightly and dry them. When the chocolate is ready, it will feel slightly sticky. Dark chocolate will lose some of its shine.

3. To shave the chocolate, hold the chocolate in one hand and use the vegetable peeler to scrape curls from the block of chocolate in a single layer onto the baking sheet. Scrape the peeler away from you. Scrape in 1$\frac{1}{2}$- to 2-inch-long strokes along the chocolate and make the curls about 1 inch wide. Scrape along all sides of the chocolate. The curls will vary in shape and size. Longer shavings will form curls and shorter shavings will form curves. You will not use all of the chocolate if preparing 4 cups of curls, but a large piece of chocolate is easy to handle. If the chocolate curls begin to flake and break, the chocolate is too hard and should be held between your hands again until it softens. Put the baking sheet in the freezer for about 30 minutes to firm the curls.

CHOCOLATE TUBES AND SMALL CURLS
6 ounces semisweet or bittersweet chocolate, Callebaut or Guittard
    preferred, chopped
2 ounces white chocolate, Callebaut or Baker's Premium preferred,
    chopped (optional)

1. Preheat the oven to 175°F. Place the dark chocolate in an ovenproof container and white chocolate in a nonreactive ovenproof container. Put the chocolate in the oven and leave it until it melts, 8 to 12 minutes. Remove the chocolate from the oven and stir it smooth.

2. Have ready a baking sheet lined with wax paper. Raise the oven heat to 275°F. Put a clean baking sheet with 1-inch-high sides in the oven until it is warm, about 5 minutes. Remove the baking sheet from the oven and turn it bot-

tom side up. Use a thin metal spatula to spread the melted chocolate in an even layer over the bottom of the baking sheet.

3. To create marbleized chocolate tubes, spread the dark chocolate on the bottom of the baking sheet. Drizzle the melted white chocolate over the dark chocolate and use the spatula to swirl the 2 chocolates together. Swirl gently so that the white chocolate shows clearly and is not mixed completely into the dark chocolate.

4. Let the chocolate sit until you can touch it with your finger and it doesn't leave a mark. The chocolate will be softly firm. The surface of the chocolate will change from shiny to dull. The time it takes for the chocolate to firm depends on the temperature of your kitchen. In a warm kitchen it could take as long as 3 hours. You can speed the cooling process by putting the baking sheet in the refrigerator for a few minutes. Check the chocolate often and remove it from the refrigerator as soon as it begins to firm.

5. Place the baking sheet chocolate side up on a damp dish towel to steady it. Use a rigid pastry scraper to scrape tubes ranging in size from $1\frac{1}{2}$ to 4 inches wide. Place the bottom edge of the scraper at a 45° angle to the baking sheet, $1\frac{1}{2}$ to 2 inches from the bottom edge of the chocolate, and $1\frac{1}{2}$ to 4 inches from the right or left edge of the chocolate. Push the scraper firmly away from you and the chocolate will roll into a tube. Spoon each tube onto the paper-lined baking sheet. Repeat to form tubes from the remaining chocolate. If the chocolate breaks as you roll it, the chocolate is too cold. If the chocolate sticks to the scraper and curls don't form, the chocolate is too warm. Put the baking sheet in the freezer for about 30 minutes to firm the tubes.

6. To make small chocolate curls, use a soup spoon to scrape the chocolate. Pull the spoon toward you and small curls will form.

DARK AND WHITE CHOCOLATE STRIPES
6 ounces white chocolate, Callebaut or Baker's Premium preferred, chopped
4 ounces semisweet or bittersweet chocolate, Callebaut or Guittard preferred, chopped

chocolate and cover the container tightly. Wrap each cold chocolate cup carefully in plastic wrap. Place the cups in a single layer in a metal or plastic freezer container and cover tightly. Label with date and contents. Freeze up to 3 months. Do not defrost the chocolate decorations before using them and they will be less likely to melt.

I. Melt the chocolate as described on page 56.

2. Turn a baking sheet bottom side up and cover it with parchment paper. Use a thin metal spatula to spread the melted white chocolate evenly over the parchment paper. Let the white chocolate sit until it firms slightly and lines remain in the chocolate when a decorating comb is drawn across it, about 15 minutes for Callebaut or Lindt white chocolate and about 5 minutes for Baker's Premium. Use the medium tines on a metal decorating comb to draw parallel lines in one direction across the white chocolate. Wipe excess white chocolate off the decorating comb. Let sit about 10 minutes, or until the chocolate is firm to the touch.

3. Spread the melted dark chocolate over the white chocolate. The dark chocolate will fill in the lines created by the decorating comb. Let the chocolate firm slightly, about 5 minutes. Use a large sharp knife to mark rectangular or square shapes in the chocolate. Press straight down with the knife to form straight, sharp edges. To make the chocolate stripes for the yule log (see page 205), cut rectangles that measure 1 × 2 inches. Put the baking sheet in the freezer for about 30 minutes to firm the chocolate. Break or cut the marked chocolate into the desired shapes.

CHOCOLATE LACE
3 ounces semisweet or bittersweet chocolate, Callebaut or Guittard preferred, chopped
1 ounce white chocolate, Callebaut or Baker's Premium preferred, chopped (optional)

I. Melt the chocolate as described on page 56.

2. Line a baking sheet with parchment paper. Use a teaspoon to drizzle thin lines of the dark chocolate over the parchment. Drizzle the chocolate in a circular motion to make a lace pattern and in crisscross lines to form a crosshatch pattern. Check to see that the lines connect to give the lace a sturdy structure. Three ounces of chocolate will cover an area about 12 × 10 inches. If desired, drizzle lines of white chocolate over the dark chocolate. Put the baking sheet in the freezer for about 30 minutes to firm the chocolate.

3. Turn the chocolate paper side up on the baking sheet and peel the paper from the chocolate. Break or cut the chocolate lace into random pieces about 3 to 4 inches in size. Turn the chocolate lace top side up to use. The lace can also be made with white chocolate.

CHOCOLATE STARS, HEARTS, TRIANGLES, AND SQUARES
6 ounces semisweet or bittersweet chocolate, Callebaut or Guittard preferred, chopped

1. Melt the chocolate as described on page 56.

2. Turn a baking sheet bottom side up and cover it with parchment paper. Use a thin metal spatula to spread the melted chocolate evenly over the parchment paper into a rectangle about 13 × 10 inches. The chocolate should cover the paper so that the paper does not show through the chocolate. The chocolate will look shiny and wet. Put the chocolate-covered baking sheet in the refrigerator and chill it just until the chocolate looks dull and dry and is soft but no longer melted, about 5 minutes for white chocolate and about 3 minutes for dark chocolate. Do not let the chocolate harden.

3. Use a sharp knife to trim the edges of each chocolate sheet into a 12 × 9-inch rectangle. Use the knife to mark twelve 3-inch squares on each sheet of chocolate. Cut each square diagonally into triangles, if desired. Do not draw the knife across the chocolate, but press down to make sharp edges. Check to see that the knife cuts completely through the chocolate. If the chocolate is too soft and runs together, chill it until it is firm enough to hold the cut marks. If the chocolate hardens and then cracks when it is cut, warm the chocolate sheet in the oven for a few seconds. Or do not trim the edges of the chocolate into a rectangle and use a heart-, star-, or half moon–shape metal cutter to cut chocolate shapes. Depending on the size of the cutter, you will have 12 to 24 chocolate shapes. Return the marked chocolate to the refrigerator to firm completely, about 30 minutes.

4. Remove the baking sheet from the refrigerator. Turn the chocolate paper side up on the baking sheet. Peel the paper from the chocolate. The chocolate

will separate easily into squares or other shapes. Use a large knife to separate any squares that stick together or to trim any hearts or other shapes that do not fall free.

INDIVIDUAL DARK CHOCOLATE CUPS
Makes 6 cups

12 ounces semisweet or bittersweet chocolate, Callebaut or Guittard preferred, chopped

I. Melt the chocolate as described on page 56.

2. Place 6 small juice glasses or tomato paste cans, about 2 inches in diameter and about 3 inches high, about 4 inches apart on a baking sheet. Cut six 8-inch squares of parchment paper. Use a thin metal spatula to spread about a sixth of the melted chocolate in a circle about 7 inches in diameter over each parchment square. Place the squares, paper side down, over the bottom of the glasses. The parchment paper will fall in gentle folds. Do not let the folds touch, or the paper will not remove easily. Because the parchment paper is only partially covered with chocolate, the paper squares are easy to handle. Refrigerate the chocolate until firm, about 1 hour. Lift a chocolate cup from the glass and carefully tear the paper from the chocolate cup. Repeat to peel the paper from the remaining cups.

Fast Chocolate Desserts for Sudden Chocolate Attacks

I have two ways of dealing with my frequent chocolate cravings. One is to grab a handful of chocolate chips for immediate gratification, and the second, even more satisfying method, is to whip up one of these easy desserts. Although there are lots of quick-and-easy desserts featured throughout this book, the ones in this chapter can be prepared in thirty minutes or less, including any baking time. Nutella Ice Cream Torte, informal Chocolate Chocolate Chip Cookies, or sophisticated Mocha Marble Mousse is less than an hour away.

These desserts are fast, not because I cut corners but because of clever techniques. Melted marshmallows thicken a mousse, storebought ladyfingers and sorbet fill a party terrine, and peanut butter makes quick work of a pie filling. Crushed Amaretti di Saronno cookies or drizzles of melted chocolate add fast decorative toppings. Other desserts employ simple homemade components that take just minutes to prepare. All that is needed for a Chocolate Cream Pie filling is some Thick Chocolate Truffle Sauce and whipped cream. If you find yourself really pressed for time, try these ready-in-no-time chocolate desserts.

CHOCOLATE CHOCOLATE CHIP COOKIES

What's better than a chocolate chip cookie? These all chocolate chocolate chip cookies, crisp on the outside and soft in the center, are a strong contender.

MAKES ABOUT SIXTEEN 3^1/$_2$-INCH COOKIES

3/4 cup plus 1 tablespoon unbleached all-purpose flour
1/3 cup unsweetened Dutch process cocoa powder, such as Droste or Hershey's European Style
1 teaspoon baking soda
1/2 teaspoon salt
1/4 pound (1 stick) unsalted butter, softened slightly for about 30 minutes
1/2 cup (firmly packed) light brown sugar
6 tablespoons granulated sugar
1 large cold egg
1 teaspoon vanilla extract
2 cups semisweet chocolate chips (12 ounces)

1. Position 2 oven racks in the middle and upper third of the oven. Preheat the oven to 325°F. Line 2 baking sheets with heavy aluminum foil.

2. Sift the flour, cocoa powder, baking soda, and salt together and set aside.

3. Put the butter, brown sugar, and granulated sugar in the large bowl of an electric mixer and beat on medium speed for about 1 minute, or until the mixture is smooth. Add the egg and vanilla and mix on low speed for about 30 seconds, or until they are blended thoroughly. Decrease the speed to low and add the flour mixture, mixing just until the flour is incorporated. Stop the mixer and scrape the bowl during this mixing. Stir in the chocolate chips.

4. Using 2 tablespoons of dough for each cookie, roll the dough between the palms of your hands into a ball about 1 3/4 inches in diameter. Place the cookie balls about 2 1/2 inches apart on the prepared baking sheets.

Good Advice
· Chocolate scorches easily, so these cookies, with their high chocolate content, can easily burn on the bottom. If you line the cookie sheets with heavy aluminum foil, and check the cookies carefully as they near the end of the baking time, you will have no problem.

· Baking the cookies at 325°F., rather than at the higher baking temperature often used for chocolate chip cookies, ensures perfectly baked cookies.

Doubling the Recipe
Use 1 1/2 teaspoons baking soda and 3/4 teaspoon salt and double the remaining ingredients.

5. Bake the cookies about 15 minutes or until the tops of the cookies change from shiny to dull. Reverse the baking sheets after 7 minutes front to back and top to bottom, to ensure even browning. Watch the cookies carefully as they near the end of their baking time. Remove the cookies from the oven when the tops become evenly dull. The center of the cookies will be soft.

6. Cool the cookies thoroughly on the baking sheets. As the cookies cool, they will flatten and the tops will wrinkle. Wrinkled tops indicate an excellent chocolate chip cookie.

To Freeze

Place the bottoms of 2 cookies together and wrap them in plastic wrap. Put the wrapped cookies in a metal or plastic freezer container and cover tightly. Label with date and contents. Freeze up to 3 months.

To Serve

Remove as many cookies from the freezer as needed and defrost the wrapped cookies at room temperature. Serve within 3 days. If you prefer cookies with warm, soft chocolate chips, unwrap the defrosted cookies, spread them in a single layer on a baking sheet, and warm them in a preheated 200°F. oven for 5 minutes.

MOCHA PIE

Two creamy layers, one chocolate and one coffee, fill a walnut–cookie crumb crust in this easy no-bake pie. Drizzle lacy lines of melted chocolate on top of the pie to make a quick, fancy finish that will also protect the soft topping from getting squashed by its wrapping.

SERVES 8

1 Graham Cracker Crumb Crust with walnuts (page 40) baked in a 10-inch pie pan, cooled or frozen

CHOCOLATE CREAM FILLING
6 ounces semisweet chocolate, chopped
1 ounce unsweetened chocolate, chopped
³/₄ cup heavy whipping cream
¹/₂ teaspoon instant decaffeinated coffee granules
6 ounces (1¹/₂ sticks) very soft unsalted butter
1 cup powdered sugar, sifted
1 teaspoon vanilla extract

1 ounce semisweet chocolate, for drizzling

COFFEE WHIPPED CREAM TOPPING
1 cup cold heavy whipping cream
1 tablespoon instant decaffeinated coffee granules
¹/₂ cup powdered sugar
1 teaspoon vanilla extract

Prepare the Chocolate Cream Filling

1. Put the 6 ounces of semisweet chocolate, the unsweetened chocolate, heavy cream, and coffee granules in a medium saucepan and cook over low heat, stirring often, until the chocolate is melted and the mixture is smooth. Pour the mixture into a small bowl. Cool to room temperature, about 75°F. To cool the mixture quickly, put the bowl in the freezer, uncovered, for about 5 minutes. Stir the mixture once to help it cool evenly.

2. Put the butter in the large bowl of an electric mixer and beat at medium speed until smooth, about 30 seconds. Decrease the speed to low and mix in the powdered sugar and vanilla. Increase the speed to medium and beat until the

· If you are in a hurry to cool down the crumb crust after baking, put it in the freezer, uncovered, for 10 minutes while you prepare the pie filling. Put the warm crust on a dish towel directly on a freezer shelf, being careful not to rest it on frozen food that it might defrost.

· The butter for the chocolate filling must be very soft. A sunny window is a good place to soften the butter.

· By using heavy whipping cream and adding a portion of the chocolate filling to the coffee whipped cream topping, you add fat and density to the whipped cream so it becomes suitable for freezing. Stop mixing the whipped cream topping as soon as firm peaks form. Overbeating will cause a grainy texture.

· Rather than turning the oven on just to melt one ounce of semisweet chocolate for the garnish, I melt it over hot water.

mixture is smooth and fluffy, about 2 minutes. Decrease the speed to low, slowly add the cooled chocolate mixture, and beat 1 minute. Stop the mixer and scrape the sides of the bowl to incorporate all of the chocolate. The mixture will look smooth and shiny. Reserve ½ cup of the chocolate cream mixture to add to the whipped cream topping and set aside. Spread the remaining chocolate cream evenly in the prepared crust.

Melt the Semisweet Chocolate

3. Put the 1 ounce of semisweet chocolate in a small heatproof container set over, but not touching, a saucepan of barely simmering water. Stir the chocolate over the hot water until it is melted and smooth. Remove from over the water to cool slightly.

Prepare the Coffee Whipped Cream Topping

4. Put the heavy cream, instant coffee, powdered sugar, and vanilla in the large bowl of an electric mixer. With the mixer on medium speed, add the reserved ½ cup of chocolate cream filling. Increase the speed to medium-high and beat to firm peaks. The mixture will thicken quickly, and the movement of the beaters will form a teardrop pattern in the cream when firm peaks form. Spread the coffee whipped cream topping evenly over the chocolate filling. Dip a fork in the melted semisweet chocolate and drizzle thin lines of chocolate in a random pattern over the top of the pie. The pie is ready to serve or it can be frozen.

Doubling the Recipe
Use two crusts and double the remaining ingredients.

To Freeze
Chill the pie, uncovered, in the freezer until the topping is firm. Wrap the pie tightly with plastic wrap then heavy aluminum foil, gently pressing the aluminum foil against the pie. Label with date and contents. Freeze up to 1 month.

To Serve
Defrost the wrapped pie in the refrigerator overnight. Serve the pie cold. Leftover pie can be covered and stored in the refrigerator up to 2 days.

CHOCOLATE CREAM PIE

Chocolate truffle sauce plays a double role in this no-cook cream pie. Pure truffle sauce makes a thin, fudgy layer between the chocolate cream and the crust while also keeping the crust crisp by separating it from the cream layer. Then truffle sauce is whipped with cream for a quick chocolate filling.

SERVES 8

¾ cup Thick Chocolate Truffle Sauce (page 50), warmed just until smooth and pourable
1 Chocolate Wafer Cookie Crumb Crust (page 40) baked in a 10-inch pie pan, cooled or frozen

CHOCOLATE CREAM FILLING
1¼ cups cold whipping cream
1 tablespoon unsweetened Dutch process cocoa powder, such as Droste or Hershey's European Style
½ teaspoon instant decaffeinated coffee granules
1 cup Thick Chocolate Truffle Sauce (page 50), cooled thoroughly or defrosted and softened over low heat just until it spoons easily

1 cup semisweet Chocolate Curls (page 55), not defrosted if using chocolate curls from the freezer

I. Pour the ¾ cup truffle sauce over the crumb crust. Use a metal spatula to carefully spread an even layer of sauce over the crust.

Prepare the Chocolate Cream Filling

2. Put the cream, cocoa powder, and coffee granules in the large bowl of an electric mixer and beat on low speed until the cocoa powder and coffee dissolve. Mix in the truffle sauce. Stop the mixer and scrape the sides of the bowl to incorporate any truffle sauce that splashes onto the sides of the bowl. As soon as the

Good Advice
· Spread the truffle sauce carefully over the crust so the crumbs in the crust are not disturbed.

· The Thick Chocolate Truffle Sauce must be cooled thoroughly or defrosted and softened over low heat just until it is soft enough to spoon easily before you whip it with the cream (about 85°F. if measured with a food thermometer). If the truffle sauce is too warm, the cream will not whip properly.

· Topping the pie with chocolate curls adds a crunchy dimension to match the crisp crust and protects the top of the pie when it is wrapped.

truffle sauce is blended with the cream, increase the speed to medium and beat just until firm peaks form.

3. Spread the chocolate cream evenly over the truffle sauce in the crust. Spoon the chocolate curls over the top of the pie. The pie is ready to serve or it can be frozen.

Doubling the Recipe
Use two crusts and double the remaining ingredients.

To Freeze
Freeze the pie, uncovered, until the topping is firm. Wrap the pie tightly with plastic wrap then heavy aluminum foil, gently pressing the aluminum foil against the pie. Label with date and contents. Freeze up to 1 month.

To Serve
Defrost the wrapped pie in the refrigerator at least 5 hours or overnight. Serve the pie cold. Leftover pie can be covered and refrigerated up to 2 days.

PEANUT BUTTER PIE WITH FUDGE TOPPING

Recently I developed a line of ready-made desserts for our local market to sell from the freezer. This peanut butter pie has become a favorite, with people stopping me every day on the street to say how much they enjoy it. The pie has a crisp chocolate crust, creamy peanut butter filling, and thick fudge topping.

SERVES 8 TO 10

PEANUT BUTTER FILLING
8 ounces cream cheese, softened about 2 hours
1 cup creamy peanut butter
1 cup powdered sugar, sifted
1 cup cold whipping cream
1 teaspoon vanilla extract

1 Chocolate Wafer Cookie Crumb Crust (page 40) baked in a 10-inch pie pan, cooled or frozen
1 cup Thick Chocolate Truffle Sauce (page 50), warmed just until smooth and pourable

Prepare the Peanut Butter Filling

I. Put the cream cheese and peanut butter in the large bowl of an electric mixer. Beat on medium speed until blended thoroughly. Decrease the speed to low and add the powdered sugar. Mix until all of the sugar is incorporated. Set aside.

2. Put the whipping cream and vanilla in a clean bowl of an electric mixer. Beat the cream on medium speed until soft peaks form. Whisk a third of the whipped cream into the peanut butter mixture. Use a rubber spatula to gently but thoroughly fold in the remaining whipped cream.

Good Advice
· Soften the cream cheese thoroughly, about 2 hours, so that it combines smoothly with the peanut butter. Cut the cream cheese into several pieces and it will soften more quickly than as a large block.

· The flavor of this pie depends on using good quality peanut butter. Use a creamy peanut butter that tastes good to you.

· The pie is so rich you can cut ten slices rather than the usual eight.

Doubling the Recipe
Use two crusts and double the remaining ingredients.

3. Spread the filling evenly in the prepared crust. Use a metal spatula to smooth the top of the pie. Freeze the pie until the filling is firm, about 10 minutes.

4. Pour the truffle sauce over the top of the pie, using the metal spatula to spread the sauce evenly. The pie is ready to serve or it can be frozen.

To Freeze

Chill the pie, uncovered, in the refrigerator or freezer until the topping is firm, about 30 minutes. Wrap the pie tightly with plastic wrap then heavy aluminum foil, gently pressing the aluminum foil against the pie. Label with date and contents. Freeze up to 2 months.

To Serve

Defrost the wrapped pie in the refrigerator at least 5 hours or overnight. Uncover the pie and let it sit at room temperature for 20 minutes before serving. Leftover pie can be covered and stored in the refrigerator up to 3 days.

MOCHA MARBLE MOUSSE

elted marshmallows play an unexpected role in this coffee and chocolate mousse. The fluffy marshmallows lighten the mousse mixture and the gelatin in them thickens the mousse as it chills.

SERVES 6 TO 8

7 ounces semisweet chocolate, chopped
1 cup whole milk
4 teaspoons instant decaffeinated coffee granules
4 cups miniature marshmallows (about 5½ ounces)
2 cups cold whipping cream
1 teaspoon vanilla extract

1. Preheat the oven to 175°F. Put the chocolate in a heatproof container and melt it in the oven, 10 to 12 minutes. Remove the chocolate from the oven as soon as it is melted and stir it smooth. Have ready a serving bowl with a 2- to 2½-quart capacity.

2. Heat the milk and instant coffee in a medium saucepan over medium heat until the coffee dissolves. Add the marshmallows and cook, stirring constantly, until the marshmallows dissolve. The mixture will look foamy. Pour the mixture into a large mixing bowl. Put the bowl in the freezer until the mixture is cool, thick, and syrupy, about 10 minutes. Stir the mixture once to ensure that it cools evenly. The mixture should not set firm.

3. While the coffee mixture is chilling, put the cream and vanilla in the large bowl of an electric mixer. Beat on medium-high speed until firm peaks form. Whisk the cooled coffee mixture smooth and fold it into the whipped cream.

4. Reserve 2 tablespoons of the melted chocolate and transfer the remaining melted chocolate to a large bowl. Add 1 cup of the coffee cream mixture to the chocolate and whisk it smooth. Use a large rubber spatula to fold 1 cup of the coffee cream mixture into the chocolate mixture. Pour the remaining coffee cream mixture over the chocolate mixture. Use the rubber spatula to swirl the

· Use miniature marshmallows for this recipe. They melt quickly in the warm liquid and eliminate the messy job of cutting large marshmallows into small pieces.

· Melt all of the chocolate at the same time but reserve a portion to garnish the top of the mousse. To avoid turning on the oven just to melt the chocolate, you can put it in a heatproof container and place it over, but not touching, a saucepan of barely simmering water. Stir the chocolate over the hot water until it melts.

· A soufflé dish makes a nice serving bowl for the mousse.

Doubling the Recipe

Double the ingredients and put the mousse in a 4- to 5-quart serving bowl or two 2- to 2½-quart serving bowls.

mixtures together slightly to marbleize them. Pour the mousse into the serving bowl. Dip the ends of a fork in the reserved melted chocolate and drizzle thin lines of chocolate over the top of the mousse. The mousse is ready to serve or it can be frozen.

VARIATION Fill 8 stemmed glasses with mousse. Drizzle some melted chocolate over each mousse. To freeze, wrap each glass with plastic wrap, then heavy aluminum foil. Individual glasses of mousse will defrost in about 3 hours.

To Freeze

Freeze the mousse until the top is firm, about 1 hour. Press plastic wrap on the top of the mousse. Gently press heavy aluminum foil over the mousse. Label with date and contents. Freeze up to 1 month.

To Serve

Defrost the wrapped mousse in the refrigerator, about 5 hours or overnight. Serve the mousse cold. Serve within 2 days. After 2 days some liquid may form on the bottom of the mousse.

CANNOLI TORTE

he filling for this no-bake torte is a classic Sicilian cannoli filling of sweetened ricotta cheese, chocolate chips, and orange. Crisp almond-flavored Amaretti di Saronno cookies line the pan, add crunch to the filling, and garnish the top of the torte.

SERVES 10

21 Amaretti di Saronno cookies, whole
1 pound whole milk ricotta cheese
1 cup powdered sugar, sifted
1 tablespoon grated orange zest
1 teaspoon orange flower water (optional)
1 teaspoon vanilla extract
½ cup miniature semisweet chocolate chips
12 Amaretti di Saronno cookies, broken into quarters
4 Amaretti di Saronno cookies, crushed into crumbs, for garnishing when the torte is served

I. Line the bottom of an 8-inch springform pan with heavy aluminum foil. Line the bottom of the pan with the 21 whole Amaretti di Saronno cookies, flat side facing down. There will be spaces between the cookies, which the ricotta filling will fill.

2. Put the ricotta cheese and powdered sugar in a large bowl and use a large spoon to mix them thoroughly. Stir in the orange zest, orange flower water, if using, vanilla, and chocolate chips. Stir in the 12 quartered Amaretti di Saronno cookies. Spread the ricotta mixture evenly over the cookies in the springform pan. Wrap the torte with plastic wrap and chill for 2 hours.

· Amaretti di Saronno cookies can be found in many supermarkets and gourmet food shops. The cookies are packed in pairs wrapped in colored paper.

· Orange flower water can be found in gourmet food shops, usually with the spices, or in well-stocked liquor stores. The orange flower water is optional, but it adds a soft, elusive orange fragrance to the torte.

· If the ricotta looks watery, put it in a clean strainer over a bowl and let it drain in the refrigerator, about 3 hours.

· The cookie crumb topping softens quickly, so add the crumb garnish when you are ready to serve the torte.

Doubling the Recipe
Double the ingredients and use two pans.

3. Use a small sharp knife to loosen the edges of the torte from the pan. Release the sides of the springform pan.

4. To serve the torte immediately, sprinkle the crushed cookie crumbs over the top of the torte and cut it into wedges. To freeze the torte, remove the spring-form bottom and aluminum foil after the torte is firmly frozen.

To Freeze

Freeze the torte firm, about 3 hours. Invert the torte onto a flat plate and carefully pull the springform bottom and aluminum foil away from the torte bottom. Place a platter or aluminum foil—wrapped cardboard cake circle on the bottom of the torte and turn the torte right side up. Wrap the torte tightly with plastic wrap. Gently press heavy aluminum foil around the torte. Label with date and contents. Freeze up to 2 weeks.

To Serve

Defrost the wrapped torte 4 to 5 hours in the refrigerator. Sprinkle the crushed cookie crumbs over the top of the torte and serve the torte cold. Leftover torte can be covered and stored in the refrigerator 1 day.

NUTELLA ICE CREAM TORTE

*S*ome people carry leather handbags or gold jewelry home from their Italian vacations, but I bring home nutella. Nutella is a creamy chocolate hazelnut spread that originated in Italy and is as popular there as peanut butter is here. When I first tried it, quite a few years ago, it wasn't available in the United States as it is now. My son, Peter, and I would eat it straight from the jar, using his old baby spoons so it would last longer. Supermarkets here usually stock it near the peanut butter.

This ice cream torte is the fastest party dessert I know—it takes only minutes to prepare and disappears just as quickly when I serve it. Layers of pistachio, strawberry, and vanilla ice cream are alternated with nutella. The nutella freezes firm between the ice cream layers but remains soft enough to cut easily.

SERVES 12

1 cup nutella chocolate hazelnut spread, at room temperature (13-ounce jar)
2 pints pistachio ice cream, softened until spreadable but not melted
2 pints strawberry ice cream, softened until spreadable but not melted
2 pints vanilla ice cream, softened until spreadable but not melted

1. Spoon 3 tablespoons of the nutella into a small resealable plastic bag. Press out the air and seal. Set aside to use for the topping.

2. Spread the pistachio ice cream evenly over the bottom of a 9-inch springform pan with sides at least 2¾ inches high. Spread the ice cream carefully to the edges. Using half of the remaining nutella, drop teaspoonfuls evenly over the ice cream. Do not spread the nutella to the edge. When the springform sides are removed, the edges of the ice cream will show as pastel layers without it. Spread the strawberry ice cream evenly in the pan. Drop teaspoonfuls of the remaining

· Store nutella in the refrigerator after opening it, but bring it to room temperature before using it so it spoons out easily.

· The pistachio, strawberry, and vanilla ice creams make a pretty pastel color contrast, but you can substitute other flavors that contrast in color and taste.

Doubling the Recipe

Double the ingredients and use two pans.

To Freeze

Freeze the torte 15 minutes to firm the nutella topping. Wrap the torte tightly with plastic wrap. Then cover with heavy aluminum foil, gently pressing the aluminum foil against the torte. Label with date and contents. Freeze at least 4 hours or up to 2 weeks.

nutella over the strawberry ice cream, but do not spread it to the edge. Spread the vanilla ice cream evenly in the pan. Use a thin metal spatula to smooth the top of the torte. Cut a small hole in one corner of the filled plastic bag. Press the nutella through the hole in the bag to form crisscrossing lines over the top of the torte. The lines should reach to the edge of the torte.

VARIATION Press 1 cup crushed hazelnut praline (see page 54) onto the sides of the torte at serving time.

To Remove the Springform Pan

Dip a dish towel in hot water and wring it out. Hold the hot towel around the sides of the pan for 15 seconds. Release the sides of the springform pan. Since the torte has no crust, leave it on the springform bottom for serving.

To Serve

Remove the torte from the freezer and let it soften at room temperature for about 5 minutes. Slide the torte, including the springform bottom, onto a serving platter. Use a large sharp knife to cut the torte into wedges.

GRANDMA TILLIE'S SORBET TERRINE WITH GRAND MARNIER CHOCOLATE SAUCE

Jeff's Grandma Tillie used to give large dinner parties, which always ended with some sort of frozen dessert. No last-minute fuss for her. This colorful terrine has three flavors of sorbet separated by dark chocolate sauce and surrounded by storebought ladyfingers.

. SERVES 10 TO 12

GRAND MARNIER CHOCOLATE SAUCE
1 cup whipping cream
½ cup sugar
2 tablespoons light corn syrup
½ cup unsweetened Dutch process cocoa powder, such as Droste or
    Hershey's European Style, sifted
2 ounces semisweet chocolate, chopped
1 teaspoon vanilla extract
1 tablespoon Grand Marnier

10 ladyfingers, split, or 26 crisp ladyfingers
1 pint each strawberry, lemon, and orange sorbet, slightly softened
    but not melted

Prepare the Grand Marnier Chocolate Sauce

1. Put the whipping cream, sugar, corn syrup, and cocoa powder in a medium saucepan. Cook over medium heat, whisking constantly, until the mixture comes to a simmer and the sugar and cocoa dissolve. Remove from the heat and stir in the chocolate. Stir the sauce until it is smooth and all of the chocolate is melted. Stir in the vanilla extract and Grand Marnier. Cool the sauce before using it. Or pour the sauce into a storage container and refrigerate, loosely covered with plastic wrap, until the sauce is cold. Cover tightly and store the sauce up to 2 weeks in the refrigerator or freeze it.

Good Advice
· An alternative to American-style ladyfingers is Italian-style ladyfingers, which are crisp rather than soft. They do not pull apart and are usually about an inch wide; you will need twenty-six crisp ladyfingers.

· If you use a standard 9 × 5-inch loaf pan, you will need fewer ladyfingers and will have ten servings.

· Serve the chocolate sauce cold or at room temperature. Stir cold sauce to smooth it.

Doubling the Recipe
Double the ingredients and use two pans.

To Freeze the Sauce
Pour the chocolate sauce into a plastic freezer container, leaving 1 inch of space at the top. Press a piece of plastic wrap onto the top of the chilled sauce and cover the container tightly. Label with date and contents. Freeze up to 2 months.

2. Line the bottom of a long narrow loaf pan measuring about 12¾ × 4¼ × 2½ inches with parchment paper, letting the ends of the paper extend over the ends of the pan. Line the bottom of the pan with 10 ladyfinger halves, flat side up, placing the ladyfingers side by side from one narrow end of the pan to the other. Spread the strawberry sorbet evenly over the ladyfingers. Spoon about ⅓ cup cooled chocolate sauce over the sorbet. Spread the sauce to the edges of the pan. Repeat with the lemon sorbet and another ⅓ cup sauce. Spread the orange sorbet evenly over the sauce. Press the remaining 10 ladyfinger halves, flat side down, onto the orange sorbet. Cover and refrigerate the remaining sauce to serve with the terrine.

VARIATION Add 1 tablespoon Grand Marnier to Dark Chocolate Sauce (page 49) and substitute for the Grand Marnier chocolate sauce.

To Serve the Sauce

Defrost the sauce in the covered container overnight in the refrigerator. Stir the sauce until it is smooth and serve cold or let it sit at room temperature for 1 hour.

To Freeze the Terrine

Wrap the terrine tightly with plastic wrap then heavy aluminum foil. Label with date and contents. Freeze until the sorbet is firm or up to 1 week.

To Serve the Terrine

Remove the terrine from the freezer and unwrap. Use a small sharp knife to loosen the sorbet from the sides of the pan. Place a serving plate on top of the terrine and invert it. Release the terrine from the pan by pulling on the ends of the parchment paper. Remove the pan and peel off the parchment paper. Serve slices with a spoonful of chocolate sauce.

COLD FUDGE
PARFAITS

· Use glasses with straight open tops for the sundaes rather than glasses that curve inward at the top as some wineglasses do. Sundae glasses, large goblets, or highball tumblers all work well. I use clear glasses rather than colored glasses to reveal the attractive layers.

· Soften the ice cream just until it is easy to scoop. Don't let the ice cream melt since it could form unpleasant ice crystals when it freezes again.

· The truffle sauce will be pleasantly firm, not rock hard, when it is frozen.

· It's fun to make the sundaes with several combinations of ice cream and offer a choice of flavors. Some combinations to try are: vanilla and chocolate ice cream, coffee and chocolate ice cream, vanilla ice cream and raspberry sorbet, mint chip or peppermint and chocolate ice cream, vanilla ice cream and orange sorbet.

I had a childhood friend who had a soda fountain in her house. It was a child's fantasy come true, and I dreamed of having one myself one day. A home soda fountain is not very practical, but these fudge parfaits are the next best thing. I fill tall glasses with different combinations of ice cream or sorbet layered with Slightly Thinner Chocolate Truffle Sauce and have my own mini ice cream shop ready in my freezer.

SERVES 6

1 1/2 cups Slightly Thinner Chocolate Truffle Sauce (page 50), warmed just until pourable.

4 pints ice cream, at least 2 flavors
(see Good Advice for suggestions) softened until spreadable but not melted

Have ready 6 ice cream sundae glasses, goblets, or tumblers of about 12-ounce capacity. Prepare 3 parfaits at a time to prevent the ice cream from melting during preparation. Put 1 teaspoon of truffle sauce in the bottom of each glass. Fill 3 of the glasses about a third full with one flavor of ice cream. Use about 1/3 cup ice cream for each layer. Spread 1 tablespoon of the sauce over the ice cream, using the back of a spoon to spread the sauce to the edges so that it shows through the glass. Spoon a second flavor of ice cream into each glass and spread another tablespoon of sauce. Add a layer of the first ice cream flavor and spread another tablespoon of sauce. Top with about 2 tablespoons of the second ice cream flavor and drizzle 1 or 2 teaspoons of sauce over the top. You will have 3 thick layers of ice cream and sauce topped with a small scoop of ice cream and sauce. The parfait may not reach the top of the glass. Wipe off any ice cream that has dripped onto the sides of the glass. Put the finished parfaits in the freezer. Repeat to prepare the 3 remaining parfaits and put them in the freezer. You will not use all of the fourth pint of ice cream.

VARIATION Sprinkle coarsely chopped toasted pecans or walnuts (see page 12) between the layers of ice cream and on top. Use about 1 cup of nuts for 6 parfaits.

Doubling the Recipe

Double or triple the ingredients.

To Freeze

Freeze the parfaits 15 minutes to firm the sauce. Cover each parfait with plastic wrap. Gently press heavy aluminum foil over each one. Label with date and contents. Freeze up to 1 week.

To Serve

Unwrap the parfaits and let sit at room temperature for 5 to 10 minutes to soften the ice cream slightly.

UNCLE HOWIE'S HOT FUDGE SUNDAES

*S*everal years ago my uncle Howie collected recipes from everyone in our family and had them printed in a cookbook. We sold books and donated the proceeds to cancer research. Many of the recipes were ones that I had grown up with, but I also discovered new treasures such as Uncle Howie's hot fudge sauce. The sauce remains soft even when frozen and reminds me of the homemade hot fudge sauce ice cream parlors used to serve.

MAKES 6 SUNDAES

UNCLE HOWIE'S HOT FUDGE SAUCE
3 ounces unsweetened chocolate, chopped
4 tablespoons (1/2 stick) unsalted butter
1 1/2 cups powdered sugar, sifted
3/4 cup whole or low fat evaporated milk (6 ounces)
1/8 teaspoon salt
1/2 teaspoon vanilla extract

2 pints ice cream, preferably vanilla, coffee, or raspberry, for serving

Prepare Uncle Howie's Hot Fudge Sauce

1. Put the chocolate, butter, powdered sugar, milk, and salt in a large heat-proof container set over, but not touching, a saucepan of barely simmering water. Stir the mixture over the hot water until the butter and chocolate are melted and smooth. Cook over the hot water for 10 minutes, stirring occasionally. The sauce will thicken and become shiny as it cooks. Remove the sauce from the heat and stir in the vanilla. The sauce is ready to serve or freeze. Makes 1 1/2 cups sauce.

2. Use shallow glass bowls or tall sundae glasses for the sundaes. If using shallow bowls, top scoops of ice cream with fudge sauce. If using tall glasses, alternate scoops of ice cream with fudge sauce. Use about 1/4 cup of sauce for each sundae.

Good Advice

Whole evaporated milk makes the richest sauce, but low fat evaporated milk produces an acceptable sauce. Sauce made with skim evaporated milk, however, is too thin. Since most evaporated milk is sold in twelve-ounce cans, doubling the recipe is a good idea.

Doubling the Recipe

Double the ingredients.

To Freeze the Sauce

Pour the sauce into plastic freezer containers, leaving 1 inch of space at the top. Loosely cover and cool for 1 hour at room temperature. Press a piece of plastic wrap onto the top of the sauce and cover the container tightly. Label with date and contents. Freeze up to 2 months.

To Serve the Sauce

Defrost the sauce overnight in the refrigerator. Warm the sauce in a medium saucepan over low heat, stirring frequently. Leftover sauce can be covered and refrigerated up to 2 weeks.

Brownies, Bars, and Chocolate Chip Cookies

Several years ago our "frozen cookie jar" appeared on national television and became famous. It's a small shelf in the freezer section of our refrigerator-freezer reserved for cookies and brownies. I'm the one who fills the shelf, but it's my husband, Jeff, who manages it. Every day he chooses a few cookies or brownies and arranges them on a plate. When friends come to the house, they invariably look for the cookie plate. Since cookies and brownies are our daily dessert, the little assortment is always there—with a few extras for drop-ins—and I never worry about disappointing anyone. And, when people ask how we both stay reasonably slim, I say it's the cookie shelf. A cookie, brownie, or even one of each satisfies our sweet cravings.

Since I'm a notorious chocolate chip lover, I set a chocolate chip cookie challenge for myself. All of these cookies had to include some sort of chocolate chip. There are mini chips in the buttery chocolate shortbread, white chocolate chips in crisp pistachio cookies, and milk chocolate chips in the crunchy peanut butter cookies. I stretched things a bit with chocolate-coated toffee chips in the oatmeal cookies, but I doubt there will be any complaints.

All of these brownies and cookies use simple mixing techniques, but they do need to be checked carefully as the end of their baking time nears. Use a toothpick to check brownies and a visual test for cookies. Insert a toothpick into the center of a batch of brownies. If the toothpick has moist batter on it, continue to bake the brownies. Run your fingers over the toothpick and it will feel wet if the brownies are not ready. When a few moist crumbs cling to the toothpick, remove the brownies from the oven. The center of a pan of brownies will always be slightly less baked than the edges. Given a choice, I, and probably most people, would choose slightly underbaked brownies to overbaked ones.

Watch cookies for the appearance of a golden brown color or browned edge, which indicates that they are finished baking. Dark-colored chocolate cookies usually lose the shine from their tops when baked sufficiently.

Cookies have a high sugar content, which makes them susceptible to burned bottoms. Since I've burned many cookies by using flimsy baking sheets, I know the value of using good quality heavy baking sheets. They provide insulation, won't warp or bend, and will see you through hundreds of batches of cookies. Sometimes, I add insulation to baking sheets by lining them with heavy aluminum foil. This makes clean-up easy too; discard the aluminum foil and the baking sheet underneath will usually be ready for your next baking day. Cookies are not harmed by opening the oven door repeatedly, so I check them often toward the end of their baking. Opening the oven door may slow down the baking slightly, but it won't affect the final result. Keeping an eye on cookies while they bake is the best way to make every batch of cookies a good one.

FUDGY CHOCOLATE BROWNIES

*B*arbara Fairchild, the executive editor of Bon Appétit maga-zine, is their resident chocolate lover. Not one to pass up a good opportunity to solicit a chocolate expert, I asked her to send me one of her favorite chocolate recipes for this book. She chose her family's special recipe for these not-too-sweet, very dark and moist chocolate brownies—a perfect choice and a perfect brownie.

MAKES 12 TO 16 BROWNIES

1/4 pound (1 stick) unsalted butter
4 ounces unsweetened chocolate, chopped
3 large eggs
1 1/2 cups sugar
1 teaspoon vanilla extract
3/4 cup plus 2 tablespoons unbleached all-purpose flour
1 cup coarsely chopped walnuts (optional)

1. Position an oven rack in the middle of the oven and preheat to 325°F. Butter a 9-inch square baking pan at least 1 1/2 inches deep.

2. Put the butter and unsweetened chocolate in a large heatproof container set over, but not touching, a saucepan of barely simmering water. Stir the mixture until the butter and chocolate are melted and smooth.

3. Put the eggs and sugar in a large bowl and whisk them together to thoroughly blend them. Whisk in the warm chocolate mixture and vanilla. Add the flour and whisk just until the flour is incorporated. Add the nuts, if using. Spread the batter in the prepared pan.

4. Bake 25 to 30 minutes, or until a toothpick inserted in the center of the brownies comes out with moist crumbs clinging to it.

5. Cool the brownies in the pan on a wire rack, about 2 hours. Cut the brownies into 12 or 16 pieces.

Good Advice

· To ensure moist brownies, bake them only to the point that a toothpick inserted in the center of the brownies has moist crumbs clinging to it. The toothpick should not come out clean.

Doubling the Recipe

Double the ingredients and use two pans.

To Freeze

Wrap individual brownies tightly in plastic wrap. Place in a metal or plastic freezer container and cover tightly. Or put the wrapped brownies in a plastic freezer bag and seal. Label with date and contents. Freeze up to 3 months.

To Serve

Remove as many brownies as you want from the freezer and defrost the wrapped brownies at room temperature for about 2 hours. Leftover brownies can be wrapped in plastic wrap and stored at room temperature up to 3 days.

WHITE CHOCOLATE BROWNIES WITH CHOCOLATE CHERRIES

When you taste these brownies, you'll think they're richer than other brownies, but they're not. It's the combination of white chocolate and chocolate cherries that gives that impression. You can find good quality chocolate cherries from a candy shop or Russell Stover, which is available at many all-purpose drug stores.

MAKES 9 BROWNIES

6 tablespoons ($^3/_4$ stick) unsalted butter
7 ounces white chocolate, Callebaut or Baker's Premium preferred, chopped
2 large eggs
$^1/_2$ cup sugar
$^1/_2$ teaspoon salt
1 teaspoon vanilla extract
$^1/_4$ teaspoon almond extract
$^3/_4$ cup unbleached all-purpose flour
16 chocolate-covered cherries, dark or a combination of dark and milk chocolate (about 7 ounces)

1. Position the oven rack in the middle of the oven and preheat to 350°F. Line an 8-inch square pan with 2-inch-high sides with parchment paper, letting the paper extend over 2 opposite sides of the pan. Butter the paper and dust lightly with flour.

2. Put the butter and white chocolate in a heatproof container and place it over, but not touching, a saucepan of barely simmering water. Stir the mixture until the white chocolate and butter are melted and smooth. Remove the container from over the water and set aside.

3. Put the eggs in the large bowl of an electric mixer and mix at medium speed for 10 seconds. Add the sugar and salt and beat for 2 minutes until the mixture thickens and the color lightens. Decrease the speed to low and mix in

· To avoid losing any of the creamy liquid filling from the chocolate cherry candy, drop the cherries into the brownie batter as you cut them. I have used dark chocolate cherries or a combination of dark and milk chocolate cherries with liquid centers with equal success.

· Line the pan with buttered and floured parchment paper so that any cherries that fall to the bottom of the pan don't stick to it.

the melted white chocolate mixture, vanilla, and almond extract. Mix in the flour. Cut the cherries in half and drop them into the batter as you cut them. Stir the cherries gently into the batter. Pour the batter into the prepared pan.

4. Bake until a toothpick inserted into the center of the brownies comes out with moist crumbs attached, 35 to 40 minutes. The center of the brownies will feel soft and the top will have an even golden color.

5. Cool the brownies in the pan on a wire rack, about 2 hours. Loosen the sides of the brownies from the pan with a small thin knife blade. Lift the paper and brownies from the pan. Invert the brownies and carefully remove the parchment paper from the bottom. Turn the brownies right side up and cut into 9 pieces.

Doubling the Recipe

Double the ingredients and use two pans.

To Freeze

Wrap individual brownies tightly in plastic wrap. Place in a metal or plastic freezer container and cover tightly. Or put the wrapped brownies in a plastic freezer bag and seal. Label with date and contents. Freeze up to 3 months.

To Serve

Defrost the wrapped brownies at room temperature for about 3 hours. Leftover brownies can be wrapped in plastic wrap and stored at room temperature up to 3 days.

CHOCOLATE-COVERED RAISIN BROWNIES

Good Advice
The brownies will be easy to cut and remove from the pan if you cool them thoroughly.

Doubling the Recipe
Double the ingredients and use two pans.

To Freeze
Wrap individual brownies in plastic wrap. Put the wrapped brownies in a metal or plastic freezer container and cover tightly. Or put the wrapped brownies in a plastic freezer bag and seal. Label with date and contents. Freeze up to 3 months.

I used to make these brownies with chocolate-covered raisins from the candy counter, but recently Nestlé introduced chocolate-covered raisins for baking. Apparently, I wasn't the only one who baked with them. The chocolate covering on the raisin melts into the brownies making them extra-fudgy, while the raisins add a nice chewy touch.

MAKES 9 BROWNIES

6 ounces (1½ sticks) unsalted butter, cut into pieces
6 ounces semisweet chocolate, chopped
1 ounce unsweetened chocolate, chopped
$2/3$ cup unbleached all-purpose flour
$3/4$ teaspoon baking powder
$1/4$ teaspoon salt
2 large eggs
$3/4$ cup sugar
1 teaspoon vanilla extract
$3/4$ cup chocolate-covered raisins (about 4 ounces)

1. Position a rack in the middle of the oven. Preheat the oven to 350°F. Butter an 8-inch square pan with 2-inch-high sides.

2. Put the butter, semisweet chocolate, and unsweetened chocolate in a heat-proof container and place it over, but not touching, a saucepan of barely simmering water. Stir the mixture until the chocolate and butter are melted and smooth. Remove from over the water and let cool 10 minutes.

3. Put the flour, baking powder, and salt in a small bowl and stir together. Set aside. Put the eggs in the large bowl of an electric mixer and mix the eggs at medium speed for 10 seconds to break up the yolks. Add the sugar and beat for 1 minute, or until the egg mixture is fluffy and lightened in color. Decrease the speed to low and mix in the melted chocolate mixture and vanilla. Add the flour

mixture and mix just until no white streaks of flour remain. Stir in the chocolate-covered raisins. Spread the batter in the prepared pan.

4. Bake until a toothpick inserted in the center of the brownies comes out with moist crumbs attached, about 30 minutes.

5. Cool the brownies in the pan on a wire rack, about 2 hours. Cut the brownies into 9 pieces.

To Serve

Remove as many brownies as you want from the freezer and defrost the wrapped brownies at room temperature for about 2 hours. Leftover brownies can be wrapped tightly in plastic wrap and stored at room temperature up to 3 days.

DOUBLE DECKER MOCHA BROWNIES

*O*ne *batch of brown sugar brownie batter is divided and flavored part with chocolate and part with coffee for these two-layered brownies. When I was testing this recipe, I took an informal poll as to whether or not to include the chocolate chips. You can guess the outcome. The chocolate chips separate the light coffee and dark chocolate layers and make the middle fudgy.*

MAKES 12 TO 16 BROWNIES

6 ounces semisweet chocolate, chopped
1 ounce unsweetened chocolate, chopped
2 cups unbleached all-purpose flour
1 teaspoon baking powder
1/2 teaspoon salt
1/2 pound (2 sticks) soft unsalted butter
1 cup granulated sugar
1 1/4 cups (packed) light brown sugar
3 large eggs
2 teaspoons vanilla extract
1 tablespoon plus 1 teaspoon instant decaffeinated coffee dissolved in 2 tablespoons hot water
2/3 cup semisweet chocolate chips (4 ounces)

I. Position an oven rack in the middle of the oven. Preheat the oven to 175°F. Butter a 13 × 9 × 2-inch baking pan.

2. Put the semisweet chocolate and unsweetened chocolate in an ovenproof container and melt it in the oven, 8 to 10 minutes. As soon as the chocolate is melted, remove it from the oven and stir it smooth. Set aside to cool slightly. Increase the oven temperature to 325°F.

3. Put the flour, baking powder, and salt in a medium bowl and stir together. Set aside. Put the butter in the large bowl of an electric mixer and mix on medium speed for 15 seconds. Add the granulated sugar and brown sugar and

Good Advice
The brownie batter is made thick so that the two layers remain separate when they are spread over each other. A thin metal spatula will spread the batter easily into even layers.

Doubling the Recipe
Use 1 1/2 teaspoons baking powder, double the remaining ingredients, and use two pans.

To Freeze
Wrap individual brownies tightly in plastic wrap. Place in a metal or plastic freezer container and cover tightly. Or put the wrapped brownies in a plastic freezer bag and seal. Label with date and contents. Freeze up to 3 months.

beat until the butter and sugar are creamed thoroughly, about 1 minute. Decrease the speed to low and mix in the eggs and vanilla, mixing until the eggs are incorporated. The mixture will look slightly curdled. Stop the mixer and scrape the sides of the bowl once during this time. Slowly add the flour mixture and mix just until the flour is incorporated and the mixture is smooth. Put 2 cups batter in a medium bowl. You can use the bowl that held the flour mixture. Stir the dissolved coffee into this batter. Stir the melted chocolate into the batter remaining in the large mixing bowl. Use a thin metal spatula to spread the chocolate batter evenly in the prepared pan. Spread the batter to the edges of the pan. Sprinkle the chocolate chips evenly over the batter. Use the thin metal spatula to spread the coffee batter evenly over the chocolate chips. A few chocolate chips may show through the coffee batter.

4. Bake until a toothpick inserted in the center no longer has liquid clinging to it but the top of the brownies still feels soft, about 35 minutes. If the toothpick penetrates a chocolate chip, test another spot.

5. Cool the brownies in the pan on a wire rack, about 2 hours. Cut the brownies into 12 or 16 pieces.

To Serve

Defrost the wrapped brownies at room temperature for about 3 hours. Leftover brownies can be wrapped tightly in plastic wrap and stored at room temperature up to 3 days.

COCONUT MACAROON BROWNIE BARS

ounds candy, chocolate-covered coconut patties, and now Coconut Macaroon Brownie Bars. Joining the list of chocolate and coconut classics, these bars have a crisp coconut topping that covers a dark, moist brownie layer.

MAKES 12 TO 16 BROWNIES

CHOCOLATE BROWNIE LAYER
6 ounces semisweet chocolate, chopped
2 ounces unsweetened chocolate, chopped
6 ounces (1½ sticks) unsalted butter, cut into pieces
¾ cup unbleached all-purpose flour
¾ teaspoon baking powder
¼ teaspoon salt
2 large eggs
1 cup sugar
2 teaspoons vanilla extract

COCONUT MACAROON TOPPING
1 cup sugar
2 large eggs
1 teaspoon vanilla extract
½ teaspoon almond extract
2 tablespoons unbleached all-purpose flour
¼ teaspoon salt
2 cups shredded sweetened coconut
⅔ cup semisweet chocolate chips (4 ounces)

Prepare the Chocolate Brownie Layer

1. Position the oven rack in the middle of the oven and preheat to 325°F. Butter an 11 × 7 × 1¾-inch baking pan or ovenproof glass baking dish.

2. Put the semisweet chocolate, unsweetened chocolate, and butter in a heatproof container and place it over, but not touching, a saucepan of barely sim-

Good Advice

I bake the brownie bars in an 11 × 7 × 1¾-inch baking pan. The pan I use is made of ovenproof glass; it can be found in most supermarkets. This size baking dish produces a thick brownie. A 13 × 9 × 2-inch baking pan works fine also, but it produces thinner brownies, which require less baking time and have more of a cakelike texture.

Doubling the Recipe

Double the ingredients and use two pans.

To Freeze

Wrap individual brownies tightly in plastic wrap. Place in a metal or plastic freezer container and cover tightly. Or put the wrapped brownies in a plastic freezer bag and seal. Label with date and contents. Freeze up to 3 months.

mering water. Stir the mixture until the chocolate and butter are melted and smooth. Remove the container from over the water. Set aside to cool slightly.

3. Stir the flour, baking powder, and salt together in a small bowl. Set aside. Put the eggs in the large bowl of an electric mixer and mix on medium speed for 10 seconds. Add the sugar and vanilla and beat for 1 minute, or until the mixture thickens and the color lightens slightly. Decrease the speed to low and mix in the melted chocolate mixture until it is combined thoroughly with the egg mixture. Add the flour mixture and mix just until the flour is incorporated. Spread the batter evenly in the prepared pan.

Prepare the Coconut Macaroon Topping

4. Put the sugar and eggs in the large bowl of an electric mixer and beat on medium speed until the mixture thickens and the color lightens, about 1 minute. Mix in the vanilla and almond extract. Add the flour and salt and mix just until the flour is incorporated. Decrease the speed to low. Reserve $1/2$ cup of coconut and mix in the remaining $1\frac{1}{2}$ cups of coconut and the chocolate chips. Use a thin metal spatula to spread the coconut mixture evenly over the chocolate batter. Sprinkle the remaining coconut over the top of the batter.

5. Bake until a toothpick inserted in the center of the brownies comes out with a few moist crumbs clinging to it, about 1 hour. If a toothpick penetrates a chocolate chip, test another spot. The coconut topping will look golden brown.

6. Cool the brownies in the pan on a wire rack, about 2 hours. Use a large sharp knife to cut the cooled brownies into 12 or 16 pieces.

To Serve

Defrost the wrapped brownies at room temperature for about 3 hours. Leftover brownies can be wrapped in plastic wrap and stored at room temperature up to 3 days.

REVIVAL CHOCOLATE CHIP MERINGUE BARS

*M*y mom often baked these brown sugar bars, which are liber-ally stuffed with chocolate chips and topped with a brown sugar meringue. As other recipes came along, I forgot about the bars, and the instructions were buried in the recipe box. Several years ago, someone brought them to a meeting and the memory of how much I like these cookies came flooding back. I went home, dug out my recipe—luckily it was still there—and baked a batch immediately. I won't forget them again.

MAKES 35 BARS

2 cups unbleached all-purpose flour
1 teaspoon baking soda
$^1/_2$ teaspoon salt
$^1/_2$ pound (2 sticks) soft unsalted butter
$^3/_4$ cup granulated sugar
2 cups (packed) light brown sugar
3 large eggs, separated
1$^1/_2$ teaspoons vanilla extract
1$^1/_2$ cups semisweet chocolate chips (9 ounces)
$^1/_4$ teaspoon cream of tartar
Powdered sugar, for dusting

I.   Position a rack in the middle of the oven. Preheat the oven to 350°F. Butter a 15$^1/_2$ × 10$^1/_2$ × 1-inch baking pan.

2.   Sift the flour, baking soda, and salt together. Set aside. Put the butter, gran-ulated sugar, and $^1/_2$ cup of the brown sugar in the large bowl of an electric mixer and beat on medium speed for about 1 minute, or until the mixture is smooth and creamy. Add the egg yolks and 1 teaspoon of the vanilla and beat for 1 minute. Stop the mixer and scrape the bowl during this time. Decrease the speed to low and add the flour mixture, mixing just until the flour is incorpo-

Good Advice
· Spread the brown sugar meringue evenly over the chocolate chips. All of the chocolate chips will be cov-ered with meringue, but some will be visible through the meringue.

· You will need two large mixing bowls for these bars. The bowl used to beat the egg whites must be clean and greasefree.

· The 15$^1/_2$ × 10$^1/_2$ × 1-inch baking sheet required for this recipe is sometimes called a jelly-roll pan.

Doubling the Recipe
Double the ingredients and use two pans.

rated. Use a thin metal spatula to spread the batter evenly in the prepared pan. Sprinkle the chocolate chips evenly over the batter.

3. Put the egg whites and cream of tartar in a clean large electric mixer bowl and beat on low speed until the egg whites are frothy. Increase the speed to medium-high and beat until soft peaks form. Reduce the speed to low and slowly beat in the remaining $1^{1}/_{2}$ cups of brown sugar, about 3 tablespoons at a time. Mix in the remaining $^{1}/_{2}$ teaspoon of vanilla. The meringue looks shiny and is soft enough to spread easily. Use a thin metal spatula to spread the brown sugar meringue evenly over the chocolate chips. Spread the meringue to the edges of the pan.

4. Bake until a toothpick inserted in the center of the bars comes out clean, about 30 minutes. If a toothpick penetrates a chocolate chip, test another spot. After 15 minutes of baking, reverse the pan front to back to ensure even baking.

5. Remove the bars from the oven and use a small sharp knife to loosen the meringue from the edges of the pan. Cool the bars in the pan on a wire rack, about 2 hours. Dust the top with powdered sugar. Cut 35 bars about 2 inches square.

To Freeze

Place 2 bars side by side and wrap them in plastic wrap. Put the wrapped bars in a metal or plastic freezer container and cover tightly. Label with date and contents. Freeze up to 3 months.

To Serve

Remove as many bars from the freezer as needed and defrost the wrapped bars at room temperature for about 2 hours. Leftover bars can be wrapped in plastic wrap and stored at room temperature up to 3 days.

OATMEAL TOFFEE CHIP COOKIES

There are two opposing camps when it comes to oatmeal cookies—the chewy and the crisp. These oatmeal cookies belong in my camp— the crisp one. Crushed toffee adds even more crunch to these cookies.

MAKES ABOUT SIXTEEN 3-INCH COOKIES

1 cup unbleached all-purpose flour
1/2 teaspoon baking soda
1/4 teaspoon salt
1/4 teaspoon ground cinnamon
1/4 pound (1 stick) soft unsalted butter
1/2 cup granulated sugar
1/2 cup (packed) dark brown sugar
1 large egg
1 teaspoon vanilla extract
1 cup oatmeal, not quick cooking
1/2 cup crushed toffee crunch candy, such as Heath Bar or Skor (about 3 ounces)

1. Position 2 oven racks in the middle and upper third of the oven. Preheat the oven to 350°F. Line 2 baking sheets with parchment paper.

2. Sift the flour, baking soda, salt, and cinnamon together. Set aside. Put the butter, granulated sugar, and brown sugar in the large bowl of an electric mixer and beat on medium speed for about 1 minute, or until the mixture is smooth. Add the egg and vanilla and mix on low speed until they are blended thoroughly, about 15 seconds. Stop the mixer and scrape the bowl during this time. Decrease the speed to low and add the flour mixture and oatmeal. Stir in the crushed toffee. Using 2 tablespoons of dough for each cookie, roll the dough between the palms of your hands to form 1 1/2-inch balls. Place the cookie balls about 2 inches apart on the prepared baking sheets.

3. Bake the cookies until golden brown, 12 to 13 minutes. After 7 minutes of baking, reverse the baking sheets front to back and top to bottom to ensure even browning. Watch the cookies carefully as they near the end of their baking time.

4. Cool the cookies on the baking sheets for 5 minutes. Transfer the cookies to 2 wire racks to cool completely.

Good Advice
· Lining the baking sheets with parchment paper will prevent the melted toffee from sticking to the baking sheet.

· The bottoms of these sweet cookies can burn easily, so watch the cookies carefully at the end of their baking time.

· To crush the toffee, leave it in its paper wrapper and crush it with the flat side of a meat pounder. Unwrap the toffee and break up any pieces larger than 1/2 inch.

Doubling the Recipe
Double the ingredients.

To Freeze
Place the bottoms of 2 cookies together and wrap them in plastic wrap. Put the wrapped cookies in a metal or plastic freezer container and cover tightly. Label with date and contents. Freeze up to 3 months.

To Serve
Remove as many cookies from the freezer as needed and defrost the wrapped cookies at room temperature. Serve within 3 days.

MILK CHOCOLATE CHIP PEANUT BUTTER COOKIES

As the peanut butter cup candy manufacturers proved long ago, milk chocolate and peanut butter make a winning combination. These are big thick cookies. They are crisp all the way through, but with a soft, crumbly texture.

MAKES ABOUT TWENTY-FOUR 3-INCH COOKIES

1 cup unbleached all-purpose flour
1 teaspoon baking soda
$1/2$ teaspoon salt
$1/4$ pound (1 stick) unsalted butter, softened
$1/2$ cup granulated sugar
$1/3$ cup (packed) light brown sugar
1 large egg
1 teaspoon vanilla extract
$3/4$ cup smooth peanut butter
2 cups milk chocolate chips (12 ounces)

1. Position 2 oven racks in the middle and upper third of the oven. Preheat the oven to 325°F. Line 2 baking sheets with heavy aluminum foil.

2. Sift the flour, baking soda, and salt together. Set aside. Put the butter, granulated sugar, and brown sugar in the large bowl of an electric mixer and beat on medium speed for about 1 minute, or until the mixture is smooth. Add the egg and vanilla and mix on low speed for about 15 seconds, or until they are blended thoroughly. Stop the mixer and scrape the bowl during this time. Add the peanut butter and mix until smooth. Decrease the speed to low and add the flour mixture, mixing just until the flour is incorporated. Stir in the chocolate chips. Use 2 level tablespoons of dough for each cookie. Place mounds of batter about 2 inches apart on the prepared baking sheets.

3. Bake the cookies until evenly light brown, 22 to 24 minutes. After 10 minutes of baking, reverse the baking sheets front to back and top to bottom to ensure even browning. Watch the cookies carefully as they near the end of their baking time. Cool the cookies thoroughly on the baking sheet. The tops of the cookies will look crinkled.

Good Advice
Watch the cookies carefully near the end of the baking time since the bottoms can burn easily.

Doubling the Recipe
Use $1 1/2$ teaspoons baking soda and $3/4$ teaspoon salt and double the remaining ingredients.

To Freeze
Place the bottoms of 2 cookies together and wrap them in plastic wrap. Put the wrapped cookies in a metal or plastic freezer container and cover tightly. Label with date and contents. Freeze up to 3 months.

To Serve
Remove as many cookies from the freezer as needed and defrost the wrapped cookies at room temperature. Serve within 3 days.

CHOCOLATE CHOCOLATE CHIP SHORTBREAD STICKS

Shortbread cookies get their good flavor from butter, but a buttery chocolate shortbread seemed an even better idea to me. I added cocoa powder to the dough and for good measure mixed in a generous helping of chocolate chips. For a fancy finish, you can coat an end of each shortbread stick with baked melted white chocolate. Very fast shortbread cookies can be prepared by pressing the dough into a pan and cutting the baked shortbread into squares.

MAKES ABOUT 48 SHORTBREAD STICKS OR
35 SHORTBREAD SQUARES

1½ cups unbleached all-purpose flour
½ cup unsweetened Dutch process cocoa powder, such as Droste or
  Hershey's European Style
½ teaspoon baking powder
¼ teaspoon salt
½ pound (2 sticks) soft unsalted butter
1 cup powdered sugar
1 cup miniature semisweet chocolate chips (6 ounces)
4 ounces white chocolate, Callebaut or Baker's Premium preferred,
  chopped

1. Position 2 oven racks in the middle and upper third of the oven. Preheat the oven to 300°F. Line 2 baking sheets with heavy aluminum foil.

2. Sift the flour, cocoa, baking powder, and salt together. Set aside. Put the butter in the large mixing bowl of an electric mixer and mix on low speed for 15 seconds. Add the powdered sugar. Increase the speed to medium and beat until the mixture is smooth, about 1 minute. Decrease the speed to low and add the flour mixture. Mix until the flour mixture is blended completely into the dough and the dough holds together, about 2 minutes. Stop the mixer and scrape the bowl during this time. Mix in the chocolate chips. Divide the dough in half and

Good Advice
· The addition of a small amount of baking powder makes this shortbread especially light textured.

· The shortbread is soft when it comes out of the oven and becomes crisp as it cools.

· To coat the cookies with white chocolate without getting cookie crumbs in it, spoon melted white chocolate over the ends of the baked shortbread rather than dipping the cookies.

· Some or all of the shortbread sticks can be dipped in melted semisweet chocolate rather than white chocolate.

Doubling the Recipe
Double the ingredients and use two pans.

place 1 piece of dough on wax paper. Press the dough into a rectangle measuring 7×5 inches and about $1/2$ inch thick. Use a large sharp knife to cut 8 strips 7 inches long by about $5/8$ inch wide. Cut each strip into 3 cookies about $2^{1}/4$ inches long. Using a wide spatula to move the cookies, place the cookies 1 inch apart on the prepared baking sheet. Repeat with the remaining dough.

3. Bake 25 minutes. The tops of the cookies change from shiny to dull.

4. Cool the shortbread on the baking sheets for 10 minutes. Transfer the cookies to 2 wire racks to cool completely.

5. While the cookies cool, melt the white chocolate. Preheat the oven to 175°F. Place the white chocolate in a small nonreactive container. Melt the white chocolate in the oven, about 8 minutes. Remove the white chocolate from the oven as soon as it is melted and stir until smooth. Hold a cookie over the white chocolate and spoon white chocolate over 1 end of the cookie, covering about $1/2$ inch of the cookie. Drag the bottom of the cookie over the top of a bowl to remove any excess chocolate. Let the cookies sit on the rack until the white chocolate is firm. To firm the white chocolate quickly, refrigerate or freeze the cookies.

VARIATION For shortbread squares, butter a $13 \times 9 \times 2$-inch baking pan and press the dough evenly into the pan. The surface of the dough will not look completely smooth. Bake 30 minutes, reversing the pan after 15 minutes to ensure even baking. The tops of the cookies change from shiny to dull. Remove the shortbread from the oven. Using a small sharp knife, immediately cut the shortbread into 35 cookies about 2 inches square and $1/2$ inch thick. Cut the shortbread while it is warm and it will cut neatly, without crumbling. Cool the shortbread thoroughly in the pan. Sift powdered sugar over the tops of the cookies. Use a long narrow spatula to remove the cookies from the pan.

To Freeze
Place 2 cookies side by side and wrap in plastic wrap. Put the wrapped cookies in a metal or plastic freezer container and cover tightly. Freeze up to 3 months.

To Serve
Remove as many cookies from the freezer as needed and defrost the wrapped cookies at room temperature. Serve within 3 days.

PISTACHIO AND WHITE CHOCOLATE CHIP CRISPS

These cookies are my entry for Most Sophisticated Chocolate Chip Cookie. Pistachio nuts and white chocolate chips replace the usual walnuts and semisweet chocolate chips, transforming a family cookie into a fancy cookie. Using margarine rather than butter gives the cookies their crisp texture.

MAKES SIXTEEN 3-INCH COOKIES

3/4 cup unbleached all-purpose flour
1/2 teaspoon baking powder
1/4 teaspoon salt
1/4 pound (1 stick) margarine, softened
1/4 cup granulated sugar
1/4 cup (packed) light brown sugar
1 large egg
1 teaspoon vanilla extract
3/4 teaspoon almond extract
1 teaspoon grated lemon zest
2/3 cup unsalted shelled pistachio nuts, roasted and chopped (see page 12) in half
3/4 cup white chocolate chips, Ghirardelli or Guittard preferred

I. Position 2 oven racks in the middle and upper third of the oven. Preheat the oven to 350°F. Line 2 baking sheets with parchment paper.

2. Sift the flour, baking powder, and salt together. Set aside. Put the margarine, granulated sugar, and brown sugar in the large bowl of an electric mixer and beat on medium-low speed for about 1 minute, or until the mixture is smooth. Add the egg, vanilla, almond extract, and lemon zest and mix on low speed for about 1 minute, or until they are blended thoroughly into the mixture. Stop the mixer and scrape the bowl during this time. The batter will have small lumps. Add the flour mixture, mixing just until the flour is incorporated. The

Good Advice

· Check to see that the white chocolate chips list cocoa butter as one of the ingredients. Ghirardelli or Guittard brand would be a good choice.

· Using margarine rather than butter produces a crisper cookie.

· Line the baking sheets with parchment paper. These cookies release easier from parchment paper than from aluminum foil.

· If you will be using these cookies for Crispy Pistachio and Orange Dream Frozen Sandwiches (page 268), form each cookie with the same amount of dough so that you have cookies of the same size to sandwich together.

· Unsalted shelled pistachio nuts are available at natural food stores and specialty food shops. Buchanan Hollow Nut Company (see page 295) ships shelled pistachio nuts.

dough will be smooth. Stir in the pistachio nuts and white chocolate chips. Use a rounded tablespoon of dough for each cookie. Place mounds of batter about 3 inches apart on the prepared baking sheets.

3. Bake the cookies until the tops are light golden brown and the edges are an even light brown, 12 to 14 minutes. After 7 minutes, reverse the baking sheets front to back and top to bottom to ensure even browning. Watch the cookies carefully as they near the end of their baking time.

4. Cool the cookies 5 minutes on the cookie sheet. Transfer the cookies to a wire rack to cool thoroughly.

Doubling the Recipe
Double the ingredients.

To Freeze
Place the bottoms of 2 cookies together and wrap them in plastic wrap. Put the wrapped cookies in a metal or plastic freezer container and cover tightly. Label with date and contents. Freeze up to 3 months.

To Serve
Remove as many cookies from the freezer as needed and defrost the wrapped cookies at room temperature. Serve within 2 days.

Pies, Tarts, and Confections

Although it's the pan that determines whether a dessert falls into the pie or tart category, I still think of pies in their tins as informal family desserts and free-standing tarts as more sophisticated. The simplest, most informal pie is a crisp with a crumb topping rather than a rolled crust.

I wanted to include a fruit crisp in this chapter, but I wasn't sure about using chocolate in this type of dessert, that is, until I came up with the Pear and Dark Chocolate Crisp. I always serve this warm with vanilla ice cream, so it becomes a warm fruit crisp sundae. The pears bake for a short time before the crisp is assembled. Prebaking fruit softens the cell walls so that they don't burst and the crisp is not waterlogged after it is baked.

With the exception of the Walnut Chocolate Chip Pie, which requires a traditional pie crust, all of the pies in this chapter are made with cookie crumb crusts. I didn't plan it this way, but these chocolate pies lend themselves to a crumb crust. I bake pies in 10-inch diameter heavy aluminum pie pans, and each pie slices into at least eight generous servings. If you substitute a 9-inch pie pan and have too much filling, pour the extra filling into an ovenproof ramekin and bake it for a snack. When these pies are baked in a 9-inch pie pan, the thicker filling may require a longer baking time than a 10-inch pie. Some desserts are flexible—the chilled filling for My Birthday Chocolate Chiffon Pie will fit in either size pan and doesn't require baking.

Tarts are usually removed from the pan before serving. Since they require a crust that will support a filling once the pan is removed, I line tart pans with a chocolate or vanilla pastry that has a tender, cookie-type texture. I bake these tarts in a dark metal tart pan with a removable bottom and shallow fluted sides, which give the crust an attractive ridged pattern. I prepare the Milk Chocolate and Caramel Pecan Tart, which has a graham cracker crumb crust, however, in a springform pan. Whenever I try to remove a crumb crust from a fluted tart pan, it crumbles. Crumb crusts release easily from the smooth sides of a springform pan.

Both of the truffles make good holiday gifts. They can be packed in decorative tins and put in the freezer until you are ready to give them away. During the holiday season, I clear out a small shelf or section of my freezer and use it to stack filled gift tins. They're instantly accessible, and I have a wonderful feeling of accomplishment when I see the stacked tins ready to go.

PEAR AND DARK CHOCOLATE CRISP

Dessert fads may come and go, but fruit crisps are here to stay. One bite of warm, bubbling fruit with a crunchy crumb topping served with a scoop of cold ice cream proves why fruit crisps remain one of America's favorite desserts. A surprise layer of chocolate just under the crunchy topping of this crisp coats the pear filling with soft warm chocolate and acts as a hot chocolate sauce for the vanilla ice cream.

SERVES 8

PEAR AND CHOCOLATE FILLING
6 cups peeled and cored ripe pears (about 6 pears)
1 tablespoon unsalted butter, melted
1 tablespoon sugar
2 tablespoons unbleached all-purpose flour
6 ounces semisweet chocolate, chopped

BROWN SUGAR CRUMB TOPPING
1 cup unbleached all-purpose flour
1 cup (packed) light brown sugar
1 teaspoon ground cinnamon
6 tablespoons (¾ stick) unsalted butter, melted

Vanilla ice cream, for serving with the crisp

Prepare the Pear and Chocolate Filling

1. Position a rack in the middle of the oven and preheat to 350°F.

2. Cut the peeled pears into ¾- to 1-inch chunks. Put the pears in a 2½-quart baking container, either a 10-inch layer pan with 2-inch-high sides or a shallow baking dish that is safe to transfer from freezer to oven. Drizzle the melted butter over the pears. Sprinkle the sugar and flour over the pears. Stir the mixture.

3. Bake, uncovered, for 20 minutes, stirring once. Remove from the oven. Use a spoon to remove any liquid that has formed and wipe the edges of the baking dish clean. Cover loosely and refrigerate until cold. When cold, sprinkle the chocolate evenly over the pears.

Good Advice

· The dessert is properly baked when the crisp is bubbling gently and a toothpick inserted into the pears offers no resistance.

· Cover the chocolate completely with the crumbs. The crumbs will insulate the chocolate and prevent it from burning.

· This dessert is prepared and frozen unbaked in its baking dish. Just pop it in the oven the day you want to serve it. A deep baking container will require a longer baking time than a shallow one.

Doubling the Recipe

Double the ingredients and use two pans.

To Freeze

Wrap the crisp tightly with plastic wrap then heavy aluminum foil, pressing the aluminum foil against the crisp. Label with date and contents. Freeze up to 1 month. Don't place anything on top of the frozen crisp.

Mix the Brown Sugar Crumb Topping

4. Put the flour, brown sugar, and cinnamon in a large bowl and stir together. Pour the melted butter over the flour mixture and use a large spoon to stir the mixture until it is evenly moistened and fine crumbs form. Break up any large clumps with a fork. Sprinkle the crumbs evenly over the chocolate. The crumbs will cover the chocolate.

To Bake and Serve

Uncover the frozen crisp. Position a rack in the middle of the oven. Preheat the oven to 325°F. Bake the frozen crisp 55 to 60 minutes, or until the mixture just begins to bubble. Or defrost the crisp in the refrigerator and bake, uncovered, at 325°F. for 40 to 45 minutes. Let the crisp cool about 15 minutes before serving or warm previously baked crisp, uncovered, in a 250°F. oven for 15 minutes. Spoon the warm crisp onto individual plates and serve with a scoop of vanilla ice cream.

MY BIRTHDAY
CHOCOLATE CHIFFON PIE

My mom likes to tell the mud pie story that took place when I was about six years old. When she asked what kind of mud pies I was making, I promptly replied, "Chocolate chiffon." Creamy chocolate chiffon pie in a crisp graham cracker crust was what I chose for every birthday when I was a child. Even as a little girl, I recognized a good chocolate pie wherever I met one.

SERVES 8

6 ounces semisweet chocolate, chopped
1 envelope gelatin ($1/4$ ounce)
$1/4$ cup cold water
$1/2$ cup whole milk
4 large eggs, separated
$1/2$ cup sugar
1 teaspoon vanilla extract
1 Graham Cracker Crumb Crust (page 40) baked in a 10-inch pie pan, cooled or frozen

1. Preheat the oven to 175°F.

2. Put the chocolate in a small heatproof container and melt it in the oven, 10 to 12 minutes. Remove the chocolate from the oven as soon as it is melted and stir it smooth. Set aside to cool slightly. Sprinkle the gelatin over the water in a measuring cup. Set aside to soften while you prepare the custard mixture. Put the milk in a medium saucepan and heat over medium-low heat until the milk is hot. The hot milk will form tiny bubbles around the edge of the pot and measure about 175°F. on a food thermometer. Do not let the milk boil.

3. Put the egg yolks in a medium bowl. Use a whisk to mix $1/4$ cup of the sugar into the egg yolks. Pour the hot milk over the egg yolk mixture while whisking constantly. Pour the mixture back into the saucepan and cook over medium heat, whisking constantly, until the mixture measures 160°F. on a food thermometer. Steam will begin to rise from the mixture. Remove from the heat and

Good Advice

· The top of the pie is soft even when cold, and plastic wrap will stick to the pie once it defrosts. The best way to cover the pie in the refrigerator is with a large plastic cake dome that doesn't touch the top of the pie. Or space a few toothpicks around the pie before covering it with plastic wrap. The toothpicks will leave a few tiny holes in the chiffon, but these are perfect for birthday candles.

· The pie filling does not get hard even when frozen and will easily defrost in only 2 hours.

Doubling the Recipe

Use two crusts and double the ingredients.

stir in the softened gelatin. Stir the mixture until it is smooth and the gelatin dissolves. Stir in the melted chocolate and vanilla. Pour the chocolate mixture into a large bowl, cover with plastic wrap, and refrigerate until slightly thickened, about 15 minutes.

4. Put the egg whites in the clean large bowl of an electric mixer and beat on medium-high speed to soft peaks. Slowly beat in the remaining $1/4$ cup of sugar. Use a rubber spatula to fold half of the egg whites into the slightly thickened chocolate mixture. Fold in the remaining egg whites until no white specks remain. Pour the filling into the prepared crumb crust.

VARIATION My aunt Elaine covers the top of the pie with whipped cream before she serves it. Whip 1 cup whipping cream with 1 tablespoon powdered sugar and 1 teaspoon vanilla extract to firm peaks. Spread the whipped cream over the pie and serve.

To Freeze

Freeze the pie until the top is firm, about 2 hours. Wrap gently with plastic wrap. Gently press heavy aluminum foil around the pie. Label with date and contents. Freeze up to 2 weeks. After 2 weeks the crumb crust may soften, but the chocolate filling will be fine.

To Serve

Remove the wrapping from the frozen pie and cover it with a plastic cake dome. Or unwrap the pie and space four or five toothpicks evenly over the top of the pie and carefully cover the pie with plastic wrap. Defrost the pie in the refrigerator, about 2 hours. Serve the pie cold. Leftover pie can be stored in the refrigerator up to 2 days, covered with a plastic cake dome or with plastic wrap supported by toothpicks.

GERMAN CHOCOLATE PIE

Chocolate, pecans, and coconut, the flavors in German chocolate cake, inspired this pie. I baked a graham cracker crumb crust, filled it with a light chocolate cream, and covered the cream with a topping of chocolate, coconut, and chopped pecans. Not quite the same, but close enough to evoke the memory of that old classic.

SERVES 8

LIGHT CHOCOLATE CREAM FILLING
1 cup cold whipping cream
1/2 cup Thick Chocolate Truffle Sauce (page 50), cooled thoroughly or defrosted and softened over low heat just until it spoons easily

1 Graham Cracker Crumb Crust (page 40) baked in a 10-inch pie pan, cooled or frozen

TOASTED COCONUT TOPPING
2 cups shredded sweetened coconut (about 5 ounces)
1 cup half-and-half
4 tablespoons (1/2 stick) unsalted butter, cut into 4 pieces
2 large eggs
1/2 cup sugar
1/8 teaspoon salt
1/2 cup semisweet chocolate chips or (3 ounces) semisweet chocolate, chopped
1 teaspoon vanilla extract

1 cup chopped toasted pecans (see page 12), for sprinkling on the pie when served

Prepare the Light Chocolate Cream Filling

I. Put the whipping cream in the large bowl of an electric mixer. With the mixer on low speed, pour in the truffle sauce. Stop the mixer and scrape the sides of the bowl to incorporate any truffle sauce that splashes onto the sides of the

· Before whipping freshly prepared warm truffle sauce with cream, it must be cooled thoroughly. Frozen truffle sauce must be defrosted and softened over low heat. The truffle sauce should be just soft enough to spoon easily (about 85°F. if measured with a food thermometer). If the truffle sauce is warm, the cream will not whip properly.

· Watch the coconut carefully at the end of the baking time. Sweetened coconut darkens quickly at the end of its baking.

· I sprinkle the pecans over the pie just before serving it. It only takes a minute, but then I know that the pecans will be crisp. If the pecans are frozen on top of the pie, they will become soft when frozen.

Doubling the Recipe

Use two crusts and double the ingredients.

bowl. As soon as the truffle sauce is blended with the cream, increase the speed to medium-high and beat until firm peaks form. Spread the chocolate cream evenly in the prepared crumb crust. Refrigerate the pie to firm the filling while you prepare the topping.

Prepare the Toasted Coconut Topping

2. Position a rack in the middle of the oven. Preheat the oven to 300°F.

3. Spread the coconut on a baking sheet. Toast for about 10 minutes, or until the coconut becomes golden, stirring once. Check toward the end of the baking time. Set aside.

4. Put the half-and-half and butter in a medium saucepan and heat over medium heat until it is hot and the butter melts, about 160°F. if measured with a food thermometer. Put the eggs, sugar, and salt in a large bowl and whisk them together until they are smooth. Whisking constantly, slowly pour the hot half-and-half mixture into the egg mixture. Return the mixture to the saucepan and cook, stirring constantly, over medium heat until the mixture thickens and reaches 165°F. on a food thermometer. Do not boil the mixture, or it will curdle. Remove from the heat. Strain the custard into a clean large bowl. Stir in the chocolate, stirring until the chocolate melts and the mixture is smooth. Stir in the vanilla and toasted coconut. Cover loosely and refrigerate until cold and slightly thickened, about 1 hour. Use a thin metal spatula to spread the topping evenly over the chocolate cream.

To Freeze
Freeze the pie, uncovered, until the topping is firm, about 30 minutes. Wrap the pie tightly with plastic wrap then heavy aluminum foil, gently pressing the aluminum foil against the pie. Label with date and contents. Freeze up to 1 month.

To Serve
Defrost the wrapped pie in the refrigerator at least 5 hours or overnight. Unwrap the pie and sprinkle the toasted pecans evenly over the top. Serve the pie cold. Leftover pie can be covered and refrigerated up to 2 days.

RAZZLE-DAZZLE RASPBERRY FUDGE PIE

The dictionary defines razzle-dazzle as a state of riotous gaiety, which is just what you'll experience when you taste this pie. It's a rich layering of chocolate crumb crust, fudge brownie, raspberries, cream cheese, and chocolate truffle. A synonym for razzle-dazzle is razzmatazz, and this pie has a lot of that too.

SERVES 10

FUDGE BROWNIE LAYER
6 tablespoons unbleached all-purpose flour
$^1/_2$ teaspoon baking powder
$^1/_8$ teaspoon salt
4 ounces semisweet chocolate, chopped
1 ounce unsweetened chocolate, chopped
$^1/_4$ pound (1 stick) unsalted butter, cut into 8 pieces
1 large egg
1 large egg yolk
$^1/_2$ cup sugar
1 teaspoon vanilla extract

1 Chocolate Wafer Cookie Crumb Crust (page 40) baked in a 10-inch pie pan, cooled or frozen
$1^1/_2$ cups raspberries, preferably fresh, or frozen unsweetened raspberries, not defrosted

CREAM CHEESE LAYER
10 ounces cream cheese, softened about 3 hours at room temperature
$^1/_3$ cup sugar
1 large egg
1 teaspoon vanilla extract
$^1/_2$ teaspoon almond extract

2 tablespoons Thick Chocolate Truffle Sauce (page 50), warmed just until smooth and pourable

Good Advice

· The pie is rich, so a 10-inch pie will easily serve ten people.

· If you are using frozen raspberries, do not defrost them before adding them to the pie.

Doubling the Recipe

Use two crusts and double the remaining ingredients.

To Freeze

Chill the pie, uncovered, in the freezer until the truffle sauce is firm, about 30 minutes. Cover the pie tightly with plastic wrap then with heavy aluminum foil, gently pressing the aluminum foil against the pie. Label with date and contents. Freeze up to 2 months.

Prepare the Fudge Brownie Layer

1. Position an oven rack in the middle of the oven. Preheat the oven to 350°F.

2. Sift the flour, baking powder, and salt together. Set aside. Put the semi-sweet chocolate, unsweetened chocolate, and butter in a heatproof container set over, but not touching, a saucepan of simmering water. Stir the chocolate and butter together until they are melted and the mixture is smooth. Remove from over the water and cool slightly.

3. Put the egg and egg yolk in the large bowl of an electric mixer and beat just to break up the egg yolks. Add the sugar and vanilla and beat on medium-low speed until the mixture thickens slightly, about 1 minute. Mix in the slightly cooled chocolate mixture. Add the flour mixture and mix on low speed just until the flour is incorporated. Pour the batter into the crumb crust.

4. Bake 17 minutes.

5. Cool 10 minutes. The brownie will deflate slightly. Spoon the raspberries evenly over the brownie layer.

Prepare the Cream Cheese Layer

6. Put the cream cheese and sugar in the large bowl of an electric mixer. Beat on low-medium speed until the mixture is smooth, about 30 seconds. Add the egg, vanilla, and almond extract and mix just until the mixture is smooth. Use a thin metal spatula to spread the cream cheese mixture evenly over the raspberries.

7. Bake until the top is set, about 15 minutes.

8. Cool the pie 1 hour, or until the cheesecake layer is firm before adding the truffle sauce.

9. Use a teaspoon to drizzle the truffle sauce in thin lines over the top of the pie.

To Serve
Defrost the wrapped pie in the refrigerator overnight. Serve the pie cold. Leftover pie can be covered and refrigerated up to 3 days.

WALNUT CHOCOLATE CHIP PIE

Jeff and I once lived in Louisville, Kentucky, for six weeks, and although it wasn't long enough to see much of bluegrass country, we did make one great discovery—derby pie. The pie is a mixture of walnuts and chocolate held together by just a bit of sticky filling that forms a sweet crisp top to the pie. It's similar to pecan pie, but less sweet and somewhat firmer. The original recipe for derby pie is a closely guarded secret, but over the years I've worked out a version that stands up to any Kentuckian's scrutiny.

SERVES 8

2 large eggs
1 cup granulated sugar
¼ cup (packed) light brown sugar
¼ cup unbleached all-purpose flour
¼ teaspoon salt
6 tablespoons (¾ stick) unsalted butter, melted
1 teaspoon vanilla extract
2 cups coarsely chopped walnuts
1 cup semisweet chocolate chips (6 ounces)
1 Easy as Pie Crust (page 38) in a 10-inch pie pan, unbaked and frozen
Whipped cream or vanilla ice cream, for serving with the pie (optional)

1. Position an oven rack in the middle of the oven. Preheat the oven to 400°F.

2. Put the eggs in a large bowl and with a large spoon or an electric mixer on low speed mix the egg yolks and whites together. Add the granulated sugar, brown sugar, flour, and salt and mix until the mixture is smooth. Mix in the melted butter and vanilla. Stir in the chopped walnuts and chocolate chips. Pour the filling into the frozen pie crust.

3. Bake 15 minutes. Reduce the oven temperature to 350°F. and continue to bake until the filling is set, about 30 minutes. Check to see that the pie is set by giving it a gentle shake; the center should remain firm.

4. Cool thoroughly at room temperature.

MILK CHOCOLATE AND CARAMEL PECAN TART

This tart is a good example of how to put together a fancy dessert from your frozen pantry. Fill a frozen baked graham cracker crumb crust with a small container of caramel filling and some toasted pecans, then drizzle melted milk chocolate over it all. Who says you can't use your frozen assets?

SERVES 10 TO 12

1½ cups Caramel Filling (page 52), warmed just until pourable
1 Graham Cracker Crumb Crust (page 40) baked in a 9-inch springform pan, cooled or frozen
2 cups pecans halves, toasted and cooled (page 12)
6 ounces milk chocolate, chopped
1 tablespoon vegetable oil

I. Gently pour 1 cup of the caramel filling evenly over the prepared crust. Tilt the pan to spread the caramel evenly. Place the pecans evenly over the caramel. Use a teaspoon to drizzle the remaining ½ cup caramel evenly over the pecans. Refrigerate the tart to firm the filling, about 15 minutes.

2. Put the chocolate and vegetable oil in a heatproof container and place it over, but not touching, a saucepan of barely simmering water. Stir the mixture until the chocolate is melted and the mixture is smooth. Remove the chocolate mixture from over the hot water. Use a teaspoon to drizzle the melted chocolate mixture over the top of the tart.

3. Refrigerate the tart until the chocolate and filling are firm and the tart is cold, about 1 hour. For faster chilling, freeze the tart for 30 minutes.

Good Advice
· Since the sides of the graham cracker crust are rather delicate, leave the tart on the bottom of the springform pan.

Doubling the Recipe
Use two crusts and double the remaining ingredients.

To Freeze
Release the sides of the springform pan and remove. Leave the tart on the springform bottom. If you need to move the tart to a serving plate or cardboard cake circle, freeze the tart firm, about 4 hours. Loosen the tart with a small sharp knife. Carefully slide the removable bottom of a tart pan under the crust and move the tart to the plate or cardboard. Wrap tightly with plastic wrap then with heavy aluminum foil. Label with date and contents. Freeze up to 2 months.

To Serve
Defrost the wrapped tart in the refrigerator overnight. Serve the tart cold. Leftover tart can be covered with plastic wrap and stored in the refrigerator up to 3 days.

PISTACHIO MARZIPAN TART WITH PURE CHOCOLATE GLAZE

When I was a little girl, my family spent summers visiting my grandfather in Brooklyn. Daily shopping on Avenue J was a lot different from shopping in the small Florida town where I lived the rest of the year. Brooklyn offered delicatessens with steaming corned beef and hot knishes, bakeries on every block offering specialties from different European countries, and Barton's candy store with my favorite candy bar, pistachio marzipan, arranged in a pyramid on top of the counter. The log-shaped, pale green marzipan was covered with a thin layer of dark chocolate to keep the lightly sweetened pistachio paste soft and moist. It seemed only natural that I turn my candy bar memory into a full-fledged dessert. I made a ground pistachio filling in the food processor, lightly baked it to keep it moist, and covered the tart with a pure chocolate and water glaze. Although it's been more than thirty years since I've had a Barton's marzipan bar, this tart brought the good taste and memory right back.

SERVES 12

PISTACHIO FILLING
2½ cups unsalted shelled pistachio nuts, roasted
½ cup powdered sugar
½ cup granulated sugar
1 tablespoon fresh lemon juice
1 teaspoon vanilla extract
¾ teaspoon almond extract
1 large egg
2 large egg whites

1 Sweet Butter Pastry (page 34) in an 11-inch tart pan, unbaked and frozen

PURE CHOCOLATE GLAZE
9 ounces semisweet or bittersweet chocolate, chopped
6 tablespoons lukewarm water, at the same temperature as melted chocolate

Good Advice

· The chocolate glaze is a mixture of melted chocolate and warm water. It is important that both the chocolate and the water be at a similar temperature. Adding cold water to the melted chocolate would harden it, while adding hot water could overheat the chocolate and cause it to become grainy. Adjust the water temperature until it feels the same as the chocolate temperature. If you use a thermometer, the water and chocolate should measure 88° to 90°F. As the water is added to the chocolate, the chocolate darkens and the glaze becomes shiny. It loses its shine as it cools on the cake and comes to look like the chocolate coating on a candy bar.

· Use the glaze as soon as you prepare it since it will firm as it stands.

Doubling the Recipe

Use two crusts, prepare the

Prepare the Pistachio Filling

1. Position an oven rack in the middle of the oven. Preheat the oven to 375°F.

2. Rub any loose skins off the pistachio nuts and discard. Put the nuts, powdered sugar, and granulated sugar in the workbowl of a food processor fitted with the steel blade and process until the nuts are finely ground, about 1 minute. With the machine running, add the lemon juice, vanilla, almond extract, egg, and egg whites. Process until a soft paste forms, about 1 minute. Stop the machine and scrape down the mixture once during this time. Pour the pistachio filling into the frozen pastry shell.

3. Bake until the filling is light brown and firm, about 20 minutes.

4. Cool the tart completely.

Prepare the Pure Chocolate Glaze and Glaze the Tart

5. Preheat the oven to 175°F. Place the chocolate in a heatproof container and melt it in the oven, about 10 minutes. As soon as the chocolate is melted, remove it from the oven. Pour the melted chocolate into a medium bowl and stir it smooth. Measure out the lukewarm water into a small bowl. Check with your fingertips that the water temperature feels similar to the chocolate temperature. Add the lukewarm water all at once and gently whisk the mixture until it is smooth. Makes about 1 cup.

6. Pour the chocolate glaze over the top of the cooled tart. Using a thin metal spatula, spread the glaze evenly.

pistachio filling in two batches, and double the chocolate glaze.

To Freeze

Chill or freeze the tart, uncovered, until the chocolate glaze is firm, about 30 minutes. Use a small sharp knife to loosen the sides of the crust from the pan. Set the tart pan on a shallow bowl, such as a soup bowl, and let the rim slide down. Slide the tart onto a serving plate or 12-inch cardboard cake circle. Wrap tightly with plastic wrap then heavy aluminum foil. Label with date and contents. Freeze up to 2 months.

To Serve

Defrost the wrapped tart in the refrigerator overnight. Uncover the tart and let it sit at room temperature 30 minutes before serving. The glaze should soften slightly. Leftover tart can be covered with plastic wrap and stored in the refrigerator up to 4 days.

WHITE MOCHA TRUFFLE TART

For a dessert that looks so sophisticated, this two-toned tart takes a surprisingly short time to prepare. Just melt white chocolate in a hot cream mixture, flavor part of the mixture with coffee, and spread the layers of white chocolate and coffee truffle in a baked chocolate crust. The two flavors of truffle, sweet white chocolate and less sweet coffee, make a good contrast. A simple technique creates a fancy web pattern for the top of the tart.

SERVES 12

1 Chocolate Butter Pastry (page 36) in an 11-inch tart pan, unbaked and frozen

WHITE CHOCOLATE AND COFFEE TRUFFLE FILLING
1 cup whipping cream
6 tablespoons (3/4 stick) unsalted butter
21 ounces white chocolate, Callebaut or Baker's Premium preferred, chopped
2 teaspoons vanilla extract
2 teaspoons instant decaffeinated coffee dissolved in 1 tablespoon whipping cream

1. Position an oven rack in the middle of the oven. Preheat the oven to 375°F.

2. Press a piece of heavy aluminum foil into the frozen tart crust and over the edges of the tart pan. Fill the aluminum foil with metal pie weights, or about 3 cups of raw rice or beans. Check to see that the weights cover the entire bottom of the crust. Place the pan on a baking sheet. Bake the tart for 15 minutes. Carefully remove the pie weights and aluminum foil. Reduce the oven temperature to 350°F. Bake for about 13 minutes, or until the pastry looks dull and is no longer shiny. Cool the crust completely.

Prepare the Truffle Filling

3. Put the cream and butter in a medium saucepan and heat just until the cream is hot and the butter is melted. The hot cream mixture will form tiny bub-

Good Advice
Use only the tip of the knife to form the web pattern on top of the tart. Try the web pattern as a decoration on other desserts, whenever you have two colors of filling, frosting, or sauce to work with.

Doubling the Recipe
Use two crusts and double the remaining ingredients.

bles around the edge of the pan and measure about 175°F. on a food thermometer. Do not let the mixture boil. Remove the pan from the heat and add the chopped white chocolate. Let the white chocolate soften in the cream for 1 minute. Stir the truffle until it is smooth and all of the white chocolate is melted. Return the saucepan to low heat for 1 minute, if necessary, to melt the white chocolate completely. Add the vanilla and stir the mixture until it is smooth and all of the chocolate is melted. Put $1\frac{1}{4}$ cups of the white chocolate mixture in a small bowl and stir in the dissolved coffee. Cool both truffle mixtures at room temperature until cool to the touch but still pourable, about 30 minutes.

4. Reserve 2 tablespoons of the white chocolate truffle mixture and pour the remaining white chocolate truffle into the baked crust, spreading evenly. Refrigerate or freeze until the white chocolate truffle is firm, about 40 minutes.

5. Pour the coffee truffle mixture evenly over the white chocolate truffle.

6. Using a teaspoon, drizzle the reserved white chocolate truffle in a spiral pattern over the top of the tart. It will look like a target pattern. Using a small sharp knife, begin at the center and draw the tip of the knife across the top of the filling toward the edge of the tart. Move the tip of the knife over about 1 inch. Begin at the edge of the tart and draw the knife toward the center of the tart. Continue pulling shallow lines, alternating the direction of the knife around the top of the tart from center to edge and edge to center, to form a web pattern.

To Freeze

Refrigerate the tart just to firm the topping, about 1 hour. Once the tart is cold, remove the tart pan. Use a small sharp knife to carefully loosen the crust from each indentation in the sides of the pan. Set the pan on a shallow bowl, such as a soup bowl, and let the rim slide down. Slide the tart onto a serving platter or 12-inch cardboard cake circle. Wrap the cold tart tightly with plastic wrap then heavy aluminum foil, gently pressing the foil against the tart. Freeze up to 2 months.

To Serve

Defrost the wrapped tart in the refrigerator overnight. Uncover the tart and let it sit at room temperature for 1 hour before serving. This will give the tart a soft consistency and bring out the flavor. Leftover tart can be covered with plastic wrap and stored in the refrigerator up to 3 days.

CRANBERRY AND WHITE CHOCOLATE LINZER TART

Look around the produce department in the middle of winter, and you'll notice a lack of colorful fruit. Cranberries are the exception, and they make a festive, bright red filling for this linzer tart. During the annual Christmas holiday delirium, it's nice to have several of these tarts tucked away in your freezer for holiday entertaining or last-minute gifts. The pastry for the tart, a press-in almond cookie dough, is filled with white chocolate and cooked cranberries. The impressive lattice topping is simply rolled ropes of the almond cookie dough.

SERVES 10

CRANBERRY FILLING
2¹/₂ cups cranberries, fresh or previously frozen and defrosted
¹/₄ cup fresh orange juice
¹/₂ cup sugar

ALMOND COOKIE CRUST
1 cup ground blanched almonds
1²/₃ cups unbleached all-purpose flour
¹/₂ cup sugar
¹/₂ teaspoon baking powder
1 teaspoon ground cinnamon
¹/₄ teaspoon ground mace
¹/₂ pound (2 sticks) cold unsalted butter, cut into 16 pieces
1 large egg
1 large egg yolk
1 teaspoon vanilla extract

6 ounces white chocolate, Callebaut or Baker's Premium preferred, chopped
Powdered sugar, for dusting the tart when it is served

Prepare the Cranberry Filling

I. Cook the cranberries, orange juice, and sugar in a medium saucepan over medium heat until the mixture comes to a boil. Reduce the heat to medium-low and simmer, stirring occasionally, until the liquid becomes thick and syrupy,

Good Advice
· Cool the cranberry filling thoroughly so that it doesn't melt the dough when you fill the tart.

· Press the dough evenly up the sides of the springform pan to form a level edge.

· Nutmeg can be substituted for the mace.

Doubling the Recipe
Double the ingredients.

To Freeze
Use a small sharp knife to loosen the sides of the crust from the pan. Release the sides of the springform pan and remove. To remove the bottom of the springform pan, use a sharp knife to loosen the tart from the bottom of the pan and a wide metal spatula to slide the tart onto a serving plate or aluminum foil—wrapped cardboard cake circle. Or carefully invert the tart onto a flat plate and remove the springform bottom. Place a serving plate or cake circle

about 10 minutes. The cranberry mixture will have a jamlike consistency. Set aside to cool thoroughly, about 30 minutes. The mixture will thicken to a firm jam when cool.

Prepare the Almond Cookie Crust

2. Position an oven rack in the middle of the oven. Preheat the oven to 350°F. Butter a 9-inch springform pan.

3. Put the almonds, flour, sugar, baking powder, cinnamon, and mace in the large bowl of an electric mixer and mix on low speed just to blend the ingredients, about 10 seconds. Add the butter and mix until most of the butter pieces are the size of peas, about 1 minute. The mixture will look crumbly and the crumbs will vary in size. With the mixer running, add the egg, egg yolk, and vanilla. Mix until the mixture clings together and pulls away from the sides of the bowl, about 30 seconds. Reserve 1 cup of the mixture for the lattice topping and refrigerate it while you prepare the crust.

4. Press the remaining dough evenly over the bottom and 1¼ inches up the sides of the prepared pan. Sprinkle the white chocolate evenly over the crust. Use a thin metal spatula to spread the cooled cranberry mixture evenly over the white chocolate.

5. Remove the reserved dough from the refrigerator. Using about 2 tablespoons of dough for the longest ropes and less for the shorter ropes, roll pieces of the dough back and forth to form ropes of dough about ½ inch in diameter. If ropes break, pinch them back together. Put a 9-inch-long rope across the middle of the tart. Spacing the ropes about 2 inches apart, place a rope about 8 inches long on either side of the center rope. Place a rope about 4½ inches long near each end of the tart. You will have 5 ropes of dough across the top of the tart. Turn the tart pan a half turn and place 5 more ropes evenly over the top of the tart for a lattice pattern.

6. Bake the tart until the top is golden brown, about 1 hour.

7. Cool the tart thoroughly in the pan.

on the bottom of the tart and turn the tart right side up. Wrap the cooled tart tightly with plastic wrap then heavy aluminum foil. Label with date and contents. Freeze up to 2 months.

To Serve

Defrost the wrapped tart at room temperature. Unwrap the tart and dust with powdered sugar. Leftover tart can be covered with plastic wrap and stored at room temperature up to 3 days.

CHOCOLATE HAZELNUT VOLCANO

*S*everal years ago my daughter, Laura, and I went back to school together. We spent an idyllic month in Avignon, France, taking a French language immersion course. When our morning classes ended, we spent the rest of the day exploring Avignon and nearby Provençal villages, and each afternoon found us at a café having tea and pastry. After testing the pastry at several cafés, we soon found one that served homemade chocolates and chocolate desserts, which were prepared on the premises in a huge basement work area. We usually shared a "volcano," a small tartlet shell filled with a thin layer of sweetened hazelnuts, covered with a mini mountain of whipped chocolate truffle, and topped with chocolate glaze. As we pulled out of the Avignon train station, carefully balancing a box of these goodies for the long trip home, I was busy writing notes about chocolate volcanoes so that we could duplicate them and the memories of our mother-daughter school days.

MAKES 8 VOLCANOES

½ recipe Sweet Butter Pastry (page 34), cold unbaked dough

HAZELNUT PASTE
½ cup hazelnuts, peeled and toasted (see page 12)
2 tablespoons powdered sugar
1 tablespoon plus 1 teaspoon whipping cream

TRUFFLE FILLING AND GLAZE
2 tablespoons unsalted butter
¾ cup whipping cream
12 ounces semisweet chocolate, chopped
1 teaspoon vanilla extract

I. Position a rack in the middle of the oven. Preheat the oven to 400°F. Have ready 8 tartlet tins, 3 inches in diameter and ½ inch deep, preferably with smooth not fluted sides.

Good Advice

· It is easiest to form the small tarts in individual round, smooth-edged metal tartlet tins. They are inexpensive and can be found in many specialty cookware shops. Previn (see page 295) ships the tartlet tins. I have baked the tart shells in muffin tins, but the tartlet tins are easier to work with and form more perfectly shaped crusts. The tart shells release easily from the tartlet tins, and the tins do not need to be buttered.

· You will need only half a recipe of Sweet Butter Pastry for eight volcanoes. Prepare a full recipe of pastry and wrap and freeze the remaining dough for another batch of tarts.

Doubling the Recipe

Use a full recipe of Sweet Butter Pastry and double the remaining ingredients.

2. Remove the dough from the refrigerator and unwrap it. If the dough has become cold and hard, let it sit at room temperature until it is easy to roll, about 10 minutes. Lightly flour the rolling surface and rolling pin. Roll the dough from the center out into a circle about 13 inches in diameter and ⅛ inch thick. Use the rim of a tartlet tin to cut out 8 circles. Lift each dough circle into a tartlet tin. Press the dough evenly into the tin and to the edge of the tin. (Dough scraps can be placed on the baking sheet, baked with the tartlet pastry, and eaten as cookies.) Put the filled tins on a baking sheet and freeze for 30 minutes. Or wrap each tin tightly in plastic wrap then heavy aluminum foil and freeze for up to 1 month.

3. Press a small square of heavy aluminum foil onto each frozen tartlet crust. Fill the aluminum foil with raw rice, dried beans, or metal pie weights.

4. Bake for 15 minutes. Carefully remove the aluminum foil and pie weights. Reduce the oven temperature to 350°F. Bake for 10 minutes more. The edges of the pastry will be light brown and the center golden.

5. Cool the pastry completely and remove the tartlet tins.

Prepare the Hazelnut Paste

6. Put the hazelnuts and powdered sugar in the workbowl of a food processor fitted with the steel blade and process until the hazelnuts are finely ground, about 30 seconds. With the motor running, pour in the cream and process until the cream is incorporated and the mixture forms a paste, about 15 seconds. Spread about 2 teaspoons of the hazelnut paste over the bottom of each cooled tartlet shell.

Prepare the Truffle Filling and Glaze

7. Put the butter and cream in a medium saucepan and heat just until the cream is hot and the butter is melted. The hot cream mixture will form tiny bubbles around the edge of the pan and measure about 175°F. on a food thermometer. Do not let the mixture boil. Remove the pan from the heat and add the

To Freeze
Freeze the tartlets, uncovered, until the frosting is firm, about 30 minutes. Wrap each tartlet in plastic wrap. Place the tartlets in a single layer in a metal or plastic freezer container and cover tightly. Label with date and contents. Freeze up to 1 month.

To Serve
Defrost the wrapped tartlets in the refrigerator at least 5 hours or overnight. Unwrap and let sit at room temperature for 1 hour before serving. Leftover tartlets can be covered with plastic wrap and stored in the refrigerator up to 3 days, but serve them at room temperature.

chopped chocolate. Let the chocolate melt in the cream for 1 minute. Stir the sauce until it is smooth and all of the chocolate is melted. Return the saucepan to low heat for 1 minute, if necessary, to melt the chocolate completely. Stir in the vanilla. Remove $1/2$ cup of sauce and set aside at room temperature. Pour the remaining sauce into the large bowl of an electric mixer and press plastic wrap onto the surface. Refrigerate the sauce until it is cold to the touch and just beginning to harden around the edges, about 1 hour. Stir occasionally to ensure that the mixture chills throughout.

8. Beat the cold truffle on medium speed until the mixture lightens from a dark to a medium chocolate color and thickens slightly, 45 seconds to 1 minute. Do not overbeat the mixture. Immediately spoon about 2 tablespoons of the mixture into the center of each tartlet shell. Use a thin metal spatula to spread the filling smooth and into a cone or mountain shape. Chill 10 minutes to firm the filling. Use a thin metal spatula to spread 1 tablespoon of the reserved, unwhipped truffle glaze over the top of each tartlet.

MANON—BELGIAN WHITE CHOCOLATE AND COFFEE TRUFFLES

Several birthdays ago a strange man appeared at my door to deliver a present of a box of truffles. They had a silken-smooth whipped coffee filling and were thickly coated with white chocolate. The candy was called Manon. It seems that any Belgian candy with the name Manon has this whipped coffee filling and is covered in white chocolate. My friend Helen Hall had somehow arranged for a box of Manons to be delivered to me from a tiny confectioner in Brussels. I never found out how she accomplished this feat, but since strange men rarely appear on my doorstep with fresh Belgian truffles, I did figure out how to make the truffles at home.

MAKES ABOUT 16 TRUFFLES

COFFEE TRUFFLE FILLING
½ cup heavy whipping cream
4 tablespoons (½ stick) unsalted butter, cut into 2 pieces
12 ounces white chocolate, Callebaut or Baker's Premium preferred, chopped
2 teaspoons instant decaffeinated coffee dissolved in 2 teaspoons water
1 teaspoon vanilla extract

WHITE CHOCOLATE COATING
8 ounces white chocolate, Callebaut or Baker's Premium preferred, chopped
5 teaspoons corn oil

Prepare the Coffee Truffle Filling

I. Put the cream and butter in a small saucepan and heat just until the cream is hot and the butter is melted. The hot cream mixture will form tiny bubbles around the edge of the pan and measure about 160°F. on a food thermometer. Do not let the mixture boil. Remove from the heat and add the chopped white chocolate. Let the white chocolate melt in the cream for 1 minute. Return the saucepan to low heat for 1 minute, if necessary, to melt the chocolate completely. Add the dissolved coffee and vanilla and stir the mixture until it is

· The truffles are formed into balls with a flat bottom, but they do not have to be uniformly smooth balls. A few bumps are appealing.

· In order to dip the truffles completely, I prepare more white chocolate coating than needed. Leftover coating can be cooled, chilled, and melted again for another use. If you pour it over ice cream, it will form a crisp shell on the ice cream.

· Let the coating cool a few minutes before trying to dip the truffles. If the coating is too warm, it may slide off the truffle filling.

· I use corn oil for the white chocolate coating. The corn oil balances well with the delicate taste of the white chocolate.

· I use a two-pronged fork to hold the truffle filling while I dip it in the white chocolate. A fondue fork or the pickle fork that came with my silverware set work equally well. A large two-pronged meat fork is too cumbersome for dipping candy. Special two- and three-pronged forks and dipping tools are available at specialty stores.

Doubling the Recipe
Double the ingredients.

To Freeze
Wrap each truffle in plastic wrap. Place the truffles in a single layer in a metal or plastic freezer container and cover tightly. Label with date and contents. Freeze up to 1 month.

To Serve
Defrost the wrapped truffles in the refrigerator at least 4 hours or overnight. Unwrap and let sit at room temperature for 15 minutes before serving. Leftover truffles can be covered with plastic wrap and stored in the refrigerator up to 3 days.

smooth. Pour the mixture into the large bowl of an electric mixer and press plastic wrap onto the surface. Refrigerate the sauce until it is firm and cold to the touch, about 3 hours or overnight.

2. Line a baking sheet with wax or parchment paper. With an electric mixer on high speed, whip the cold truffle until the mixture lightens in color, about 20 seconds. The mixture will look very smooth. Use a tablespoon to drop 16 tablespoons of the mixture onto the baking sheet to form mounds about 1 1/4 to 1 1/2 inches in diameter. The mounds will not be completely smooth. Freeze the truffle filling until it is firm, about 45 minutes.

Prepare the White Chocolate Coating

3. Put the white chocolate and corn oil in a heatproof container and place it over, but not touching, a saucepan of barely simmering water. Stir the mixture until the chocolate is melted and the mixture is smooth. Pour the coating into a small bowl (a soup bowl works well) and let it sit 5 minutes to cool slightly.

4. Remove the truffle fillings from the freezer. Lift the truffles and paper from the baking sheet. Use a thin metal spatula to loosen each truffle mound from the paper. Line the baking sheet with a clean piece of wax or parchment paper. Slide a two- or three-pronged candy dipping fork under the bottom of a cold truffle mound. Dip the truffle in the white chocolate coating and spoon the coating over the truffle. Lift out the coated truffle, let the excess white chocolate drip into the bowl, and tap the fork over the rim of the bowl to remove excess white chocolate. Use the metal spatula to slide the truffle off the fork and onto the paper-lined baking sheet, flat side down. Repeat to coat all of the truffles. Remove any excess coating that forms around the bottom edge of the truffle with the spatula. The coating will firm quickly. As soon as the coating is firm, dip a clean fork in the remaining coating and wave it over each truffle to form thin lines of white chocolate crisscrossing back and forth over the top. Move the fork quickly to create thin lines. If the white chocolate coating has become too firm to drizzle easily, pour it back in the heatproof container and warm it over hot water. Refrigerate or freeze the truffles to firm the coating thoroughly, about 30 minutes. Cover and refrigerate any leftover coating up to 1 week.

CRANBERRY, WALNUT, AND WHITE CHOCOLATE TRUFFLES

All year long I think about a special, but easy gift from my kitchen to give as holiday gifts. One year I nestled these fruit-and-nut white chocolate truffles in shiny holiday tins for my sweet offerings. The creamy white chocolate truffle filling holds tart red cranberries, orange zest, and toasted walnuts. After the soft truffles were rolled in ground walnuts for a simple, yet professional decorative finish, I felt like a fancy French confectioner.

MAKES ABOUT 24 TRUFFLES

1 cup cranberries, fresh or previously frozen and defrosted
¼ cup freshly squeezed orange juice
¼ cup sugar
4 tablespoons (½ stick) unsalted butter
½ cup whipping cream
12 ounces white chocolate, Callebaut or Baker's Premium preferred, chopped
2 teaspoons grated orange zest
½ teaspoon vanilla extract
1 tablespoon Grand Marnier liqueur
¾ cup walnuts, toasted, cooled, and finely chopped (see page 12)
1½ cups walnuts, toasted, cooled, and ground (see page 12)

1. Line a plate with a double thickness of paper towels. Heat the cranberries, orange juice, and sugar in a medium saucepan over medium heat until the cranberries soften and pop and the sugar is dissolved, about 5 minutes. Stir the cranberries several times while they are cooking. Drain the cranberries and discard the liquid. Spread the drained cranberries on the paper towels to cool and dry.

2. Put the butter and cream in a small saucepan and heat just until the cream is hot and the butter is melted. The hot cream mixture will form tiny bubbles around the edge of the pan and measure about 175°F. on a food thermometer. Do not let the mixture boil. Remove from the heat and add the chopped white

Good Advice
· These truffles are quite soft at room temperature and should be served cold. When chilled, the consistency remains soft and creamy.

· Defrost frozen cranberries overnight in the refrigerator, and they will hold their shape. Once cooked, drain and dry the cranberries thoroughly so that they do not streak the white chocolate filling and turn it pink (which doesn't affect the taste, but the filling loses the red and white contrast).

Doubling the Recipe
Double the ingredients.

Leave the truffles on the baking sheet and put them in the freezer to firm, about 1 hour. Wrap pairs of truffles in plastic wrap. Place the truffles in a single layer in a metal or plastic freezer container and cover tightly. Label with date and contents. Freeze up to 1 month.

To Serve

Defrost the wrapped truffles in the refrigerator at least 3 hours or overnight. Unwrap and serve cold. Leftover truffles can be covered with plastic wrap and stored in the refrigerator up to 3 days.

chocolate. Let the white chocolate melt in the cream for 1 minute. Return the saucepan to low heat for 1 minute, if necessary, to melt the chocolate completely. Stir in the orange zest, vanilla, Grand Marnier, cranberries, and finely chopped walnuts. Pour the mixture into a medium bowl and cover and refrigerate until firm, about 3 hours or overnight.

3. Line a baking sheet with wax or parchment paper. Roll tablespoon-size portions of the truffle mixture between the palms of your hands to form balls, $1\frac{1}{4}$ to $1\frac{1}{2}$ inches in diameter. Roll the balls in the ground walnuts to coat them completely. Place the finished truffles on the baking sheet. The truffles will be soft so handle them gently. Chill the truffles for 1 hour. Serve immediately or freeze.

Mousse Desserts

I was halfway through writing this book when I suddenly realized that there was no recipe for chocolate mousse. Can you imagine a chocolate cookbook that didn't have one of the world's most popular chocolate desserts? I couldn't. I rectified my mistake and made a chocolate mousse that would freeze and defrost well. Since the major ingredients for a mousse are chocolate and whipped cream, it contains enough fat to freeze successfully.

Many of these desserts have interesting but simple finishes. Plain storebought cookies form geometric designs in slices of Gillian's Chocolate Pudding–Mousse Cake, and raspberry mousse is cleverly enrobed in a thin layer of chocolate to form a Chocolate-covered Raspberry Mousse Mountain. It takes just minutes to enclose tiramisù in a chocolate band, and an orange-filled jelly roll makes a fancy spiral edge for an Orange and White Chocolate Charlotte.

Classic recipes for mousse are not cooked and often contain raw eggs. Several years ago when some eggs were thought to be carriers of salmonella bacteria, it became advisable not to use raw eggs in recipes. Since salmonella is killed at 160°F., I cook egg yolks in mousse recipes to this temperature. And since egg whites contain little protein and make a poor environment for salmonella, I use raw egg whites in some of my mousse recipes. Handle eggs carefully by keeping them refrigerated until you use them. Use fresh eggs and discard any with cracked shells. I use egg whites cold, rather than at room temperature, in unbaked mousse desserts. Tiramisù usually contains raw eggs but my recipe omits them entirely without giving up one whit of the expected creamy, rich texture. The final decision, however, rests with you as to whether or not to use uncooked eggs.

PURE CHOCOLATE MOUSSE

I still remember the first time I tasted chocolate mousse. After Jeff and I were married, we took a trip to France. One evening we ordered a dessert called mousse au chocolat. *I had no idea what we were getting, but since it was chocolate, how bad could it be? The waiter brought a big crock filled with a creamy, dark chocolate mixture to the table and served us directly from the crock. He made the big mistake of leaving the crock on the table so we could help ourselves to seconds. Boy, did we choose the right place for our chocolate mousse initiation. Ever since, any chocolate mousse I make is dark, rich, and always served in a large bowl so everyone can take as much as they want. This recipe makes about four and a half cups of mousse and will probably serve six people, but the number of servings depends on who you are serving.*

SERVES ABOUT 6

8 ounces semisweet chocolate, chopped
3 ounces unsweetened chocolate, chopped
$^1/_3$ plus $^1/_4$ cup sugar
$^1/_4$ cup hot water
3 large eggs, separated
$^1/_4$ teaspoon cream of tartar
$^3/_4$ cup cold whipping cream
1 teaspoon vanilla extract
$^1/_2$ teaspoon instant decaffeinated coffee granules

Whipped cream, for serving with the mousse

I. Have ready a $1^1/_2$- to 2-quart serving bowl. A soufflé dish works well. Put the semisweet chocolate, unsweetened chocolate, the $^1/_4$ cup of sugar, and water in a heatproof container and place it over, but not touching, a saucepan of gently simmering water. Stir the mixture together until the chocolate melts and the mixture is smooth. Remove the heatproof container from over the water and

Good Advice

· When cooking the egg yolks with the melted chocolate, stir the mixture constantly.

· The chocolate mixture must be soft and creamy when you add the beaten egg whites to it. It should be cool to the touch (about 110°F.). If the chocolate mixture has become too firm from chilling in the refrigerator, stir it until it becomes creamy.

· I pass a bowl of whipped cream to spoon over the mousse. My son, Peter, claims it cuts the richness of the mousse.

Doubling the Recipe

Double the ingredients and use a 3-quart serving bowl.

whisk in the egg yolks. Protect your hands from any steam that escapes. Place the chocolate mixture back over the simmering water and, stirring constantly, cook just until the temperature reaches 160°F. on a food thermometer, about 8 minutes. The chocolate mixture will thicken and look a bit grainy when the egg yolks are added, then become shiny and smooth as it reaches 160°F. Transfer the chocolate mixture to a large bowl and refrigerate just until the mixture is cool to the touch, about 20 minutes. Stir the mixture occasionally while it is cooling so that it cools evenly. The mixture will have a temperature of about 110°F. if measured with a food thermometer. The mixture can also be chilled in the freezer for about 10 minutes.

2. Put the egg whites and cream of tartar in a clean large bowl of an electric mixer and with clean dry beaters, beat on low speed until the egg whites are foamy. Increase the speed to medium-high, and beat just until soft peaks form. Slowly add the 1/3 cup of sugar, 1 tablespoon at a time. Remove the cooled chocolate mixture from the refrigerator and whisk about half of the beaten egg whites into the chocolate mixture until the mixture is smooth. Use a large rubber spatula to fold the remaining egg whites into the chocolate mixture.

3. Put the whipping cream, vanilla, and coffee in a clean large bowl of an electric mixer. Beat the cream at medium speed until soft peaks form. Fold the whipped cream into the chocolate mixture. Pour the mousse into the serving bowl. Smooth the top of the mousse.

To Freeze

Freeze the mousse, uncovered, until the top is cold and firm, about 2 hours. Press plastic wrap onto the surface of the mousse then wrap the bowl with heavy aluminum foil. Label with date and contents. Freeze up to 3 weeks.

To Serve

Remove the mousse from the freezer and remove the plastic wrap that is resting on top of the mousse. Wrap the bowl with plastic wrap or aluminum foil in such a way that the wrapping does not sit on the mousse. Defrost the wrapped mousse in the refrigerator at least 5 hours or overnight. Serve the mousse cold. Pass a bowl of whipped cream. Leftover mousse can be covered and refrigerated up to 2 days.

HOT CHOCOLATE MOUSSE

I *f desserts have destinies, Hot Chocolate Mousse is destined to become a classic. I freeze a simple chocolate mousse in ramekins, then put them in the oven to bake when we sit down to dinner. The mousse puffs up as it bakes and has the texture of a dense, dark chocolate soufflé, but unlike a soufflé, it is virtually foolproof. You can create additional flavors by adding nut praline, orange zest, or even raspberry jam to the chocolate mousse.*

SERVES 6

6 ounces semisweet chocolate, chopped
6 tablespoons (³/4 stick) unsalted butter
3 large eggs, separated
¹/4 teaspoon cream of tartar
¹/4 cup sugar
1 teaspoon vanilla extract

1. Have ready six 6-ounce ramekins that are safe to transfer from freezer to oven. Put the chocolate and butter in a heatproof container and place it over, but not touching, a saucepan of barely simmering water. Stir the chocolate and butter together until the chocolate melts and the mixture is smooth. Transfer the mixture to a large bowl to cool slightly.

2. Put the egg whites and cream of tartar in the clean large bowl of an electric mixer and with clean dry beaters, beat the egg whites with the cream of tartar on low speed until the egg whites are foamy and the cream of tartar is dissolved. Increase the speed to medium-high and beat just until soft peaks form. Slowly add the sugar, 1 tablespoon at a time.

3. Use a large mixing spoon to mix the egg yolks thoroughly into the chocolate mixture. Stir in the vanilla. Stir about a fourth of the beaten egg whites into

Good Advice

· Leave ¹/2 inch of space at the top of each ramekin since the mousse will rise as it bakes. Let the baked mousse cool for about 10 minutes before serving. It will retain its puffy texture and be pleasantly warm rather than burning hot.

· The plastic wrap may disturb the top of the mousse in the freezer, but baking will restore a smooth surface.

Doubling the Recipe

Double the ingredients.

To Freeze

Wrap each ramekin tightly with plastic wrap then heavy aluminum foil. Label with date and contents. Freeze up to 1 month.

the chocolate mixture. Use a rubber spatula to fold the remaining egg whites into the chocolate mixture. Pour a scant $\frac{1}{2}$ cup of the chocolate mixture into each of the ramekins, leaving at least $\frac{1}{2}$ inch of space at the top.

VARIATIONS

· Fold 2 tablespoons seedless raspberry jam or 1 tablespoon grated orange zest into the prepared mousse mixture.

· Fold 2 tablespoons almond or hazelnut praline powder (see page 54) into the mousse mixture and sprinkle $\frac{1}{2}$ teaspoon praline powder over the top of the mousse in each ramekin, then freeze as directed.

To Bake and Serve the Mousse

Position an oven rack in the middle of the oven. Preheat the oven to 325°F. Remove as many ramekins from the freezer as you want to bake, unwrap them, and place them on a baking sheet or pie tin. Bake 25 minutes. The mousse will rise slightly above the rim of the ramekin as it bakes. Cool the mousse 10 minutes and serve. A leftover ramekin can be rewarmed for about 10 minutes in a 275°F. oven.

ORANGE AND WHITE CHOCOLATE CHARLOTTE

One sheet of Hot Milk Sponge Cake does double duty in this elegant dessert. Part of the sponge cake sheet is used to line the bottom of a springform pan. The remainder is spread with orange marmalade, rolled up jelly-roll fashion, and cut into thin slices to line the sides of the pan. The spiraled cake slices make a fancy edge and hold the charlotte filling, which is then topped with white chocolate curls.

SERVES 12

1 Hot Milk Sponge Cake Sheet, 17 × 12 inches (page 44), baked and cooled
   or defrosted
1/3 cup orange marmalade

ORANGE AND WHITE CHOCOLATE MOUSSE
1 envelope gelatin (1/4 ounce)
1/4 cup cold water
1 cup whole milk
4 large egg yolks
1/3 cup sugar
8 ounces white chocolate, Callebaut or Baker's Premium preferred,
   chopped
1 tablespoon grated orange zest
1 teaspoon vanilla extract
1 tablespoon Grand Marnier
1 1/4 cups cold whipping cream

3 cups White Chocolate Curls (page 55)

I. Have ready a 9-inch springform pan. Unroll the sponge cake sheet onto a clean dish towel and remove any paper wrapping. The long side of the cake should be parallel to the edge of the counter. Using the bottom of the springform pan as a guide, cut a 9-inch circle from the cake. Line the bottom of the pan with the cake circle. From the remaining cake, cut a strip 7 inches wide and about 12 inches long. Spread the cake strip evenly with the orange marmalade. Roll the cake up tightly like a jelly roll. Use a serrated knife to cut the cake roll

Good Advice
· The baked cake sheet should measure about 17 × 12 inches. This size is large enough to cut a 7-inch-wide strip of cake to roll with the marmalade and a 9-inch circle to line the bottom of the pan.

· You can remove the charlotte from the springform pan bottom to a serving plate after it is frozen. Don't attempt to move the charlotte to another plate after it defrosts. It's risky and not worth taking the chance that it will break.

Doubling the Recipe
Use two baked sponge sheets and double the remaining ingredients.

into approximately ½-inch slices. Line the inside of the pan with cake slices placed flat against the side of the pan and standing upright. You will need about 12 slices to go around the pan completely.

Prepare the Orange and White Chocolate Mousse

2. Sprinkle the gelatin over the water in the measuring cup and let the gelatin soften while you prepare the custard mixture. Put the milk in a medium saucepan and heat over medium-low heat until the milk is hot. The hot milk will form tiny bubbles around the edge of the pan and measure about 175°F. on a food thermometer. Do not let the milk boil.

3. Put the egg yolks in a medium bowl and use a whisk to mix the sugar into the egg yolks. Pour the hot milk over the egg yolk mixture while whisking constantly. Pour the mixture back into the saucepan and cook over medium heat, stirring constantly, until the mixture measures 165°F. on a food thermometer. Remove the mixture from the heat and stir in the softened gelatin. Stir the mixture until it is smooth and the gelatin dissolves. Mix in the white chocolate and stir to dissolve. Return the mixture to low heat if needed to dissolve the white chocolate. Stir in the orange zest, vanilla, and Grand Marnier. Pour the white chocolate mixture into a large bowl, cover with plastic wrap, and refrigerate until thickened slightly, about 30 minutes. Stir the mixture occasionally to ensure it cools evenly.

4. Put the cream in the clean large bowl of an electric mixer and beat on medium-high speed to soft peaks. Use a rubber spatula to fold half of the cream into the cooled and slightly thickened white chocolate mixture. Fold in the remaining cream. Pour the filling into the prepared pan and refrigerate until the filling is firm enough to support the white chocolate curls, about 1 hour.

5. Spoon the white chocolate curls over the top of the charlotte. Return the charlotte to the refrigerator for at least 5 hours to firm completely or put it in the freezer to firm more quickly, about 2 hours. You can remove the sides of the springform pan after the filling is firm or after it is frozen.

To Freeze
Freeze the charlotte, uncovered, for about 2 hours, until it is cold and firm. Wrap with plastic wrap then with heavy aluminum foil. Label with date and contents. Freeze up to 3 weeks. Once the charlotte is frozen, you can remove the sides of the springform pan. Either leave the charlotte on the springform bottom or use a large spatula to slide it onto a serving plate. Rewrap the charlotte with the plastic wrap and aluminum foil.

To Serve
Defrost the wrapped charlotte in the refrigerator about 4 hours. Do not slide the charlotte off the springform bottom once it defrosts. Use a large sharp knife to cut the charlotte into slices. Serve the charlotte cold. Leftover charlotte can be covered with plastic wrap and stored in the refrigerator up to 2 days.

INDIVIDUAL CHOCOLATE-ORANGE MOUSSE CAKES

These little mousse cakes may look as if they came from a French pâtisserie, but they're actually quite easy to prepare. Mounds of intensely flavored chocolate-orange mousse sit on top of circles of chocolate soufflé cake, and chocolate glaze covers the mousse and cake.

SERVES 6

½ Chocolate Soufflé Cake Sheet (page 46), cooled thoroughly or defrosted
   just until soft enough to cut easily
2 teaspoons Grand Marnier

CHOCOLATE-ORANGE MOUSSE
4 ounces semisweet chocolate, chopped
1 ounce unsweetened chocolate, chopped
¼ cup plus 2 tablespoons sugar
2 tablespoons hot water
2 large eggs, separated
⅛ teaspoon cream of tartar
½ cup cold whipping cream
1 teaspoon vanilla extract
1 teaspoon grated orange zest
1 teaspoon Grand Marnier

CHOCOLATE GLAZE
½ cup whipping cream
4 tablespoons (½ stick) soft unsalted butter
¼ cup light corn syrup
4 ounces semisweet chocolate, chopped

2 teaspoons grated orange zest, for serving with
   the cakes (optional)

I. Use a 3-inch round metal cutter to cut 6 circles from the cake sheet. Cut the scraps left from the cake into approximately ½-inch pieces. Measure 1 cup of

Good Advice
· If you have a chocolate soufflé cake sheet in the freezer, cut the cake in half while it is frozen and return half of the cake to the freezer for another use. Defrost the frozen chocolate soufflé cake just until it can be cut easily, about 15 minutes. Cold cake cuts easily into neat rounds.

· Chill the mousse thoroughly before adding the chocolate glaze, and the mousse will hold its shape when the glaze is applied.

Doubling the Recipe
Use a whole soufflé cake sheet and double the remaining ingredients.

cake pieces and put them in a small bowl. Sprinkle the 2 teaspoons of Grand Marnier over the cake pieces and stir together. Set aside.

Prepare the Chocolate-Orange Mousse

2. Put the semisweet chocolate, unsweetened chocolate, the 2 tablespoons of sugar, and hot water in a heatproof container and place it over, but not touching, a saucepan of gently simmering water. Stir the chocolate and water together until the chocolate is melted and the mixture is smooth. Remove the heatproof container from over the water and whisk in the egg yolks. Protect your hands from any steam that escapes. Place the chocolate mixture back over the simmering water and, stirring constantly, cook just until the temperature measures 160°F. on a food thermometer, about 5 minutes. The chocolate mixture may thicken and look a bit grainy when the egg yolks are added, then become shiny and smooth as it reaches 160°F. Transfer the chocolate mixture to a large bowl and refrigerate the mixture just until it is cool to the touch, about 10 minutes. Stir the mixture once while it is cooling to ensure that it cools evenly. The mixture will have a temperature of about 110°F., if measured with a food thermometer. Or chill the mixture in the freezer for about 5 minutes.

3. Put the egg whites and cream of tartar in a clean large bowl of an electric mixer and with clean dry beaters, beat on low speed until the egg whites are foamy. Increase the speed to medium-high, and beat just until soft peaks form. Slowly add the 1/4 cup of sugar, 1 tablespoon at a time.

4. Remove the cooled chocolate mixture from the refrigerator, and whisk about half of the beaten egg whites into the chocolate mixture until the mixture is smooth. Use a large rubber spatula to fold the remaining egg whites into the chocolate mixture.

5. Put the 1/2 cup cold whipping cream and vanilla in a clean bowl of an elec-

Carefully lift each cake from the cake rack and wrap with plastic wrap. Place the cakes in a single layer in a metal or plastic freezer container and cover tightly. Label with date and contents. Freeze up to 1 month.

To Serve
Defrost as many wrapped cakes as you need in the refrigerator at least 4 hours or overnight. Remove the plastic wrap and sprinkle the top of each cake with grated orange zest, if desired. Serve cold. Leftover cakes can be covered with plastic wrap and stored in the refrigerator up to 3 days.

tric mixer. Beat the cream at medium speed until soft peaks form. Fold the whipped cream, orange zest, and Grand Marnier into the chocolate mixture. Fold the Grand Marnier–flavored cake pieces into the mixture. Chill the mousse in the refrigerator until it firms slightly, about 8 minutes.

6. Put the cake circles on a cake rack. Mound a generous $1/2$ cup of mousse on each cake circle. Smooth the mousse with a thin metal spatula, forming the mousse into a conical shape. Put the rack of cakes in the freezer and freeze until the mousse is firm, $1\frac{1}{2}$ to 2 hours.

Prepare the Chocolate Glaze

7. Put the cream, butter, and corn syrup in a small saucepan and stir over medium heat until the mixture is hot and the butter melts. The hot cream mixture will form tiny bubbles around the edge of the pan and measure about 175°F. on a food thermometer. Do not let the mixture boil. Remove the pan from the heat and add the chopped chocolate. Let the chocolate melt for about 30 seconds. Gently stir the glaze until all of the chocolate is melted and the glaze is smooth. Let the glaze cool until it thickens slightly, about 30 minutes.

8. Remove the cakes from the freezer. Put a piece of wax paper under the rack to catch and recycle any glaze that drips off the cakes. Pour enough glaze over each cake to cover it. Smooth any unglazed spots with a thin metal spatula. Return the cakes and rack to the freezer to firm the glaze, about 30 minutes.

GILLIAN'S CHOCOLATE PUDDING—MOUSSE CAKE

When I told Gillian Lewis, our English cousin, that I wanted to use her cake in this book, she protested that she was not a baker and seldom made desserts. I answered that her recipe proved you don't have to be a baker to make good homemade desserts.

The cake is an English version of our American chocolate icebox cakes. Broken plain biscuits, as the English call their cookies, are mixed into a bittersweet chocolate mixture. Social Tea cookies are perfect. Cocoa powder lends a dark color and chocolate pudding taste to the cake, while semisweet chocolate provides the rich chocolate flavor.

SERVES 10 TO 12

$3/4$ cup warm water
4 tablespoons plus 1 teaspoon unsweetened Dutch process cocoa powder, such as Droste or Hershey's European Style, sifted
$3/4$ teaspoon instant decaffeinated coffee granules
6 ounces semisweet chocolate, chopped
3 large eggs
6 ounces ($1^1/2$ sticks) soft unsalted butter
$3/4$ cup superfine sugar
1 teaspoon vanilla extract
24 Social Tea cookies or similar plain cookie, broken in half (about 4 ounces)

I. Cut a long piece of parchment paper to fit the bottom and extend over the ends of a long, narrow loaf pan with a 7- to 8-cup capacity. Use a pan that measures about $12^3/4 \times 4^1/4 \times 2^1/2$ inches. Press the parchment paper strip onto the bottom and over the ends of the pan.

2. Put the water, cocoa powder, and coffee in a heatproof container and stir the mixture until the cocoa and coffee dissolve. Place the container over, but not touching, a saucepan of gently simmering water. Add the chopped chocolate and stir until the chocolate melts and the mixture is smooth. Remove the heatproof container from over the water and whisk in the eggs. Protect your hands from any steam that escapes. Place the chocolate mixture back over the simmer-

Good Advice

· The cake will fill a 7-cup loaf pan only about halfway so the cake slices will be thin and have a rectangular shape. I use a long loaf pan, $10^1/2$ inches long by 4 inches wide. Any size loaf pan with a capacity over 5 cups will work, but different size pans will produce different size slices of cake.

· Use superfine sugar, which dissolves more easily in the filling than normal granulated sugar.

· The cake is easy to slice since the cookies soften in the chocolate mixture.

Doubling the Recipe

Double the ingredients and use two loaf pans.

Loosen the sides of the cake from the pan with a small sharp knife. Place a long, narrow serving plate or long piece of cardboard covered with heavy aluminum foil on top of the cake and invert it. Release the cake from the pan by pulling on the ends of the parchment paper. Remove the pan and discard the parchment paper. Wrap the cake tightly with plastic wrap then heavy aluminum foil. Label with date and contents. Freeze up to 1 month.

To Serve

Defrost the wrapped cake in the refrigerator at least 4 hours or overnight. Use a large sharp knife to slice the cake into approximately ½-inch slices and serve 2 slices per serving. Serve cold. Leftover cake can be covered with plastic wrap and stored in the refrigerator up to 2 days.

ing water and cook, stirring constantly just until the temperature measures 160°F. on a food thermometer, about 6 minutes. Put the warm chocolate mixture in a medium bowl and refrigerate until cool to the touch, about 30 minutes. Stir occasionally to ensure that the mixture cools throughout. It should be cool enough that it doesn't melt the butter when it is added to the creamed mixture.

3. Put the butter and sugar in the large bowl of an electric mixer and beat on medium speed until the mixture is creamy, about 2 minutes. Stir in the vanilla. Remove the chocolate mixture from the refrigerator and whisk it smooth. Decrease the mixer speed to low and mix the cooled chocolate mixture into the butter mixture. Increase the speed to medium and beat for 1 minute. Stop the mixer and scrape the sides of the bowl once during this time.

4. Use a large spoon to stir the cookies into the chocolate mixture. Pour the mixture into the prepared pan and smooth the top.

5. Refrigerate the cake until firm, about 6 hours. Or freeze the cake until firm, about 1½ hours. The cake must be chilled thoroughly before it can be removed from the pan.

RASPBERRY-FILLED CHOCOLATE MOUSSE

There's a surprise in the middle of this chocolate mousse—raspberries. Simply fill a bowl with half of the chocolate mousse, scatter raspberries over the mousse, and top with more mousse. Use a glass bowl to show off the red raspberry layer.

SERVES 8

9 ounces semisweet chocolate, chopped
1 ounce unsweetened chocolate, chopped
1/2 cup plus 1 tablespoon sugar
3 tablespoons water
2 tablespoons light corn syrup
3 large egg whites, at room temperature
1/4 teaspoon cream of tartar
1 1/2 cups cold whipping cream
1 teaspoon vanilla extract
2 cups (1 pint) fresh raspberries or unsweetened frozen raspberries, not defrosted
Whipped cream, for serving (optional)
Fresh raspberries, for serving (optional)

1. Preheat the oven to 175°F. Have ready a serving bowl, preferably glass, with a 2 1/2- to 3-quart capacity.

2. Put the semisweet and unsweetened chocolate in a small ovenproof container and melt it in the oven, 10 to 12 minutes. Remove the chocolate from the oven as soon as it is melted and stir it smooth. Set aside to cool slightly.

3. Put the sugar, water, and corn syrup in a small saucepan. Cover the saucepan and cook the syrup over low heat until all of the sugar is dissolved, stirring occasionally to help the sugar dissolve. Do not let the syrup boil until the sugar dissolves. Uncover the saucepan, increase the heat to high, and boil the mixture, without stirring, until the syrup measures 240°F. (soft ball stage) on a candy thermometer. Wipe down the sides of the pan with a pastry brush dipped in hot water to dissolve any sugar crystals that form on the side of the pan.

Good Advice

· When adding the raspberry layer, put a ring of raspberries around the edge of the mousse so that the raspberries show through the sides of the glass bowl.

· This mousse is prepared with an Italian meringue, which produces a dense, stable mousse. For more detail on Italian meringue, see page 10.

Doubling the Recipe

Double the ingredients and put the mousse in a 4- to 5-quart serving bowl or two 2 1/2- to 3-quart bowls.

Freeze the mousse until the top is firm, about 1 hour. Press plastic wrap on the top of the mousse. Gently press heavy aluminum foil over the mousse. Label with date and contents. Freeze up to 1 month.

To Serve

Remove the aluminum foil from the frozen mousse. Rewrap the plastic wrap over the top of the bowl so that it does not touch the mousse. Defrost the mousse in the refrigerator at least 6 hours or overnight. A double recipe of mousse in a large bowl will need to defrost overnight. Serve the mousse cold. Serve with whipped cream topped with fresh raspberries, if desired.

4. Begin beating the egg whites when the sugar syrup begins to boil. Put the egg whites and cream of tartar in a clean large bowl of an electric mixer and beat with clean dry beaters on low speed until the egg whites are foamy and the cream of tartar is dissolved. Increase the speed to medium-high and beat the egg whites to soft peaks. Add 1 tablespoon sugar. As soon as the syrup reaches 240°F., with the mixer on low speed, slowly pour the hot syrup in a thin stream onto the softly beaten egg whites. If the syrup reaches 240°F. before the egg whites are ready, remove the syrup from the heat for a few seconds and finish beating the egg whites. Pour the syrup in the space between the sides of the bowl and the beaters to prevent as much sugar syrup as possible from splashing onto the sides of the bowl and the beaters. Continue beating the meringue at medium-low speed for 5 minutes. The outside of the bowl will be lukewarm and the meringue will be stiff and have a temperature of about 72° to 78°F. if measured with a food thermometer.

5. Put the melted chocolate in a large bowl. Whisk a third of the egg whites into the melted chocolate. Fold in the remaining egg whites.

6. Put the whipping cream and vanilla in the clean large bowl of an electric mixer. Beat on medium-high speed until soft peaks form. Fold the whipped cream into the chocolate mixture.

7. Spoon half of the mousse mixture into the bottom of the glass bowl. Spread the raspberries evenly over the mousse, placing a ring of raspberries around the edge of the bowl. Spread the remaining mousse over the raspberries. The mousse is ready to serve. If you have used frozen raspberries, refrigerate the mousse until they soften.

VARIATION Fill 8 stemmed glasses with mousse and raspberries. To freeze, wrap each glass with plastic wrap. Gently press heavy aluminum foil over the top of each glass. Individual glasses of mousse will defrost in about 4 hours.

CHOCOLATE-COVERED RASPBERRY MOUSSE MOUNTAIN

*N**ever will you spend so little time to produce such a spectacular dessert. The mountain of raspberry mousse rests on a chocolate soufflé cake layer and is enclosed in an impressive sheet of chocolate. Although the chocolate covering looks difficult, it is actually formed by an easy, clever technique.*

SERVES 10

One 9-inch Chocolate Soufflé Cake Layer (page 46), cooled or defrosted

RASPBERRY MOUSSE
1½ cups fresh raspberries or unsweetened frozen raspberries, defrosted and drained
2 tablespoons granulated sugar
¼ cup cold water
1 envelope gelatin (¼ ounce)
2 cups cold whipping cream
¼ cup powdered sugar
1 tablespoon framboise or other raspberry-flavored liqueur
1 teaspoon vanilla extract

CHOCOLATE COVERING
6 ounces semisweet chocolate, chopped

1. Fit the chocolate cake layer into the bottom of an 8-inch springform pan. Set aside.

Prepare the Raspberry Mousse

2. Put the raspberries and granulated sugar in a small bowl and stir them together, crushing the raspberries slightly. Let the mixture sit for about 5 minutes until some juice forms. Put the water in a small saucepan and sprinkle the gelatin over the water. Let the gelatin soften.

3. Put the cream, powdered sugar, framboise, and vanilla in the large bowl of

· If you are using frozen raspberries, measure them while frozen.

· A 9-inch baked and cooled chocolate soufflé cake layer will shrink as it cools and fit easily into an 8-inch springform pan.

· To make the chocolate covering, cover two paper triangles with melted chocolate and press one paper triangle over one side of the mousse, letting it harden. When the chocolate sheet is firm, peel the paper from the chocolate. Then wrap the second chocolate sheet over the other side of the mousse. Firm the chocolate, peel off the paper, and you have a chocolate covered mousse mountain. The chocolate will not be a tight covering, but will have attractive gentle curves. This method can be used for other desserts, and smaller triangles can be used to cover individual pastries.

· If the parchment paper has been rolled, the triangles will curl up on one side of the paper. Lay the triangles curled side down, and they will be easy to handle when you wrap the cake. Spread the chocolate carefully on the parchment paper triangles. Any thin spots can cause the chocolate to break, although this can be patched with a bit of melted chocolate.

· Use semisweet baking chocolate, not chocolate chips. Melted semisweet baking chocolate is thinner than melted chocolate chips and spreads easily over the paper.

Doubling the Recipe

Use two cake layers, double the mousse ingredients, and prepare four triangles of chocolate.

an electric mixer and beat on medium speed just until the cream begins to thicken and lines begin to form in the cream. When you begin beating the cream, put the saucepan of gelatin over low heat and melt the softened gelatin, stirring to melt it evenly. Stir the melted gelatin into the raspberries. With the mixer running, immediately pour the raspberry mixture into the cream. Continue to beat until firm peaks form. The gelatin will thicken the cold cream and firm peaks will form quickly.

4. Pour the raspberry mousse into the cake-lined pan. Spread the mixture to the edges of the pan and spread the center of the mousse into a mound. The center of the mousse will be about 5 inches above the bottom of the pan. Put the mousse in the freezer until it is firm, about 30 minutes.

Prepare the Chocolate Covering

5. Preheat the oven to 175°F.

6. Place the semisweet chocolate in a ovenproof container. Melt the chocolate in the oven, about 6 to 8 minutes. Stir the chocolate smooth. Cut a 14-inch square of parchment paper and cut the paper into 2 triangles. Put the triangles on a large piece of parchment paper to protect the kitchen counter. Spread the triangles flat. There will be one long side that will wrap around the bottom of the cake. Use a thin metal spatula to spread the chocolate in an even layer over the 2 paper triangles. Check to see that there are no thin spots with paper showing through. Set aside the container that held the melted chocolate, which will have a bit of melted chocolate left in it.

7. Remove the filled springform pan from the freezer. Use a small sharp knife to loosen the mousse from the sides of the pan and remove the sides. Use a large flat spatula to slide the cake onto a serving platter or cardboard cake circle. Holding the ends of 2 triangle points, carefully pick up one of the chocolate-covered papers and with the long side of the triangle edge around the bottom of the cake, wrap the paper, chocolate side against the mousse, around half of the cake. The paper will curve slightly, but don't let it fold back onto itself since this will make the paper hard to remove when the chocolate hardens. A triangle

point will drape over the center of the mousse. Check to see that the bottom of the chocolate triangle covers the bottom of the cake. Return the cake to the freezer until the chocolate hardens, about 10 minutes. Remove the cake from the freezer and carefully peel the paper from the chocolate, beginning at a bottom corner and tearing off and discarding the paper as soon as several inches of it are free. Continue to peel all of the paper from the chocolate. If you must touch the chocolate, protect it from your warm fingers with a small piece of parchment paper. Wrap the remaining triangle of chocolate around the other side of the cake. This second chocolate triangle will overlap the edges of the first piece of chocolate. Freeze the chocolate covering until firm, about 10 minutes. Remove the cake from the freezer and carefully remove the paper. If the chocolate should crack, spread a bit of melted chocolate, from the container that held the melted chocolate, over the crack to patch it.

To Freeze

Wrap the cake carefully with plastic wrap, then gently with heavy aluminum foil. Label with date and contents and freeze up to 3 weeks. The chocolate covering is fragile so do not stack anything on top of the cake or push frozen items against the cake.

To Serve

Defrost the wrapped cake in the refrigerator overnight. Use a large sharp knife to cut the cake into wedges. Warm the knife under hot water and dry it for easier cutting of the chocolate covering. Serve cold. Leftover cake can be wrapped with plastic wrap and stored in the refrigerator up to 1 day.

EBONY AND IVORY MOUSSE SANDWICHES

One of the great pleasures of baking is that you get to taste the dessert while you prepare it. When I was making some dark and white chocolate striped squares for garnishing a Winter White Yule Log, I munched on a few chocolate scraps. As soon as I tasted the dark and white chocolates together, I knew I wanted to create a dessert that highlighted the combination, and these playful, yet sophisticated, mousse sandwiches are the result. Thin squares of dark and white chocolate hold a dense chocolate mousse filling, and thin lines of dark chocolate piped over the white chocolate make an artistic finish.

SERVES 12

CHOCOLATE SQUARES
6 ounces semisweet chocolate, chopped
8 ounces white chocolate, Callebaut or Baker's Premium preferred, chopped

DENSE CHOCOLATE MOUSSE FILLING
7 ounces semisweet chocolate, chopped
1 ounce unsweetened chocolate, chopped
3 tablespoons unsalted butter
$\frac{1}{2}$ cup whipping cream
1 teaspoon vanilla extract
2 large egg whites
$\frac{1}{8}$ teaspoon cream of tartar
$\frac{1}{3}$ cup sugar

1 ounce semisweet chocolate, chopped

Prepare the Chocolate Squares

1. Turn 2 baking sheets bottom side up. Cover the bottom of each baking sheet with wax or parchment paper. Preheat the oven to 175°F.

2. Place the semisweet chocolate in an ovenproof container and the white chocolate in a nonreactive ovenproof container. Melt the chocolates in the oven,

Good Advice

· When cooling the chocolate prior to cutting it into squares, watch it carefully and remove it from the refrigerator while it is still soft, but not runny. If it should harden, warm it for a few seconds in a 175°F. oven to soften it slightly. If the chocolate is too soft, it will not hold the cut marks. If it is too hard, it will be difficult to cut into even squares.

· Keep the prepared chocolate squares cold as you work with them. Since cold chocolate is less fragile than warm chocolate, this prevents the chocolate squares from breaking or bending.

· Keep the sandwiches cold until they are served. The squares of chocolate will soften if held at room temperature. The easiest way to eat the sandwiches is to pick them up and eat them with your hands, but you can serve them with a knife and fork.

about 12 minutes. Stir each chocolate smooth. Use a thin metal spatula to spread the white chocolate evenly over 1 paper-lined baking sheet into a rectangle about 13 × 10 inches. Spread the semisweet chocolate over the paper on the second baking sheet into another rectangle. The chocolate should cover the paper so that the paper does not show through the chocolate. The chocolate will look shiny and wet. Put both chocolate-covered baking sheets in the refrigerator and chill just until the chocolate looks dull and dry and is soft but no longer melted, about 5 minutes for the white chocolate and about 3 minutes for the dark chocolate. Do not let the chocolate harden.

3. Use a large sharp knife to trim the edges of each chocolate sheet into a 12 × 9-inch rectangle. Use the knife to mark twelve 3-inch squares on each sheet of chocolate. Press down to make sharp edges without drawing the knife across the chocolate. Check to see that the knife cuts completely through the chocolate. If the chocolate is too soft and runs together, chill it until it is firm enough to hold the cut marks. If the chocolate hardens and then cracks when it is cut, warm the chocolate sheet in the oven for a few seconds. Return the marked chocolate to the refrigerator to firm completely, about 30 minutes.

Prepare the Dense Chocolate Mousse Filling

4. Put the semisweet chocolate, unsweetened chocolate, and butter in a heatproof container and place it over, but not touching, a saucepan of barely simmering water. Stir the chocolate and butter together until the chocolate melts and the mixture is smooth. Remove the mixture from over the hot water and put it in a large bowl to cool slightly.

5. Put the whipping cream and vanilla in the large bowl of an electric mixer. Beat the cream on medium speed until soft peaks form. Cover with plastic wrap and refrigerate while you beat the egg whites.

6. Put the egg whites and cream of tartar in a clean large bowl of an electric mixer and with clean dry beaters, beat the egg whites with the cream of tartar on low speed until the egg whites are foamy and the cream of tartar is dissolved.

Doubling the Recipe
Double the ingredients. Spread the melted chocolate over four baking sheets.

To Freeze
Return the baking sheets to the freezer to firm the chocolate topping, about 15 minutes. Wrap each sandwich in plastic wrap. Place the sandwiches in a single layer in a metal or plastic freezer container and cover tightly. Label with date and contents. Freeze up to 1 month.

To Serve
Defrost as many sandwiches as you need in the refrigerator at least 3 hours or overnight. Unwrap the sandwiches and serve them cold. Use an offset spatula to transfer the sandwiches to serving plates. Either serve the sandwiches with a knife and fork or pick them up and eat them with your hands. Leftover mousse sandwiches can be covered with plastic wrap and stored in the refrigerator up to 3 days.

Increase the speed to medium-high and beat just until soft peaks form. Slowly add the sugar, 1 tablespoon at a time. Whisk about a fourth of the beaten egg whites into the chocolate mixture. Use a rubber spatula to fold in the remaining egg whites. Fold the reserved whipped cream into the chocolate mixture.

7. Remove the chocolate and baking sheets from the refrigerator. Turn the chocolate paper side up on the baking sheet and peel off the paper. The chocolate will separate easily into squares. Use a large knife to separate any squares that stick together. Return half of each color of chocolate squares to the refrigerator. Turn the baking sheets right side up and line them with wax or parchment paper. Spread 6 dark chocolate squares on a baking sheet. Spoon about ¼ cup of the chocolate mousse in a mound in the center of each chocolate square. The mousse will not cover the chocolate squares. Place a white chocolate square on top of each mound of mousse. Press gently to level the white chocolate square. Put the baking sheets in the freezer to firm the mousse, about 15 minutes. Or refrigerate for 30 minutes to firm the mousse. Repeat to form 6 more sandwiches.

8. Preheat the oven to 175°F.

9. Place the 1 ounce of semisweet chocolate in an ovenproof container. Melt the chocolate in the oven, about 6 minutes. Stir the chocolate smooth. Remove the baking sheets from the freezer. Dip a fork into the melted chocolate and wave it over each white chocolate square to form thin lines. The lines will form an abstract pattern.

CHOCOLATE-WRAPPED TIRAMISÙ

The Villa Cipriani in the tiny hilltop village of Asolo, Italy, has been our special place for many years. Milestone birthdays and anniversaries make good excuses to visit and enjoy the classical Italian views from every window, sip tea on a wintry day in the glass-enclosed sun room, and indulge in the glorious Italian food. Any dish they prepare always seems to be the best of its kind, including tiramisù. Lush layers of mascarpone cream and coffee-drenched sponge cake separated by thin, crisp layers of chocolate are found in the Cipriani rendition of this Italian classic. I've reproduced their elegant yet simple dessert, and with every creamy spoonful I relive happy Cipriani celebrations.

SERVES 8 TO 10

COFFEE SYRUP
2 teaspoons instant decaffeinated espresso or coffee granules
2 teaspoons sugar
3/4 cup warm water

6 ounces semisweet chocolate, chopped, for layering in the tiramisù

MASCARPONE FILLING
1 pound mascarpone
1/4 cup whipping cream
3 tablespoons Kahlúa or coffee-flavored liqueur
2 teaspoons vanilla extract
4 large egg whites
1/4 teaspoon cream of tartar
1/2 cup sugar

One 9-inch Hot Milk Sponge Cake Layer (page 44), cooled or defrosted
4 ounces semisweet chocolate, chopped, for the chocolate band

Prepare the Coffee Syrup

I. Stir the coffee, sugar, and warm water in a small bowl until the coffee and sugar dissolve. Set aside.

Good Advice

· Trim a 9-inch Hot Milk Sponge Cake Layer to fit an 8-inch springform pan.

· I layer the tiramisù in a springform pan and freeze it. After unmolding the frozen dessert, I wrap it in a band of chocolate. The chocolate band is an easy and spectacular finish. To determine the length of the chocolate band, measure the circumference of the unmolded tiramisù with a clean tape measure. After wrapping the chocolate band around the tiramisù, use clean scissors to trim any uneven edges while the chocolate is soft.

· When serving the dessert, use a large sharp knife to cut through the band of chocolate, then a large spoon to scoop out each serving. Because this dessert is soft, it may not cut into uniform slices.

· The chocolate band serves as a box to hold the soft mascarpone filling when it defrosts. If you choose to omit the chocolate band, layer the tiramisù in a round or rectangular serving dish with a 2-quart capacity. Freeze and serve the tiramisù in the same dish.

Doubling the Recipe

Use two baked sponge layers and double the remaining ingredients.

To Freeze the Tiramisù Before Adding the Chocolate Band

Cover the springform pan tightly with plastic wrap then with heavy aluminum foil. Label with date and contents. Freeze at least overnight or up to 2 weeks. Once the tiramisù is frozen, you can remove the springform pan and add the chocolate band.

To Remove the Springform Pan

Dip a dish towel in hot water and wring it out. Hold the hot towel around the sides of the pan for 15 seconds. Release the sides of the springform pan. Slide the tiramisù

2. Preheat the oven to 175°F. Turn a baking sheet bottom side up. Cover the bottom of the baking sheet with wax or parchment paper.

3. Place the 6 ounces semisweet chocolate in an ovenproof container. Melt the chocolate in the oven, about 12 minutes. Stir the chocolate smooth and use a thin metal spatula to spread it evenly over the paper on the baking sheet into a rectangle about 13×10 inches. The chocolate should cover the paper so that the paper does not show through. Put the baking sheet in the refrigerator and chill until the chocolate hardens.

Prepare the Mascarpone Filling

4. Have ready an 8-inch springform pan with sides at least $2^3/4$ inches high.

5. Put the mascarpone, whipping cream, Kahlúa, and vanilla in a large bowl and use a large whisk to mix smooth.

6. Put the egg whites and cream of tartar in a large clean bowl of an electric mixer and with clean dry beaters, beat on low speed until the egg whites are foamy. Increase the speed to medium-high and beat just until soft peaks form. Slowly add the sugar, 1 tablespoon at a time. Whisk about a fourth of the beaten egg whites into the mascarpone mixture. Use a large rubber spatula to fold in the remaining egg whites.

7. Using the bottom of the springform pan as a guide, trim the sponge layer to 8 inches in diameter. The cake trimmings can be used to fill any uneven spaces as you layer the tiramisù. Replace the springform bottom in the pan. Use a serrated knife to cut the trimmed cake into 3 horizontal layers. Place the bottom of the sponge layer in the bottom of the springform pan. Spoon $1/4$ cup of the coffee syrup evenly over the cake. Remove the chocolate-lined baking sheet from the refrigerator and peel the paper from the chocolate. Divide the chocolate into 3 large pieces. Break one of the large pieces into several smaller pieces and place them over the cake. Spread a third of the mascarpone mixture evenly over the chocolate. Cover with the middle sponge layer and repeat the layering. Cover with the top sponge layer and repeat with a third layering, ending with a smooth layer of the mascarpone mixture. The mascarpone mixture will come to the top of the pan.

Add the Chocolate Band

8. Use a tape measure to measure the circumference and height of the tiramisù. The circumference will be about 25 inches and the height about 3 inches. Cut a piece of parchment 1 inch longer than the circumference of the tiramisù.

9. Preheat the oven to 175°F. Place the 4 ounces semisweet chocolate in an ovenproof container and melt it in the oven, about 10 minutes. As soon as the chocolate is melted, remove it from the oven and stir it smooth. Lay the parchment strip flat on a piece of parchment or wax paper on the kitchen counter. Use a thin metal spatula to spread a thin layer of chocolate over the strip of parchment paper, leaving a scant 1/2-inch plain edge for easier handling of the parchment strip. You may have chocolate left over. Immediately lift the chocolate-coated paper onto a clean section of the paper-lined counter. This forms a smooth chocolate edge on the paper strip. Let the chocolate firm for 3 to 5 minutes, just until it does not drip off the paper when you move it.

10. Remove the tiramisù from the freezer. Wrap the chocolate-coated paper, chocolate side touching the dessert, around the tiramisù. Use clean scissors to trim the ends of the paper so the seam meets evenly. Return the tiramisù to the freezer until the chocolate is firm, about 15 minutes. Carefully peel the paper from the chocolate. The tiramisù can be defrosted and served or returned to the freezer.

VARIATION Layer the tiramisù in a round soufflé-type dish or rectangular serving dish with at least 2-quart capacity. Wrap the dessert with plastic wrap and heavy aluminum foil and freeze up to 2 weeks. Defrost the wrapped dessert in the refrigerator at least 5 hours or overnight. The tiramisù can be garnished with 10 chocolate triangles (see page 55) placed on the top of the dessert.

Put chocolate back in frig between layers on assembly

onto a cardboard cake circle or serving plate. Return the dessert to the freezer while you prepare the chocolate band.

To Freeze the Tiramisù with the Chocolate Band

Carefully wrap the tiramisù with plastic wrap then with heavy aluminum foil. The total time tiramisù should remain in the freezer is 2 weeks.

To Serve

Defrost the wrapped tiramisù in the refrigerator at least 5 hours or overnight. Serve the tiramisù cold. Use a large sharp knife to cut the chocolate band and a large serving spoon to serve the tiramisù. Shallow bowls are good serving dishes for this dessert. Put any leftover tiramisù in a bowl and refrigerate up to 1 day.

Cheesecakes and Steamed Puddings

One day a friend confided to me that she had never baked a cheesecake because it was so difficult. Cheesecakes may look hard to prepare, but they're actually one of the easiest desserts you can bake. Remembering to take the cream cheese out of the refrigerator to soften is the most difficult part. The mixing time is short and simple.

Sometimes the top of a cheesecake cracks, but that doesn't affect the taste. After baking hundreds of cheesecakes, some with giant earthquake-type cracks across the center but most without any cracks at all, I've tried almost every cheesecake crack cure ever printed. I discovered that baking cheesecakes in a water bath usually prevents any cracks. The small cracks that form near the sides of the pan toward the end of the baking time indicate that the cheesecake is done and will disappear as the cheesecake cools.

When making a cheesecake, soften the cream cheese thoroughly so that it combines smoothly with other ingredients. Small lumps of cream cheese in the batter will not smooth out as the cheesecake bakes; they will remain as white specks.

I tested the cheesecakes with both regular cream cheese with a total fat content of 45 percent and reduced-fat cream cheese with a total fat content of 29 percent. Regular cream cheese produced the usual excellent results, and while the reduced-fat cream cheese made a good cheesecake, several points should be noted. Reduced-fat cream cheese is softer than regular cream cheese and softens quickly; an hour is sufficient. Using reduced-fat cream

CLOCKWISE FROM TOP:
Coconut Macaroon Brownie Bar *(page 90)*,
Chocolate Chocolate Chip Shortbread Stick *(page 96)*, and Chocolate Pecan Rugelach *(page 246)*

Ebony and Ivory Mousse Sandwich (page 142)

*White Chocolate and Raspberry Ripple Cheesecake (page 162) with a
Chocolate Wafer Cookie Crumb Crust (page 41.)*

Dark Chocolate Cake with Fudge Frosting (page 178) and a scoop of vanilla ice cream

Winter White Yule Log (page 205)

If You Only Live Once Chocolate Cake (page 174)

Chocolate Cinnamon Twist (page 259)

LEFT TO RIGHT:
Chocolate Chocolate Chip Cookie Ice Cream Sandwich *(page 269)*
and Crispy Pistachio and Orange Dream Frozen Sandwich *(page 268)*

cheese produces a thinner batter, and any solid additions to the batter, such as chopped chocolate or cherries, sink to the bottom of the cheesecake, but this will not affect the taste. The crust absorbs some of the additional moisture from the batter as the cheesecake bakes, and since a soft crust is difficult to move from the springform bottom, I leave reduced-fat cheesecakes on it for freezing and serving. Reduced-fat cheesecakes have a lighter texture than those made with regular cream cheese, and they freeze successfully, with the exception of the Mochaccino Cheesecake, which has an unacceptable soft and runny texture when made with reduced-fat cream cheese.

Steamed puddings are moist cakes that are cooked by steam rather than by dry oven heat. They cook in a covered pudding mold that sits in a pot of steaming water. Deep, round steamed pudding molds are fluted or ridged and have a center tube, which helps the cake cook evenly. I have an metal pudding mold with a snap-on lid that is easy to put on and take off when I want to check to see if the pudding is done. These metal molds are preferable to smooth-sided ceramic pudding basins. Ceramic molds lack a center tube to help cook the pudding throughout, are difficult to cover tightly, and almost impossible to uncover and check without risking a burn. Since steamed pudding molds have a ridged side and bottom, you can't line the bottom with paper. If you butter the mold carefully and coat it with powdered sugar, you should have no trouble removing the steamed pudding.

If you're unsure if a pudding is done, cook it for an additional ten minutes. It's hard to overcook a steamed pudding, but an undercooked pudding with a wet center is undesirable.

Serve steamed puddings warm. When cool, they can become dense. These cakes lend themselves to being served with a sauce. Traditional sauces for steamed puddings are more like thick spreads or frostings, but I prefer a sauce with a pouring consistency.

VANILLA AND CHOCOLATE TRUFFLE CHEESECAKE

Simple is often best and it doesn't get much simpler or better than a creamy vanilla cheesecake rippled with plenty of fudgy chocolate.

SERVES 16

1 Graham Cracker Crumb Crust (page 40) baked in a 9-inch springform
   pan with sides at least 2¾ inches high, cooled
2 pounds cream cheese, softened 3 to 4 hours at room temperature (60° to
   70°F. if measured with a food thermometer)
1¼ cups plus 2 tablespoons sugar
2 tablespoons unbleached all-purpose flour
4 large eggs, at room temperature
2 teaspoons vanilla extract
1 tablespoon fresh lemon juice
2 tablespoons whipping cream
¾ cup Thick Chocolate Truffle Sauce (page 50), warmed just until smooth
   and pourable

I. Position an oven rack in the middle of the oven. Preheat the oven to 350°F. Wrap the outside of the springform pan with crust with a large piece of heavy aluminum foil and place it in a large baking pan with sides at least 2 inches high.

2. Put the cream cheese in the large bowl of an electric mixer. Mix on low speed until smooth, about 1 minute. Add the sugar and mix until smooth and creamy, about 1 minute. Mix in the flour. Add the eggs, two at a time, mixing the batter smooth after each addition. Stop the mixer and scrape the sides of the bowl twice during this mixing. Mix in the vanilla and lemon juice. Mix in the whipping cream. Put ¾ cup of the batter into a small bowl. Stir in the chocolate truffle sauce.

3. Pour about half of the vanilla batter into the prepared springform pan. Reserve ¼ cup of the chocolate batter and pour the remaining chocolate batter slowly over the vanilla batter. Pour the remaining vanilla batter on top.

Good Advice
· Warm the chocolate truffle sauce just until it is smooth and pourable, and it will combine smoothly with the cheesecake batter.

· Swirl the top of the cheesecake with some of the chocolate mixture to form a marbleized pattern.

Doubling the Recipe
Double the ingredients and use two pans. Mix the batter in a 5-quart bowl.

4. Use a small spoon to drizzle the reserved chocolate batter over the top of the cheesecake, leaving a 1-inch plain edge. Use the spoon to gently swirl the chocolate batter in a marbleized pattern over the top of the cheesecake.

5. Put the cheesecake in the oven and pour hot water into the large baking pan to reach 1 inch up the sides of the springform pan. Bake about 1 hour, or until when you give the cheesecake a gentle shake, the top looks firm.

6. Cool the cheesecake, covered loosely with paper towels, in the water bath for 1 hour on a wire rack. Remove the cheesecake from the water bath. Remove the paper towels and cool 1 hour more. The cheesecake should feel cool to the touch. Cover with plastic wrap and chill thoroughly in the refrigerator, at least 6 hours or overnight.

To Freeze

Use a small sharp knife to loosen the cheesecake from the sides of the springform pan. Release the sides of the pan. Either leave the cheesecake on the springform bottom, or use the knife to loosen the crust from the bottom of the pan. Slide the removable bottom of a tart pan under the crust and move the cheesecake to a serving plate or cardboard cake circle. Wrap tightly in plastic wrap then heavy aluminum foil. Label with date and contents. Freeze up to 1 month.

To Serve

Defrost the wrapped cheesecake in the refrigerator overnight. Uncover the cheesecake and let it sit at room temperature 1 hour before serving. Leftover cheesecake can be covered with plastic wrap and stored in the refrigerator up to 5 days.

Good Advice
· Keep the hazelnut praline frozen and spoon out only what you need for the cheesecake.

· Since the oven temperature must be at 350°F. for the crust and cheesecake, melt the milk chocolate over hot water, rather than in the oven.

· One batter produces both flavors. Reserve a portion of the batter and add melted milk chocolate to the one portion.

· When pouring the vanilla praline mixture over the partially baked cheesecake, pour it slowly and carefully around the edge of the cheesecake. The mixture will gently flow toward the center, and the center will not collapse.

Doubling the Recipe
Double the ingredients and use two pans. Mix the batter in a 5-quart bowl.

LAYERED MILK CHOCOLATE AND HAZELNUT PRALINE CHEESECAKE

This is a stunning cheesecake. The easy press-in hazelnut praline crust holds a generous layer of milk chocolate hazelnut praline cheesecake, which is covered with a thinner layer of vanilla hazelnut praline cheesecake. The dark and light layers make a visual—and flavorful—contrast.

SERVES 12 TO 16

HAZELNUT PRALINE CRUST
1 cup unbleached all-purpose flour
1 tablespoon sugar
1/4 cup hazelnut praline powder (see page 54)
1/4 pound (1 stick) cold unsalted butter, cut into 8 pieces

HAZELNUT PRALINE FILLING
6 ounces milk chocolate, chopped
2 pounds cream cheese, softened 3 to 4 hours at room temperature (60° to 70°F. if measured with a food thermometer)
1 cup sugar
2 tablespoons unbleached all-purpose flour
4 large eggs, at room temperature
2 teaspoons vanilla extract
2 tablespoons whipping cream
3/4 cup hazelnut praline powder (see page 54)

Mix the Hazelnut Praline Crust

1. Position an oven rack in the middle of the oven. Preheat the oven to 350°F. Butter a 9-inch springform pan with sides at least 2¾ inches high.

2. Put the flour, sugar, and praline powder in the small bowl of an electric mixer. Mix on low speed just to blend the ingredients together. Add the butter and mix just until pea-size crumbs form. The largest crumbs will be ½ inch in

size. Transfer the crust mixture to the prepared springform pan and press it evenly over the bottom and 1 inch up the sides of the pan. Bake for 20 minutes. The crust will shrink slightly. Cool the crust 15 minutes. Wrap the outside of the pan with a large piece of heavy aluminum foil and place it in a large baking pan with sides at least 2 inches high.

Mix the Hazelnut Praline Filling

3. Put the chocolate in a heatproof container set over, but not touching, a saucepan of barely simmering water. Stir the chocolate until it is melted and smooth. Remove from over the water and cool slightly.

4. Put the cream cheese in the large bowl of an electric mixer. Mix on low speed until smooth, about 1 minute. Add the sugar and mix until smooth and creamy, about 1 minute. Mix in the flour. Add the eggs, two at a time, mixing the batter smooth after each addition. Stop the mixer and scrape the sides of the bowl twice during this mixing. Mix in the vanilla. Mix in the whipping cream and praline powder. Put 2 cups of the batter in a medium bowl and set aside. Mix the melted chocolate into the batter in the large bowl, stirring just until the chocolate is incorporated. Pour the chocolate batter into the prepared springform pan.

5. Put the cheesecake in the oven and pour hot water into the large baking pan to reach 1 inch up the sides of the springform pan. Bake 40 minutes. Carefully slide the oven rack out several inches. Pour the reserved 2 cups of batter all around the inside edge of the pan. The batter will flow evenly over the top of the cake. Bake 20 minutes, or until when you give the cheesecake a gentle shake, the top looks firm.

6. Cool the cheesecake, covered loosely with paper towels, in the water bath for 1 hour on a wire rack. Remove the cheesecake from the water bath. Remove the paper towels and cool 1 hour more. The cheesecake should feel cool to the touch. Cover with plastic wrap and chill thoroughly in the refrigerator, at least 6 hours or overnight.

CHOCOLATE-CHERRY CHEESECAKE

*F*resh cherry season is all too short, and I used to face the dilemma of finding good cherries to use for desserts. Then dried cherries became readily available, and my cherry problem was solved. These cherries are harvested at their peak, then dried to preserve the intense cherry flavor. I fill this cheesecake with a generous measure of dried cherries, add chopped chocolate, and my cherry predicament vanishes.

SERVES 12 TO 16

¾ cup dried pitted cherries (about 3 ounces)
1 Chocolate Wafer Cookie Crumb Crust (page 40), baked in a 9-inch springform pan with sides at least 2¾ inches high, cooled
2 pounds cream cheese, softened 3 to 4 hours at room temperature (60° to 70°F. if measured with a food thermometer)
1¼ cups plus 2 tablespoons sugar
2 tablespoons unbleached all-purpose flour
4 large eggs, at room temperature
2 teaspoons vanilla extract
½ teaspoon almond extract
1 tablespoon fresh lemon juice
2 tablespoons whipping cream
6 ounces semisweet chocolate, chopped into approximately ½-inch pieces

1. Put the cherries in a small bowl and pour boiling water over them, just to cover the cherries. Let the cherries sit in the hot water for 30 minutes. Drain the cherries and pat dry with paper towels.

2. Position an oven rack in the middle of the oven. Preheat the oven to 350°F. Wrap the outside of the springform pan with crust with a large piece of heavy aluminum foil and place it in a large baking pan with sides at least 2 inches high.

3. Put the cream cheese in the large bowl of an electric mixer. Mix on low speed until the cream cheese is smooth, about 1 minute. Add the sugar and mix until smooth and creamy, about 1 minute. Mix in the flour. Add the eggs, two at a time, mixing the batter smooth after each addition. Stop the mixer and scrape

the sides of the bowl twice during this mixing. Mix in the vanilla, almond extract, and lemon juice. Mix in the whipping cream. Stir in the soaked and drained cherries and chopped chocolate. Pour the batter into the prepared springform pan.

4. Put the cheesecake in the oven and pour hot water into the large baking pan to reach 1 inch up the sides of the springform pan. Bake about 1 hour, or until when you give the cheesecake a gentle shake, the top looks firm.

5. Cool the cheesecake, covered loosely with paper towels, in the water bath for 1 hour on a wire rack. Remove the cheesecake from the water bath. Remove the paper towels and cool 1 hour more. The cheesecake should feel cool to the touch. Cover with plastic wrap and chill thoroughly in the refrigerator, at least 6 hours or overnight.

To Freeze

Use a small sharp knife to loosen the cheesecake from the sides of the springform pan. Release the sides of the pan. Either leave the cheesecake on the springform bottom, or use the knife to loosen the crust from the bottom of the pan. Slide the removable bottom of a tart pan under the crust and move the cheesecake to a serving plate or cardboard cake circle. Wrap tightly in plastic wrap then heavy aluminum foil. Label with date and contents. Freeze up to 1 month.

To Serve

Defrost the wrapped cheesecake in the refrigerator overnight. Uncover the cheesecake and let it sit at room temperature 1 hour before serving. Leftover cheesecake can be covered with plastic wrap and stored in the refrigerator up to 5 days.

PEANUT BUTTER CUP CHEESECAKE

Several years ago I wrote a dessert article for Bon Appétit *magazine that featured a candy bar in each of the desserts. It became one of the most popular articles that I have ever written, and this no-holds-barred cheesecake actually received fan mail. It has a crisp peanut crust and a peanut butter filling loaded with chunks of peanut butter cups.*

SERVES 16

PEANUT CRUST
1 cup cake flour
1/4 cup (packed) light brown sugar
1/2 cup (1 stick) cold unsalted butter, cut into pieces
Pinch of salt
1/2 cup roasted unsalted peanuts, coarsely chopped

PEANUT BUTTER CUP FILLING
2 pounds cream cheese, softened 3 to 4 hours at room temperature (60° to 70°F. if measured with a food thermometer)
1 1/2 cups (packed) light brown sugar
1/2 cup creamy peanut butter, at room temperature
1 teaspoon vanilla extract
4 large eggs, at room temperature
1/4 cup whipping cream, at room temperature
1 1/2 cups peanut butter cups, cut into 3/4-inch pieces (about 6 1/2 ounces)

Prepare the Peanut Crust

I. Position a rack in the center of the oven. Preheat the oven to 350°F. Butter a 9-inch springform pan with sides at least 2 3/4 inches high.

2. Put the flour, brown sugar, butter, and salt in the large bowl of an electric mixer and mix on low speed just until small crumbs form. The mixture should not form a ball. Stir in the peanuts. Press the mixture onto the bottom and 1/2 inch up the sides of the prepared pan. Bake until the crust is just golden, about 15

Good Advice
The crust is a crumbly mixture that is pressed into the springform pan. Mix the crust mixture only to the crumbly stage, not a smooth dough.

Doubling the Recipe
Double the ingredients and use two pans. Mix the batter in a 5-quart bowl.

To Freeze
Use a small sharp knife to loosen the cheesecake from the sides of the springform pan. Release the sides of the pan. Either leave the cheesecake on the springform bottom, or use the knife to loosen the crust from the bottom of the pan. Slide the removable bottom of a tart pan under the crust and move the cheesecake to a serving plate or cardboard cake circle. Wrap tightly in plastic wrap then heavy aluminum foil. Label with date and contents. Freeze up to 1 month.

minutes. Cool the crust while you prepare the filling. Leave the oven on at 350°F.

Prepare the Peanut Butter Cup Filling

3. When the springform pan is cool enough to handle, wrap the outside of it with a large piece of heavy aluminum foil and place it in a large baking pan with sides at least 2 inches high.

4. Put the cream cheese in the large bowl of an electric mixer. Mix on low speed until smooth, about 1 minute. Add the brown sugar and mix until smooth and creamy, about 1 minute. Add the peanut butter and vanilla and mix just until blended. Add the eggs, two at a time, mixing the batter smooth after each addition. Stop the mixer and scrape the sides of the bowl twice during this mixing. Mix in the whipping cream. Stir in the peanut butter cup pieces. Pour the filling into the prepared springform pan.

5. Put the cheesecake in the oven and pour hot water in the large baking pan to reach 1 inch up the sides of the springform pan. Bake about 1 hour, or until when you give the cheesecake a gentle shake, the top looks firm.

6. Cool the cheesecake, covered loosely with paper towels, in the water bath for 1 hour on a wire rack. Remove the cheesecake from the water bath. Remove the paper towels and cool 1 hour more. The cheesecake should feel cool to the touch. Cover with plastic wrap and chill thoroughly in the refrigerator, at least 6 hours or overnight.

CHOCO-COLADA CHEESECAKE

ring on tropical nights, the rhumba, and Choco-Colada Cheese-cake. While the tropical nights and rhumba might prove elusive, this cheesecake filled with lots of coconut and swirled with chocolate takes just a few minutes to put together. And it just might inspire some romantic tropical nights, the rhumba, and who knows what else? Good cheesecakes can do that.

Good Advice
Swirl the chocolate gently into the cheesecake batter, being careful not to disturb the crumb crust.

Doubling the Recipe
Double the ingredients and use two pans. Mix the batter in a 5-quart bowl.

To Freeze
Use a small sharp knife to loosen the cheesecake from the sides of the springform pan. Release the sides of the pan. Either leave the cheesecake on the springform bottom, or use the knife to loosen the crust from the bottom of the pan. Slide the removable bottom of a tart pan under the crust and move the cheesecake to a serving plate or cardboard cake circle. Wrap tightly in plastic wrap then heavy aluminum foil. Label with date and contents. Freeze up to 1 month.

SERVES 12 TO 16

1 Chocolate Wafer Cookie Crumb Crust (page 40) baked in a 9-inch springform pan with sides at least 2¾ inches high, cooled
6 ounces semisweet chocolate, chopped
2 pounds cream cheese, softened 3 to 4 hours at room temperature (60° to 70°F. if measured with a food thermometer)
1¼ cups plus 2 tablespoons sugar
2 tablespoons unbleached all-purpose flour
4 large eggs, at room temperature
2 teaspoons vanilla extract
½ teaspoon almond extract
2 tablespoons whipping cream
2 cups shredded sweetened coconut

I. Position an oven rack in the middle of the oven. Preheat the oven to 175°F. Wrap the outside of the springform pan with crust with a large piece of heavy aluminum foil. Place the springform pan in a large baking pan with sides at least 2 inches high.

2. Put the chocolate in an ovenproof container and melt it in the oven, about 8 minutes. As soon as the chocolate is melted, remove it and stir it smooth. Increase the oven temperature to 350°F. Set the chocolate aside to cool slightly.

3. Put the cream cheese in the large bowl of an electric mixer. Mix on low speed until smooth, about 1 minute. Add the sugar and mix until smooth and creamy, about 1 minute. Mix in the flour. Add the eggs, two at a time, mixing the batter smooth after each addition. Stop the mixer and scrape the sides of the bowl twice during this mixing. Mix in the vanilla and almond extract. Mix in the whipping cream. Stir in the coconut. Pour the batter into the prepared spring-form pan.

4. Use a small spoon to drizzle the melted chocolate over the batter, leaving a 1-inch plain edge. Dip the spoon gently into the batter and swirl some of the chocolate into the batter, leaving some swirls of chocolate on top of the batter in a marbleized pattern. Do not disturb the crumb crust.

5. Put the cheesecake in the oven and pour hot water into the large baking pan to reach 1 inch up the sides of the springform pan. Bake about 1 hour or un-til when you give the cheesecake a gentle shake, the top looks firm.

6. Cool the cheesecake, covered loosely with paper towels, in the water bath for 1 hour on a wire rack. Remove the cheesecake from the water bath. Remove the paper towels and cool 1 hour more. The cheesecake should feel cool to the touch. Cover with plastic wrap and chill thoroughly in the refrigerator, at least 6 hours or overnight.

To Serve

Defrost the wrapped cheesecake in the refrigera-tor overnight. Uncover the cheesecake and let it sit at room temperature 1 hour before serving. Leftover cheesecake can be covered with plastic wrap and stored in the refrigerator up to 5 days.

MOCHACCINO CHEESECAKE

This is the creamiest, smoothest cheesecake in the world. Strong words, but this cheesecake earns them. In addition to cream cheese, the batter contains a large amount of sour cream which lightens the cheesecake to create a mousselike, silken texture. Since the batter is quite liquid, it is difficult to incorporate even well-softened cream cheese smoothly into the mixture with an electric mixer. I prepare the batter in the food processor, which produces a smooth mixture in less than three minutes.

SERVES 16

1 Chocolate Wafer Cookie Crumb Crust (page 40) baked in a 9-inch springform pan, cooled
4 tablespoons (1/2 stick) unsalted butter, cut into 4 pieces
6 ounces semisweet chocolate, chopped
2 tablespoons unsweetened Dutch process cocoa powder, such as Droste or Hershey's European Style, sifted
3 cups sour cream
3 tablespoons instant decaffeinated coffee granules
2 teaspoons vanilla extract
2 teaspoons ground cinnamon
3 large eggs, at room temperature
3/4 cup plus 2 tablespoons sugar
1 1/2 pounds cream cheese, softened 3 to 4 hours at room temperature (60° to 70°F. if measured with a food thermometer)

I. Position an oven rack in the middle of the oven. Preheat the oven to 350°F. Wrap the outside of the springform pan with crust with a large piece of heavy aluminum foil and place it in a large baking pan with sides at least 2 inches high.

2. Put the butter, chocolate, and cocoa powder in a heatproof container and place it over, but not touching, a saucepan of barely simmering water. Stir the mixture until the chocolate and butter melt and the mixture is smooth. Remove from over the water and set aside to cool slightly.

Good Advice

· This cheesecake takes about 1 1/2 hours to bake and set properly, about 30 minutes longer than most cheesecakes.

· Even when chilled thoroughly, this cheesecake is somewhat soft. If you decide to remove it from the springform bottom, loosen the crust carefully from the bottom of the pan. As you move the cheesecake, be sure to support the bottom of it with the removable bottom of a tart pan.

· Do not use reduced-fat cream cheese for this cheesecake. It makes the cheesecake too soft.

Doubling the Recipe

Use two crusts and mix the cheesecake batter in two separate batches.

3. Put the sour cream, coffee, vanilla, and cinnamon in a large mixing bowl and stir them together just to blend the ingredients.

4. Put the eggs and sugar in the workbowl of a food processor fitted with the steel blade and process for 1 minute. The egg mixture will lighten in color. Add the cream cheese and process with a few short bursts to break it up. Process until the mixture is smooth, about 15 seconds. Add the chocolate mixture and process until the chocolate is incorporated, about 5 seconds. The mixture will be smooth. Use a rubber spatula to stir the chocolate mixture into the sour cream mixture. Pour the batter into the prepared springform pan and smooth the top.

5. Put the cheesecake in the oven and pour hot water into the large baking pan to reach 1 inch up the sides of the springform pan. Bake about 1½ hours, or until when you give the cheesecake a gentle shake, the top looks firm.

6. Cool the cheesecake, covered loosely with paper towels, in the water bath for 1 hour on a wire rack. Remove the cheesecake from the water bath. Remove the paper towels and cool 1 hour more. The cheesecake should feel cool to the touch. Cover with plastic wrap and chill thoroughly in the refrigerator overnight.

To Freeze

Use a small sharp knife to loosen the cheesecake from the sides of the springform pan. Release the sides of the pan. Either leave the cheesecake on the springform bottom or use the knife to loosen the crust carefully from the bottom of the pan. Carefully slide the removable bottom of a tart pan under the crust and move the cheesecake to a serving plate or aluminum foil–wrapped cardboard cake circle. Wrap tightly in plastic wrap then heavy aluminum foil. Label with date and contents. Freeze up to 1 month.

To Serve

Defrost the wrapped cheesecake in the refrigerator overnight. Uncover the cheesecake and let it sit at room temperature 2 hours before serving to make sure the cheesecake is soft and creamy. Leftover cheesecake can be covered with plastic wrap and stored in the refrigerator up to 5 days.

WHITE CHOCOLATE AND RASPBERRY RIPPLE CHEESECAKE

*C*heesecakes make good party desserts. They're luxurious in feeling, appealing to everyone, and easy to serve. When I want a pull-out-all-the-stops party cheesecake, this one, flavored with white chocolate and swirled with raspberry sauce, is my pick.

SERVES 12 TO 16

1 Chocolate Wafer Cookie Crumb Crust (page 40) baked in a 9-inch springform pan with sides at least 2¾ inches high, cooled

RASPBERRY SAUCE
1½ cups fresh raspberries or unsweetened frozen raspberries, defrosted and drained
1 tablespoon sugar
1 teaspoon fresh lemon juice

WHITE CHOCOLATE CHEESECAKE
8 ounces white chocolate, Callebaut or Baker's Premium preferred, chopped
2 pounds cream cheese, softened 3 to 4 hours at room temperature (60° to 70° F. if measured with a food thermometer)
1¼ cups sugar
2 tablespoons unbleached all-purpose flour
4 large eggs, at room temperature
2 teaspoons vanilla extract
½ teaspoon almond extract
2 tablespoons whipping cream

1 cup fresh raspberries, for serving with the cheesecake (optional)

I. Wrap the outside of the springform pan with crust with a large piece of heavy aluminum foil and place it in a large baking pan with sides at least 2 inches high.

· Lightly sweetened raspberry sauce adds more raspberry flavor to the cheesecake than unsweetened raspberry puree.

· If using frozen raspberries, defrost them before pureeing them.

· Swirl the raspberry sauce gently into the cheesecake batter, being careful not to disturb the crumb crust.

Doubling the Recipe

Double the ingredients and use two pans. Mix the batter in a 5-quart bowl.

Prepare the Raspberry Sauce

2.   Puree the raspberries in a food processor. Use the back of a spoon to press the raspberries through a strainer to remove the seeds. Measure $\frac{1}{2}$ cup strained puree into a small bowl and mix with the 1 tablespoon sugar and the lemon juice. Set the sauce aside and save any additional puree for another use.

Prepare the Cheesecake

3.   Position an oven rack in the middle of the oven. Preheat the oven to 175°F. Place the white chocolate in a nonreactive ovenproof container and melt it in the oven, 8 to 10 minutes. As soon as the white chocolate is melted, remove it from the oven and stir it smooth. Increase the oven temperature to 350°F. Set the white chocolate aside to cool slightly.

4.   Put the cream cheese in the large bowl of an electric mixer. Mix on low speed until smooth, about 1 minute. Add the $1\frac{1}{4}$ cups sugar and mix until smooth and creamy, about 1 minute. Mix in the flour. Add the eggs, two at a time, mixing smooth after each addition. Stop the mixer and scrape the sides of the bowl twice during this mixing. Mix in the vanilla and almond extract. Mix in the whipping cream. Stir in the melted white chocolate. Pour the batter into the prepared springform pan.

5.   Use a small spoon to drizzle the raspberry sauce over the batter, leaving a 1-inch plain edge. Dip the spoon gently into the batter and swirl some of the sauce into the batter, leaving some swirls of sauce on top of the batter in a marbleized pattern. Do not disturb the crumb crust.

6.   Put the cheesecake in the oven and pour hot water into the large baking pan to reach 1 inch up the sides of the springform pan. Bake about 1 hour, or until when you give the cheesecake a gentle shake, the top looks firm.

7.   Cool the cheesecake, covered loosely with paper towels, in the water bath for 1 hour on a wire rack. Carefully remove the cheesecake from the water bath. Remove the paper towels and cool 1 hour more. The cheesecake should feel cool to the touch. Cover with plastic wrap and chill thoroughly in the refrigerator, at least 6 hours or overnight.

CRANBERRY, ORANGE, AND WHITE CHOCOLATE STEAMED PUDDING

Steamed puddings are cakes that are cooked in a water bath like a custard or pudding. These cakes are light and exceptionally moist since they are steamed in a large pot of simmering water rather than baked in a dry oven. Steamed puddings are served warm, which gives them a cozy quality that is just right for winter holiday dinners. Pudding molds shape the steamed cakes into pretty shapes and add sophistication. Fresh winter cranberries, orange marmalade, and white chocolate flavor this pudding with a seasonal flourish, and the bright red cranberry-orange coulis adds festive color.

SERVES 10

STEAMED PUDDING
6 ounces white chocolate, Callebaut or Baker's Premium preferred, chopped
1¼ cups unbleached all-purpose flour
1½ teaspoons baking powder
½ teaspoon salt
¼ pound (1 stick) soft unsalted butter
1 cup sugar
3 large eggs
1 teaspoon vanilla extract
1 tablespoon Grand Marnier liqueur or other orange-flavored liqueur
⅓ cup orange marmalade
1 cup coarsely chopped cranberries, fresh or previously frozen and defrosted

CRANBERRY-ORANGE COULIS
1½ cups cranberries, fresh or previously frozen and defrosted
½ cup fresh orange juice
¼ cup water
6 tablespoons sugar

Good Advice
· Leave at least 1 inch of space at the top of the mold to allow the cake to rise.

· When removing the cover from the hot pudding, use the cover as a shield to block the steam so that it escapes without burning you. Oven mitt potholders are good protection from the steam.

· To cook the pudding evenly, keep the water at a gentle boil. There will be bubbles, but since the mold sits on a cake rack or tuna cans, it won't be disturbed by the boiling water. A rolling boil could jiggle the pudding or cook it unevenly.

· Special steamed pudding molds that come with their own lid are the best type of container to use for these cakes. Pudding molds are found in cookshops, mail order catalogs that feature cookware, and hardware stores with kitchen departments. Just like Santa Claus, they seem to appear magically a few months before Christmas.

Prepare the Steamed Pudding

1. Put a small cake rack or 2 clean tuna cans with the top and bottom removed in the bottom of a large pot. The pot should be large enough to allow for 1 inch of space between the pudding mold and the sides of the pot. It should be tall enough so that the pot lid fits tightly after the pudding mold is placed in the pot. Fill the pot with enough water to come halfway up the sides of the pudding mold when it is placed in the pot. Cover the pot and bring the water to a gentle boil. After the water boils, adjust the heat to medium or medium-low to maintain the water at a gentle boil. Generously butter the bottom, sides, and center tube of a 2- to 2½-quart pudding mold. Lightly coat the inside of the mold and center tube with powdered sugar.

2. Preheat the oven to 175°F.

3. Put the white chocolate in a small nonreactive ovenproof container and melt it in the oven, 8 to 10 minutes. Remove the white chocolate from the oven as soon as it is melted and stir until smooth. Set aside to cool.

4. Sift the flour, baking powder, and salt together and set aside. Put the butter in the large bowl of an electric mixer. Add the sugar and beat on medium speed until the mixture lightens in color and looks fluffy, about 1½ minutes. Add the eggs, one at a time, mixing smooth after each addition, then beat for 1 minute, or until the mixture is smooth. Stop the mixer and scrape the sides of the bowl during this mixing. Add the vanilla and Grand Marnier. Mix in the melted white chocolate. Decrease the speed to low and mix in the flour mixture just until the flour is incorporated. Mix in the orange marmalade and the cranberries. Pour the batter into the prepared mold and cover tightly with the pudding mold lid.

5. Protect your hands with potholder mitts and place the mold evenly on the cake rack or tuna cans. Cover the pot. Check every 20 minutes to see that the water is boiling gently. Steam over medium heat for 2 hours, or until a toothpick inserted into the center of the pudding comes out clean. When done, the top of the pudding will pull away from the sides of the mold. To check for doneness, wear potholder mitts to remove the mold from the pot. Open the lid of the mold so that the steam escapes away from you.

· I use all-fruit orange marmalade, without added sugar, for this cake.

· A coulis is a pureed sauce. I use the term here to distinguish this pureed cranberry sauce from the usual cranberry sauce prepared with whole cranberries.

Doubling the Recipe

Use 2½ teaspoons baking powder and ¾ teaspoon salt and double the remaining ingredients. Steam the pudding in two molds in two pots.

To Freeze the Pudding

Wrap the cooled pudding tightly with plastic wrap then with heavy aluminum foil. Label with date and contents. Freeze up to 2 months.

To Freeze the Cranberry-Orange Coulis

Place the cold coulis in a plastic freezer container and press plastic wrap onto the surface. Cover the container. Label with date and contents. Freeze up to 1 month. Defrost the coulis in the refrigerator at least 4 hours or overnight. Stir the coulis with a whisk to smooth it. Leftover coulis can be covered and stored in the refrigerator up to 5 days.

To Serve

Defrost the wrapped pudding at room temperature at least 5 hours or overnight. Preheat the oven to 300°F. Remove the plastic wrap from the pudding and rewrap tightly with the foil that wrapped the frozen pudding. Place the wrapped pudding on a baking sheet or pie tin. Bake about 35 minutes, or until the pudding feels warm to the touch. Cut the warm pudding into thin slices and serve 2 slices on each plate. Spoon the Cranberry-Orange Coulis around one side of the pudding slices. Or fill a plastic ketchup-type bottle with the coulis and draw zigzag lines of sauce across the plate. Arrange the pudding slices on the plate so the sauce pattern is displayed. The pudding is best served the same day.

6. When done, remove the lid and place the pudding on a wire rack for 10 minutes. Use a small sharp knife to loosen the pudding from the top of the sides and center tube of the mold. Invert the pudding onto the rack. Let the pudding cool for 30 minutes and serve or cool thoroughly and freeze.

Prepare the Cranberry-Orange Coulis

7. Put the cranberries, orange juice, water, and sugar in a medium saucepan. Cook over medium heat until the cranberries pop and soften, about 7 minutes. Remove from the heat. Skim off most of the foam. Place the sauce in the workbowl of a food processor fitted with the steel blade. Process the mixture to a puree. Strain into a serving bowl, cover, and chill until serving time. The coulis can be refrigerated up to 5 days or frozen. Makes 1 cup.

LEMON AND WHITE CHOCOLATE STEAMED PUDDING

After a big holiday dinner, a lemon-flavored dessert is a refreshing ending. I serve this steamed pudding with a warm white chocolate sauce flavored with lots of lemon zest.

SERVES 10

STEAMED PUDDING
4 ounces white chocolate, Callebaut or Baker's Premium preferred, chopped
1¼ cups unbleached all-purpose flour
1½ teaspoons baking powder
½ teaspoon salt
¾ cup blanched almonds
1 cup sugar
¼ pound (1 stick) soft unsalted butter
3 large eggs
¼ cup fresh lemon juice
1 teaspoon vanilla extract
½ teaspoon almond extract
1 tablespoon grated lemon zest

LEMON AND WHITE CHOCOLATE SAUCE
½ cup whipping cream
1 tablespoon unsalted butter
4 ounces white chocolate, Callebaut or Baker's Premium preferred, chopped
1½ teaspoons grated lemon zest

Prepare the Steamed Pudding

1. Put a small cake rack or 2 clean tuna cans with the top and bottom removed in the bottom of a large pot. The pot should be large enough to allow for 1 inch of space between the pudding mold and the sides of the pot. It should be tall enough so that the pot lid fits tightly after the pudding mold is placed in the pot.

Good Advice

· Grind the almonds for the steamed pudding with some of the sugar that is used in the recipe, so they can be ground fine without becoming a paste.

· Wash the lemons and grate the zest before squeezing the lemon juice.

· For details on cooking the pudding, see page 164.

· If you don't have time to defrost the frozen sauce, run hot water over the covered container and remove the sauce. Warm it in a heatproof container placed over, but not touching, barely simmering water, stirring occasionally.

Doubling the Recipe

Use 2½ teaspoons of baking powder, and ¾ teaspoon salt, and double the remaining ingredients. Steam the pudding in two molds in two pots.

To Freeze the Pudding

Wrap the cooled pudding tightly with plastic wrap then with heavy aluminum foil. Label with date and contents. Freeze up to 2 months.

To Freeze the Sauce

Pour the sauce into a plastic freezer container, leaving 1 inch of space at the top of the container. Loosely cover and cool for 1 hour at room temperature. Press a piece of plastic wrap onto the sauce and cover the container tightly. Label with date and contents. Freeze up to 2 months. Defrost the sauce in the refrigerator overnight. Warm the sauce in a small saucepan over low heat, stirring frequently.

Fill the pot with enough water to come halfway up the sides of the pudding mold when it is placed in the pot. Cover the pot and bring the water to a gentle boil. After the water boils, adjust the heat to medium or medium-low to maintain the water at a gentle boil. Generously butter the bottom, sides, and center tube of a 2- to 2½-quart pudding mold. Lightly coat the inside of the mold and center tube with powdered sugar.

2. Preheat the oven to 175°F.

3. Put the white chocolate in a small nonreactive ovenproof container and melt it in the oven, 6 to 8 minutes. Remove the white chocolate from the oven as soon as it is melted and stir until smooth. Set aside to cool.

4. Sift the flour, baking powder, and salt together and set aside. Put the almonds and 2 tablespoons of the sugar in the workbowl of a food processor fitted with the steel blade and process until the almonds are finely ground.

5. Put the butter in the large bowl of an electric mixer. Add the remaining sugar and beat on medium speed until the mixture lightens in color and looks fluffy, about 1½ minutes. Add the eggs, one at a time, mixing smooth after each addition, then beat for 1 minute, or until the mixture is smooth. Stop the mixer and scrape the sides of the bowl during this mixing. Add the lemon juice, vanilla, almond extract, and lemon zest. The mixture will look curdled. Mix in the melted white chocolate. Decrease the speed to low and mix in the flour mixture. Beat for 30 seconds until the mixture looks smooth. Mix in the ground almonds. Pour the batter into the prepared mold and smooth the top. Cover tightly with the pudding mold lid.

6. Protect your hands with potholder mitts and place the mold evenly on the cake rack or tuna cans. Cover the pot. Check every 20 minutes to see that the water is boiling gently. Steam over medium heat for 2 hours, or until a toothpick inserted into the center of the pudding comes out clean. When done, the top of the pudding will pull away from the sides of the mold. To check for doneness, wear potholder mitts to remove the mold from the pot. Open the lid of the mold so that the steam escapes away from you.

7. When done, remove the lid and place the pudding on a wire rack for 10 minutes. Use a small sharp knife to loosen the pudding from the top of the sides and center tube of the mold. Invert the pudding onto the cake rack. Let the pudding cool for 30 minutes and serve or cool thoroughly and freeze.

Prepare the Lemon and White Chocolate Sauce

8. Put the cream and butter in a small saucepan and heat over medium-low heat until the cream is hot and the butter is melted. The hot cream mixture will form tiny bubbles around the edge of the pan and measure about 175°F. on a food thermometer. Do not let the mixture boil. Remove the pan from the heat. Add the white chocolate and let it melt in the hot cream mixture for about 30 seconds. Add the lemon zest and stir until the sauce is smooth and all of the white chocolate is melted. Makes ¾ cup. Leftover sauce can be stored in the refrigerator up to 3 days.

To Serve
Defrost the wrapped pudding at room temperature at least 5 hours or overnight. Preheat the oven to 300°F. Remove the plastic wrap from the pudding and rewrap tightly with the foil that wrapped the frozen pudding. Place the wrapped pudding on a baking sheet or pie tin. Bake about 35 minutes, or until the pudding feels warm to the touch. Cut the warm pudding into thin slices and serve 2 slices on each plate. Spoon the sauce around one side of the pudding slices. The pudding is best served the same day.

STEAMED CHOCOLATE PUDDING WITH BRANDIED BROWN SUGAR SAUCE

*C*arolyn and Keith May own the restaurant where I baked professionally for many years. Keith remembers his mother steaming this pudding on their woodstove. Both stove and pudding warmed them through the long, cold New England winters. Carolyn inherited Keith's mother's handwritten recipes and graciously shares this winter-warming tradition.

SERVES 10

CHOCOLATE STEAMED PUDDING
6 ounces semisweet chocolate, chopped
4 tablespoons (1/2 stick) unsalted butter, cut into 4 pieces
1 1/4 cups unbleached all-purpose flour
1 1/4 teaspoons baking powder
1/4 teaspoon salt
2 large eggs
2/3 cup granulated sugar
1 teaspoon vanilla extract
3/4 cup whole milk

BRANDIED BROWN SUGAR SAUCE
1 cup heavy whipping cream
3/4 cup (packed) light brown sugar
1 teaspoon instant decaffeinated coffee granules
1 tablespoon brandy

Prepare the Chocolate Steamed Pudding

I. Put a small cake rack or 2 clean tuna cans with the top and bottom removed in the bottom of a large pot. The pot should be large enough to allow for 1 inch of space between the pudding mold and the sides of the pot. It should be tall enough so that the pot lid fits tightly after the pudding mold is placed in the pot. Fill the pot with enough water to come halfway up the sides of the pudding mold when it is placed in the pot. Cover the pot and bring the water to a gentle boil. After the water boils, adjust the heat to medium or medium-low to maintain the water at a gentle boil. Generously butter the bottom, sides, and center

Good Advice
· This pudding cooks in about half the time as most steamed puddings (frugal New Englanders were not ones to waste fuel) and will be done in about an hour.

· Use heavy whipping cream rather than whipping cream for the sauce. The heavy cream gives the sauce a thick, syrupy quality.

Doubling the Recipe
Double the ingredients. Steam the pudding in two molds and two pots.

To Freeze the Pudding
Wrap the cooled pudding tightly with plastic wrap then with heavy aluminum foil. Label with date and contents. Freeze up to 2 months.

To Freeze the Sauce
Pour the sauce into a plastic freezer container, leaving 1 inch of space at the top of the container. Loosely cover

tube of a 2- to 2½-quart pudding mold. Lightly coat the inside of the mold and center tube with powdered sugar.

2. Put the semisweet chocolate and butter in a heatproof container and place it over, but not touching, a saucepan of barely simmering water. Stir the mixture until the chocolate and butter are melted and smooth. Remove from over the water and set aside to cool.

3. Sift the flour, baking powder, and salt together and set aside. Put the eggs in the large bowl of an electric mixer and mix on medium speed just to combine the yolks and whites. Add the granulated sugar and beat until the mixture lightens in color and looks fluffy, about 1½ minutes. Mix in the vanilla. Decrease the speed to low and stir in the chocolate mixture. Alternately add the flour mixture and the milk in 3 additions (3 flour, 2 milk), beginning and ending with the flour mixture. Stop the mixer and scrape the sides of the bowl during this mixing. Pour the batter into the prepared mold and smooth the top. Cover tightly with the steamed pudding mold lid.

4. Protect your hands with potholder mitts and place the mold evenly on the rack or tuna cans. Cover the pot. Check every 20 minutes to see that the water is boiling gently. Steam over medium heat for 1 hour, or until a toothpick inserted into the center of the pudding comes out clean. When done, the top of the pudding will pull away from the sides of the mold. To check for doneness, wear potholder mitts to remove the mold from the pot. Open the lid of the mold so that the steam escapes away from you.

5. When done, remove the lid and place the pudding on a wire rack for 10 minutes. Use a small sharp knife to loosen the pudding from the top of the sides and center tube of the mold. Invert the pudding onto the cake rack. Let the pudding cool for 30 minutes and serve or cool thoroughly and freeze.

Prepare the Brandied Brown Sugar Sauce

6. Stir the cream, brown sugar, and coffee together in a medium saucepan. Heat over medium heat, stirring, until the brown sugar dissolves. Simmer gently, uncovered, for 30 minutes. The sauce will reduce to about 1½ cups. Remove the saucepan from the heat and stir in the brandy. Return the saucepan to the heat and simmer for 1 minute.

and cool for 1 hour at room temperature. Press a piece of plastic wrap onto the sauce and cover the container tightly. Label with date and contents. Freeze up to 2 months. Defrost the sauce in the refrigerator overnight. Warm the sauce in a small saucepan over low heat, stirring frequently. Leftover sauce can be stored in the refrigerator up to 1 week.

To Serve

Defrost the wrapped pudding at room temperature at least 5 hours or overnight. Preheat the oven to 300°F. Remove the plastic wrap from the pudding and rewrap tightly with the foil that wrapped the frozen pudding. Place the wrapped pudding on a baking sheet or pie tin. Bake about 40 minutes, or until the pudding feels warm to the touch. Cut the warm pudding into thin slices and serve 2 slices on each plate. Spoon the sauce over the pudding slices. The pudding is best served the same day.

Outrageous Chocolate Cakes

I have a surefire way to turn any event into a special occasion: Serve chocolate cake. Whether it's a simple Dark Chocolate Cake with Fudge Frosting or a sophisticated 80th Birthday Strawberry and White Chocolate Cake, these cakes will announce happy birthdays, welcome home the weary traveler, salute the graduate, or trumpet the arrival of a new baby.

Although some of these cakes look as if they are quite a production to make, most are surprisingly easy. The cake for the Chocolate Chestnut Satin Torte is mixed in a food processor, and its chocolate glaze topping takes minutes to prepare. Lisa's Chocolate Chip Birthday Cake has a fast chocolate whipped cream frosting, and the Milk Chocolate and Hazelnut Praline Truffle Cake is mixed together quickly; all it takes is a sifting of powdered sugar to finish it off.

If cake layers require splitting, I defrost the cake to the point that I can cut through it easily. Meringues and cake layers that do not need to be split before they are filled require no defrosting. After filling and frosting the frozen layers, you can return the finished cake to the freezer. Any slight defrosting of the cake layer will not affect the flavor of the cake. Remember that if cake layers are frozen prior to frosting, store them only for two months, rather than the usual three, since they will be frozen again with the frosting for up to one month more.

The structure of a cake is developed by beating air into the batter; this takes place during the creaming of the butter and sugar and after the addition of the eggs. During these two steps, beat the batter thoroughly. When I've been in a hurry and skimped on this beating time, I may have saved two minutes, but the result was never as high or as light as a carefully beaten cake. The final step is to add the dry ingredients alternately with the liquid ingredients. This is just a process of incorporating these ingredients into the batter; they do not require long beating.

Place the oven rack in the middle of the oven to ensure evenly baked cakes. Check cakes as they bake and rotate the pans front to back if they appear to be baking unevenly. If you must use two racks for four layers, place the racks in the lower middle and upper middle of the oven. Space the pans on the rack so they are not placed directly over each other and rotate them front to back and top to bottom after the batter is set and about halfway through their baking time.

Ovens differ in how they bake, and the baking times given are approximate. Toward the end of the baking time, test the cake to see if it is done. To test a dense or fairly firm cake, first touch the center; if it feels firm, insert a wooden toothpick into the center of the cake. If the toothpick comes out clean, the cake is done. When checking a delicate sponge cake, use only the toothpick.

When splitting cakes into thinner layers, I use a serrated knife to split them and the removable bottom of a tart pan to separate them. The smooth pan bottom slides in easily and supports the whole layer so there is no chance of it breaking apart when you move it.

I often brush a cake layer with a lightly flavored sugar syrup, matching the flavor of the syrup with the flavor of the cake. Liqueurs and dissolved coffee make good flavorings. Framboise and kirsch go well with raspberries, amaretto with peach and white chocolate, crème de cacao with white chocolate, coffee with dark chocolate. Besides adding flavor and moistness, these syrups help frostings and fillings stick to the cake.

IF YOU ONLY LIVE ONCE CHOCOLATE CAKE

I started with the name of this cake, then created a chocolate cake that would live up to it. It had to include three of my favorite chocolate ingredients—chocolate cake, chocolate mousse, and thick chocolate glaze. I scooped out the center of a chocolate cake layer, crumbled it, and baked it into crisp crumbs. After filling the hollowed-out cake with chocolate mousse, I topped it with the big crisp chocolate crumbs and drizzles of thick chocolate glaze. I would never claim that this is the best chocolate cake, but if you only live once . . .

SERVES 12 TO 14

One 10-inch Devilish Chocolate Cake Layer (page 42),
  cooled or defrosted just until soft enough to split

THICK CHOCOLATE GLAZE
$^1/_2$ cup whipping cream
2 tablespoons unsalted butter, softened
2 tablespoons light corn syrup
8 ounces semisweet chocolate, chopped

CHOCOLATE MOUSSE FILLING
9 ounces semisweet chocolate, chopped
2 ounces unsweetened chocolate, chopped
4 tablespoons ($^1/_2$ stick) unsalted butter
$^3/_4$ cup whipping cream
1 teaspoon vanilla extract
3 large egg whites
$^1/_4$ teaspoon cream of tartar
$^1/_2$ cup sugar

1. Position a rack in the middle of the oven. Preheat the oven to 300°F.

2. Leaving a 1-inch border, mark a circle around the top of the cake. Leaving a $^3/_4$-inch cake base and the 1-inch border, spoon out the center of the cake. Break the cake center into crumbs about $^3/_4$ inch in size and spread them in a single layer on a baking sheet. Bake 10 minutes. Cool the crumbs thoroughly.

Prepare the Thick Chocolate Glaze

3. Put the cream, butter, and corn syrup in a medium saucepan and stir over medium heat, until the mixture is hot and the butter is melted. The hot cream

Good Advice
· Since the mousse filling firms quickly, fill the cake immediately.

· Freeze this cake only up to 2 weeks if you want the crumb topping to remain crisp. After 2 weeks in the freezer, the crumbs soften, but otherwise the cake will be fine if left in the freezer for up to 1 month.

Doubling the Recipe
Use two cake layers and double the remaining ingredients.

To Freeze
Freeze the cake, uncovered, to firm the chocolate glaze, about 1 hour. Cover tightly with plastic wrap. Gently press heavy aluminum foil around the cake. Label with date and contents. Freeze up to 2 weeks.

mixture will form tiny bubbles around the edge of the pan and measure about 175°F. on a food thermometer. Do not let the mixture boil. Remove the saucepan from the heat. Add the chopped chocolate and let it melt in the hot cream mixture for about 30 seconds. Gently stir the mixture until all of the chocolate is melted and the glaze is smooth. Set the glaze aside to cool and thicken slightly. The glaze can be transferred to a small bowl, covered, and refrigerated up to 1 week. To soften cold glaze, warm it in a medium saucepan over low heat, stirring frequently. Makes about 1 1/3 cups.

Prepare the Chocolate Mousse Filling

4. Put the semisweet chocolate, unsweetened chocolate, and butter in a heatproof container and place it over, but not touching, a saucepan of barely simmering water. Stir the chocolate and butter together until the chocolate melts and the mixture is smooth. Remove the mixture from over the hot water and pour into a large bowl to cool slightly.

5. Put the cream and vanilla in the large bowl of an electric mixer. Beat at medium speed until soft peaks form. Cover with plastic wrap and refrigerate.

6. Put the egg whites and cream of tartar in a clean large bowl of an electric mixer and with clean dry beaters, beat on low speed until the egg whites are foamy and the cream of tartar is dissolved. Increase the speed to medium-high, and beat just until soft peaks form. Slowly add the sugar, 1 tablespoon at a time. Whisk about a fourth of the beaten egg whites into the chocolate mixture. Use a rubber spatula to fold in the remaining egg whites. Fold in the whipped cream.

7. Immediately pour the mousse into the hollowed-out center of the cake, spreading a thin layer of mousse over the top edge of the cake. The mousse will fill the hollowed-out center of the cake. Mound the mousse slightly to the center of the cake. Use a thin metal spatula to spread about half of the glaze on the sides of the cake. Press about 3/4 cup of the baked cake crumbs onto the glaze. Sprinkle the remaining cake crumbs over the mousse, mounding the crumbs higher in the center of the cake. The crumbs should not cover the mousse completely. Drizzle the remaining chocolate glaze over the cake crumbs and mousse, but do not cover them completely.

To Serve

Defrost the wrapped cake in the refrigerator at least 6 hours or overnight. Unwrap and let the cake sit at room temperature about 1 hour before serving. Leftover cake can be covered with plastic wrap and refrigerated up to 2 days.

CHOCOLATE CAKE WITH WHITE CHOCOLATE AND RASPBERRY MOUSSE

I consider this one of my fanciest cakes as far as presentation goes, but the preparation is remarkably simple. I fill a chocolate cake layer with white chocolate mousse and raspberries, cover it with a shiny chocolate glaze, and have a cake ready for the grandest of splurges in short order. This version of white chocolate mousse, which is a creamy white chocolate mixture whipped with cream, is especially easy to prepare.

SERVES 12

FRAMBOISE OR KIRSCH SYRUP
1 tablespoon hot water
1 tablespoon sugar
2 tablespoons framboise or kirsch

SIMPLE WHITE CHOCOLATE AND RASPBERRY MOUSSE
1¼ cups cold whipping cream
1 tablespoon unsalted butter
6 ounces white chocolate, Callebaut or Baker's Premium preferred, chopped
1 teaspoon vanilla extract
1 cup raspberries, preferably fresh, or frozen unsweetened raspberries, not defrosted

One 10-inch Devilish Chocolate Cake Layer (page 42), cooled or defrosted just until soft enough to split
1 cup Shiny Chocolate Glaze (page 212), cooled until thickened slightly
1 ounce white chocolate, Callebaut or Baker's Premium preferred, chopped, for garnish
1 cup fresh raspberries, for garnishing the cake (optional)

Prepare the Syrup

1. Put the water and sugar in a small saucepan and mix over low heat just until the sugar dissolves. Remove from the heat, stir in the framboise or kirsch, and cool the syrup. The syrup may be covered and stored in the refrigerator for up to 1 week.

Good Advice

· Cool the white chocolate mixture for the mousse thoroughly before whipping it with the cream. A warm mixture will prevent the cream from whipping to a firm stage.

· If you are using frozen raspberries for the mousse, do not let them defrost.

· The glaze should be pourable but thick enough to spread on and cling to the sides of the cake.

· If your toaster oven can be kept at a low temperature, you can melt the white chocolate for the garnish there rather than in a large oven.

Doubling the Recipe

Use two cake layers and double the remaining ingredients.

Prepare the White Chocolate and Raspberry Mousse

2. Put ¼ cup of the cream and the butter in a medium saucepan and heat over medium-low heat until the cream is hot and the butter melts. The hot cream mixture will form tiny bubbles around the edge of the pan and measure about 175°F. on a food thermometer. Do not let the mixture boil. Remove the pan from the heat. Add the white chocolate and let it melt in the hot cream mixture for about 30 seconds. Stir until smooth and all of the white chocolate is melted. Pour the mixture into a bowl, cover, and refrigerate until cool to the touch, about 45 minutes. Stir the mixture occasionally to ensure it cools evenly. The mixture should be pourable.

3. Put the remaining 1 cup of cream, the vanilla, and the cooled white chocolate mixture in the large bowl of an electric mixer. Mix on low speed just to combine. Increase the speed to medium-high and beat until firm peaks form, about 1 minute. Gently fold in the raspberries. Assemble the cake immediately.

4. Place the chocolate cake layer on a serving plate or cardboard cake circle that has the edges covered with overhanging strips of wax paper. Use a serrated knife to cut the cake into 2 layers. Slide the removable bottom of a tart pan under the top layer and move it to the side. Use a pastry brush to lightly brush the top of each layer with the syrup. Spread the white chocolate mousse evenly over the bottom layer. Top with the second cake layer. Use a thin metal spatula to smooth the edges of the mousse filling. Pour about three fourths of the glaze over the cake, spreading a thin layer over the sides of the cake and lifting any glaze that drips onto the wax paper back onto the sides of the cake. Spread the remaining glaze over the sides of the cake. Remove the wax paper. Refrigerate the cake to firm the glaze while you melt the white chocolate for the garnish.

5. Preheat the oven to 175°F.

6. Place the white chocolate in a small nonreactive ovenproof container and melt it in the oven, about 5 minutes. Remove the white chocolate as soon as it is melted and stir it smooth. Remove the cake from the refrigerator. Dip a fork into the melted white chocolate and wave it over the cake to form thin lines of white chocolate crisscrossing back and forth over the top of the cake. Move the fork quickly to create thin lines.

To Freeze
Chill the cake, uncovered, in the freezer for about 1 hour until the white chocolate and the glaze are firm. Cover tightly with plastic wrap. Gently press heavy aluminum foil around the cake. Label with date and contents. Freeze up to 1 month.

To Serve
Defrost the wrapped cake in the refrigerator at least 6 hours or overnight. Unwrap the cake and let it sit at room temperature 30 minutes before serving. Garnish slices of the cake with fresh raspberries, if desired. Leftover cake can be covered with plastic wrap and stored in the refrigerator up to 2 days.

DARK CHOCOLATE CAKE WITH FUDGE FROSTING

Ice cream and chocolate cake—one of the dessert world's ideal combinations. To pair chocolate cake and frosting with ice cream, there should be a good proportion of cake to frosting, and the frosting must be dark and fudgelike. This two-inch-high square cake slathered with dark fudge frosting fits the bill.

SERVES 9

FUDGE FROSTING
1/4 pound (1 stick) unsalted butter, cut into 6 pieces
1/2 cup granulated sugar
1/2 cup half-and-half
4 ounces semisweet chocolate, chopped
4 ounces unsweetened chocolate, chopped
2 cups powdered sugar, sifted
1 teaspoon vanilla extract
2 teaspoons instant decaffeinated coffee dissolved in 1 tablespoon water

One 9-inch square Devilish Chocolate Cake (page 42), cooled or taken from the freezer, but not defrosted
Ice cream, for serving with the cake

Prepare the Fudge Frosting

I. Put the butter, granulated sugar, and half-and-half in a medium saucepan and heat over medium heat until the butter melts and the sugar dissolves, stirring occasionally. Increase the heat to medium-high and simmer the mixture for 1 minute, stirring constantly. Small bubbles will form around the edge of the pan. Remove the saucepan from the heat. Add the semisweet and unsweetened chocolate and stir the mixture until it is smooth and all of the chocolate is melted. Return the saucepan to low heat for 1 minute, if necessary, to melt the chocolate completely.

· Chop the chocolate into small pieces, 1/4 to 1/2 inch, so it melts evenly in the hot mixture.

· When the powdered sugar is mixed with the warm chocolate mixture, it melts the powdered sugar slightly and produces a frosting with a smooth texture.

· If you have a frozen 9-inch square cake in the freezer, you can spread the frosting over the frozen cake.

· The fudge frosting will be the same dark, rich chocolate color as the cake.

Doubling the Recipe
Use two cakes and double the remaining ingredients.

2. Pour the chocolate mixture into the large bowl of an electric mixer. Add the powdered sugar, vanilla, and dissolved coffee and mix on low speed just to incorporate the powdered sugar. Press plastic wrap onto the surface of the mixture and refrigerate until it is cool to the touch, about 35 minutes. Stir occasionally to ensure the mixture cools throughout. Makes about 2½ cups.

3. Beat the cooled chocolate mixture on medium-high for 1 minute, or until the frosting is creamy and lightens slightly in color. Use a thin metal spatula to spread the frosting over the top of the cake. Run the rounded tip of the spatula across the top of the frosting, in one direction, to form a ridged pattern on the frosting. Slide the cake onto a serving plate or piece of cardboard covered with aluminum foil.

To Freeze

Freeze the cake, uncovered, until the frosting is firm. Wrap the cake tightly with plastic wrap. Gently press heavy aluminum foil around the cake. Label with date and contents. Freeze up to 1 month.

To Serve

Defrost the wrapped cake in the refrigerator overnight. Unwrap the cake and let it sit at room temperature for about 1 hour before serving. Serve with a scoop of ice cream. Coffee or vanilla are good choices. Leftover cake can be covered with plastic wrap and refrigerated up to 3 days.

CHOCOLATE GANACHE CAKE

anache is a combination of chocolate and cream. It is a fudgy mixture that becomes creamy when whipped. The filling for this cake is a whipped ganache while the thick chocolate glaze that covers it is unwhipped ganache; both are prepared from the same mixture.

When the cake bakes, it forms a crunchy topping. Invert the cake before adding the ganache to have a crisp cake bottom in contrast to the creamy filling and soft glaze. Serve the cake at room temperature.

SERVES 10

CHOCOLATE CAKE
9 ounces semisweet chocolate, chopped
6 ounces (1½ sticks) unsalted butter
5 large eggs, separated
1 cup sugar
1 teaspoon vanilla extract
¾ cup unbleached all-purpose flour
¼ teaspoon cream of tartar

GANACHE FILLING AND GLAZE
2 tablespoons unsalted butter
1 cup whipping cream
2 tablespoons sugar
1 pound semisweet chocolate, chopped
1 teaspoon vanilla extract

Prepare the Chocolate Cake

1. Position a rack in the middle of the oven. Preheat the oven to 350°F. Butter a 9-inch cake pan with 1¾- to 2-inch-high sides. Line the bottom of the pan with parchment or wax paper and butter the paper.

2. Put the chocolate and butter in a heatproof container and place it over, but not touching, a saucepan of barely simmering water. Stir the mixture until the chocolate and butter mixture is melted and smooth. Set aside to cool slightly.

3. Put the egg yolks in the large bowl of an electric mixer and mix at medium speed for 10 seconds to break up the yolks. Add ½ cup of the sugar and beat for 1 minute, or until the egg mixture thickens and lightens in color. Decrease the speed to low and mix in the melted chocolate mixture and vanilla. Add the flour and mix just until no white streaks of flour remain.

· The chilled ganache is ready to be whipped when it is cold and thick but before it hardens. The edges of the ganache in the bowl will be firm.

· Beat ganache for a short time, just until the color lightens from dark brown to medium brown and the mixture thickens slightly.

· When beaten, the taste of ganache changes from fudgelike to creamlike. If it is not whipped enough, it will still taste fine but more like the glaze on top of the cake.

· If ganache is whipped too much, it will be grainy. To save overwhipped ganache, melt it over low heat, chill it, and whip it again. Whisking the ganache by hand makes it difficult to overbeat.

· Use whipped ganache immediately, as it firms up quickly and becomes difficult to spread.

4. Put the egg whites and cream of tartar in a clean large bowl of an electric mixer and with clean dry beaters, beat on low speed until the egg whites are foamy and the cream of tartar is dissolved. Increase the speed to medium and beat the egg whites to soft peaks. Slowly beat in the remaining ½ cup sugar, 1 tablespoon at a time. Fold a third of the egg white mixture into the chocolate mixture. Fold in the remaining egg whites. Pour the batter into the prepared pan.

5. Bake just until a toothpick inserted in the center comes out clean, about 35 minutes.

6. Cool the cake in the pan. Use a sharp knife to loosen the cake from the pan. Line the edges of a serving platter with overhanging strips of wax paper. Invert the cake onto the platter. Remove the paper from the bottom of the cake.

Prepare the Ganache Filling and Glaze

7. Put the butter, cream, and sugar in a medium saucepan and heat over medium-low heat just until the cream is hot and the butter is melted. The mixture will form tiny bubbles around the edge of the pan and measure about 175°F. on a food thermometer. Do not let the mixture boil. Remove the pan from the heat and add the chopped chocolate. Let the chocolate melt for a minute. Add the vanilla and stir the ganache until it is smooth and all of the chocolate is melted. Remove 1 cup of ganache and set it aside at room temperature to cool to lukewarm and thicken. Pour the remaining ganache into a large mixing bowl and press plastic wrap onto the surface. Refrigerate the ganache until it is cold to the touch and just beginning to harden around the edges, about 30 minutes. Stir occasionally to ensure the mixture chills throughout.

8. Whisk the cold ganache until it changes from a dark chocolate to a medium chocolate color and thickens slightly, about 30 seconds. Immediately, spread the ganache cream over the top of the cake. Refrigerate the cake until the ganache is firm, about 30 minutes.

9. Pour about ¾ cup of the reserved lukewarm ganache glaze over the top of the cake, spreading it evenly with a thin metal spatula. Spread the remaining glaze over the sides of the cake. Remove the wax paper strips. The cake is now ready to serve or freeze.

Double the ingredients and use two pans. The ganache may take longer to chill and whip.

To Freeze
Freeze the cake, uncovered, to firm the glaze, about 1 hour. Wrap tightly with plastic wrap. Gently press heavy aluminum foil around the cake. Label with date and contents. Freeze up to 1 month.

To Serve
Defrost the wrapped cake in the refrigerator overnight. Unwrap the cake and let it sit at room temperature about 1 hour before serving. Leftover cake can be covered with plastic wrap and refrigerated up to 3 days.

TRIPLE TRUFFLE
CELEBRATION CAKE

W̶hen I created this cake, I wanted to use a simple chocolate truffle mixture in many incarnations—fudgy chocolate truffle, creamy whipped truffle, and chocolate truffle glaze. This cake is my idea of how to celebrate.

SERVES 16

COFFEE SYRUP
3 tablespoons hot water
2 tablespoons sugar
1½ teaspoons instant decaffeinated coffee granules

CHOCOLATE TRUFFLE
2 cups whipping cream
4 tablespoons (½ stick) unsalted butter, cut into 4 pieces
¼ cup sugar
2 pounds semisweet or bittersweet chocolate, chopped
2 teaspoons vanilla extract

One 10-inch Devilish Chocolate Cake Layer (page 42), cooled or defrosted just until soft enough to split

Prepare the Coffee Syrup

1. Put the water, sugar, and coffee in a small saucepan and stir over low heat just until the sugar dissolves. Set the syrup aside to cool while you prepare the cake. The syrup may be covered and stored in the refrigerator for up to 1 week.

Prepare the Chocolate Truffle

2. Put the cream, butter, and sugar in a medium saucepan and heat over medium-low heat until the cream is hot, the butter is melted, and the sugar dissolved. The hot cream mixture will form tiny bubbles around the edge of the pan and measure about 175°F. on a food thermometer. Do not let the mixture boil. Remove the pan from the heat. Add the chopped chocolate and let it melt

Good Advice
· Spread the whipped truffle filling on the cake immediately as it will firm up quickly.

· The cake is rich and I cut the cake into sixteen servings rather than the usual twelve.

· Let the cake come to room temperature before serving so the chocolate truffle is soft and creamy. This will also bring out the flavor of chocolate.

Doubling the Recipe
Use two cake layers and double the ingredients. Cook the mixture in a large saucepan.

To Freeze
Freeze the cake, uncovered, to firm the chocolate glaze, about 1 hour. Cover tightly with plastic wrap. Gently press heavy aluminum foil around the cake. Label with date and contents. Freeze up to 1 month.

about 30 seconds to soften. Whisk the mixture smooth. If all of the chocolate is not melted, return the mixture to low heat for 1 minute and stir. Remove the pan from the heat and stir in the vanilla. Makes 5 cups.

3. Pour 1 cup of truffle into a small bowl for the fudge truffles. Cover and chill until firm, about 1 hour. Pour 2½ cups of truffle into a large mixing bowl for the whipped truffle and press plastic wrap onto the surface. Refrigerate the truffle until it is cold to the touch, thick, and just beginning to harden around the edges, about 1 hour. Stir once to ensure the mixture chills throughout. The mixture should not be hard. Set the remaining truffle mixture aside.

4. Use a serrated knife to cut the cake into 2 horizontal layers. Slide the removable bottom of a tart pan under the top layer and move it to the side. Place the bottom layer on a serving plate or cardboard cake circle that has the edges covered with overhanging strips of wax paper. Use a pastry brush to lightly brush the top of each cake layer with coffee syrup.

5. Form small truffle balls from the cold firm truffle. Use a teaspoon to scoop out some truffle then roll it into a ball about ¾ inch in diameter between your hands. A slightly oval shape is preferable to a round ball. The truffles do not have to be perfectly shaped. As you form the truffles place them evenly spaced on the cake layer. You should have about 28 truffles.

6. Remove the cold, but still soft, truffle for the whipped truffle from the refrigerator. Whisk the truffle mixture until the chocolate lightens from dark to medium brown, about 1 minute. Or beat the truffle with an electric mixer on medium speed about 30 seconds. Immediately spread the whipped truffle over the truffle balls to form a smooth layer of filling on the cake. Spread the whipped truffle carefully to the edges of the cake. Place the top layer on the cake.

7. Pour about ¾ cup of the cooled glaze over the top of the cake and spread the glaze evenly with a thin metal spatula. If the glaze has cooled and thickened too much to pour, warm it for about 1 minute over low heat until pourable but still thick. Use the metal spatula to smooth any glaze that has dripped onto the sides of the cake, then use the spatula to spread the remaining glaze on the sides of the cake. Carefully remove and discard the wax paper strips.

To Serve

Defrost the wrapped cake in the refrigerator overnight. Unwrap the cake and let it sit at room temperature about 1 hour before serving. Leftover cake can be covered with plastic wrap and refrigerated up to 4 days.

LISA'S CHOCOLATE CHIP BIRTHDAY CAKE

*W*hen Lisa Ekus, my friend and cookbook publicist, first read Bake and Freeze Desserts, *she pegged me immediately as a fellow chocolate chip lover. Lisa's mother made this cake for every one of Lisa's birthdays. It was her "one and only favorite birthday and special occasion cake"—a convincing recommendation if ever I heard one.*

The chocolate chips in this cake are pieces of grated chocolate, which permeate the cake with tiny chocolate flakes. The light chocolate whipped cream frosting is simply cream whipped with Slightly Thinner Chocolate Truffle Sauce.

SERVES 12

CHOCOLATE CHIP CAKE
2 cups cake flour
1 teaspoon baking soda
1/4 pound (1 stick) soft unsalted butter
2 cups (packed) light brown sugar
3 large eggs, separated
1/2 cup sour cream
1/2 teaspoon vanilla extract
1/2 cup whole milk
2 ounces (about 1/2 cup plus 2 tablespoons) grated semisweet chocolate

CHOCOLATE WHIPPED CREAM FROSTING
1 1/2 cups cold whipping cream
3 tablespoons powdered sugar
1/2 cup Slightly Thinner Chocolate Truffle Sauce (page 50), at room temperature (about 75°F. if measured with a food thermometer)

Prepare the Chocolate Chip Cake

I. Position an oven rack in the middle of the oven. Preheat the oven to 350°F. Butter the bottom and sides of two 9-inch layer pans with 1 3/4- to 2-inch-high sides. Line the bottom of each pan with parchment or wax paper and butter the paper.

2. Sift the flour and baking soda together and set aside. Put the butter in the large bowl of an electric mixer and mix on low speed for 15 seconds. Add the brown sugar. Increase the speed to medium and beat the butter and brown sugar for 1 minute, or until the mixture is creamy. Stop the mixer and scrape the sides of the bowl once during this mixing. Add the egg yolks, one at a time, and beat for 1 minute at medium speed. Stop the mixer and scrape the sides of the bowl once during this mixing. Decrease the speed to low and mix in the flour mixture just until all of the flour is incorporated. At this stage the batter will be thick. Mix in the sour cream. Mix in the vanilla. Slowly pour in the milk and mix until the batter is smooth. Stop the mixer and scrape the sides of the bowl once during this mixing.

3. Put the egg whites in a clean large bowl of an electric mixer and with clean dry beaters, beat on low speed until the egg whites are foamy. Increase the speed to high and beat just until soft peaks form. Fold about a third of the egg whites into the batter mixture. Fold in the remaining whites. Sprinkle the grated chocolate over the mixture and fold it into the batter. Pour the batter into the prepared pans, dividing the batter evenly. Smooth the top of the batter.

4. Bake the cake about 30 minutes. Gently press your fingers on the middle of the top of the cake. It should feel firm. If the cake feels firm, insert a toothpick in the center of the cake. When the toothpick comes out clean, the cake is done.

5. Cool the cake thoroughly in the baking pan on a wire rack.

Prepare the Chocolate Whipped Cream Frosting

6. Put the cream, powdered sugar, and chocolate sauce in the large bowl of an electric mixer. Beat on medium-high speed until firm peaks form. The movement of the beaters will form teardrop shapes in the whipped cream.

7. Place 1 cake layer on a cardboard circle or cake plate that has the edges covered with strips of wax paper. Spread about 1 cup frosting over the top of the cake layer. Top with the second layer. Spread the remaining frosting over the top and sides of the cake. Use a long, narrow spatula to swirl the top of the frosting. Carefully slide out the wax paper strips.

To Freeze

Freeze the cake until the frosting is firm, about 1 hour. Wrap tightly with plastic wrap. Gently press heavy aluminum foil around the cake. Label with date and contents. Freeze up to 1 month.

To Serve

The whipped cream frosting is soft and must be protected in the refrigerator. Remove the wrapping from the frozen cake. Cover the cake with a plastic cake dome or stick 5 or 6 toothpicks in the top of the cake, spacing them evenly over the cake, and carefully suspend plastic wrap over the cake. Or, top the cake with chocolate curls (see page 55) or grated chocolate and wrap the cake carefully with plastic wrap. Defrost the recovered cake in the refrigerator overnight. Serve the cake cold. Leftover cake can be covered with a plastic cake dome or with plastic wrap supported by toothpicks and stored in the refrigerator up to 2 days.

SUMMERTIME PEACH AND WHITE CHOCOLATE BUTTERCREAM CAKE

Ripe peaches are available all summer long as the harvest begins In the southern states then follows the sun northward and even west to California. So there's no rush; you have the whole summer to make this light sponge cake filled with a fresh peach and white chocolate buttercream.

SERVES 12

AMARETTO SYRUP
1/4 cup hot water
1/4 cup sugar
1/4 cup amaretto

PEACH AND WHITE CHOCOLATE BUTTERCREAM
5 to 6 large ripe peaches (about 2 pounds)
8 ounces white chocolate, Callebaut or Baker's Premium preferred, chopped
3/4 cup plus 2 tablespoons sugar
1/4 cup water
1 tablespoon light corn syrup
5 large egg whites
1/2 teaspoon cream of tartar
1/2 pound plus 4 tablespoons (2 1/2 sticks) unsalted butter, softened to about the same temperature as the cooled meringue (72° to 78°F. if tested with an instant-read thermometer)
1/2 teaspoon almond extract
1 tablespoon amaretto

Two 9-inch Hot Milk Sponge Cake Layers (page 44), cooled or defrosted just until soft enough to split
1 cup white chocolate curls (see page 55)

Prepare the Amaretto Syrup

I. Put the water and sugar in a small saucepan and mix over low heat just until the sugar dissolves. Remove from the heat, stir in the amaretto, and cool the syrup. The syrup may be covered and stored in the refrigerator for up to 1 week.

· The peach flavor of the buttercream will only be as good as the peaches, so use ripe, sweet peaches.

· Drain the peeled peaches thoroughly to remove excess water and juice from the fruit.

· The sponge cake layers are firm and easy to move around; just lift them up and move them as needed. They won't break.

· The buttercream is made with Italian meringue. For more detail on preparing Italian meringue, see page 10.

Doubling the Recipe

Use four sponge layers. Double the ingredients for the buttercream. Use a heavy duty mixer with a 5-quart bowl and beat the Italian meringue for 8 to 10 minutes rather than 5 minutes; otherwise prepare two batches of buttercream. Double the amount of white chocolate curls.

Prepare the Peach and White Chocolate Buttercream

2. Fill a large bowl with ice cubes and water. Have ready a saucepan of boiling water large enough to cover the peaches. Use a slotted spoon to gently place the peaches in the boiling water. Boil for 30 seconds. Use the slotted spoon to transfer the peaches to the ice water. Leave the peaches in the ice water just until they are cool enough to handle, about 5 minutes. Drain and peel the peaches, remove the pits, and cut the peaches into quarters. Pat the peaches with a paper towel to remove excess water. Put the peach slices in a food processor fitted with the metal blade and process to a puree. Measure out 2 cups of puree and put it in a medium frying pan, preferably nonstick. Cook gently over medium-low heat for about 30 minutes, or until the puree is reduced to 1 cup, stirring occasionally. Put the puree in a small bowl, loosely cover, and refrigerate until cool to the touch.

3. Preheat the oven to 175°F.

4. Put the white chocolate in a small nonreactive heatproof container and melt in the oven, about 10 to 12 minutes. Remove the white chocolate from the oven as soon as it is melted and stir until smooth. Set aside to cool.

5. Put the ¾ cup sugar, water, and corn syrup in a saucepan. Cover the saucepan and cook the syrup over low heat until all of the sugar is dissolved, stirring occasionally to help the sugar dissolve. Do not let the syrup boil until the sugar dissolves. Uncover the saucepan, increase the heat to high, and boil the mixture, without stirring, until the syrup measures 240°F. (soft ball stage) on a candy thermometer. Wipe down the sides of the pan with a pastry brush dipped in hot water to dissolve any sugar crystals that form on the side of the pan.

6. Begin beating the egg whites when the sugar syrup begins to boil. Put the egg whites and cream of tartar in a clean large bowl of an electric mixer and beat with clean dry beaters on low speed until the egg whites are foamy and the cream of tartar is dissolved. Increase the speed to medium-high and beat the egg whites to soft peaks. Add the 2 tablespoons of sugar, 1 tablespoon at a time. As soon as the syrup reaches 240°F., with the mixer on low speed, slowly pour the hot syrup in a thin stream onto the softly beaten egg whites. If the syrup reaches 240°F. before the egg whites are ready, remove the syrup from the heat

To Freeze
Chill the frosted cake, uncovered, in the freezer for about 1 hour, or until the buttercream is firm. Cover tightly with plastic wrap. Gently press heavy aluminum foil around the cake. Label with date and contents. Freeze up to 1 month.

To Serve
Defrost the wrapped cake in the refrigerator at least 6 hours or overnight. Unwrap the cake and let it sit at room temperature 30 minutes before serving. Leftover cake can be covered with plastic wrap and stored in the refrigerator up to 2 days.

for a few seconds and finish beating the egg whites. Pour the syrup in the space between the sides of the bowl and the beaters to prevent as much sugar syrup as possible from splashing onto the sides of the bowl and the beaters. Continue beating the meringue at medium-low speed for 5 minutes: The outside of the bowl will be lukewarm and the meringue will be stiff and have a temperature of 72° to 78°F. if measured with an instant-read food thermometer.

7. Beat in the softened butter, 2 tablespoons at a time. Stop the mixer and scrape the bowl once, but do not scrape any sugar syrup that may have splashed onto the side of the bowl and hardened. The meringue will deflate slightly when the butter is added. On low speed, mix in the slightly cooled melted white chocolate, peach puree, the almond extract, and amaretto. If the buttercream seems too soft to spread, refrigerate it for about 20 minutes to firm slightly, then whisk for a few seconds until smooth.

8. Place 1 cake layer on a serving plate or cardboard cake circle that has the edges covered with overhanging strips of wax paper. With a serrated knife, split the cake into 2 horizontal layers. Lift up the top layer and move it to the side. Use a pastry brush to lightly brush the bottom cake layer with amaretto syrup. Use a thin metal spatula to spread about 1 cup of the buttercream over the bottom layer. Lift the top layer and carefully place it on the cake. Brush with amaretto syrup and spread with 1 cup of buttercream. Split the remaining cake layer and separate the layers. Put the bottom layer on the cake. Brush with amaretto syrup and spread with 1 cup buttercream. Top with the remaining layer and brush the cake with the remaining syrup. Smooth the sides of the cake with the spatula.

9. Place the cake on a serving plate or cardboard cake circle. Spread a thin layer of buttercream on the top and sides of the cake to help the crumbs adhere to the cake. Spread the remaining buttercream over the top and sides of the cake. Spoon white chocolate curls in a circle in the center of the cake. Touch the curls as little as possible since the heat of your hand can melt them. Gently remove the wax paper strips from under the cake.

PISTACHIO PRALINE MERINGUE CAKE WITH LEMON AND WHITE CHOCOLATE BUTTERCREAM

This cake could serve as a model for a crunchy, creamy dessert. Three crisp pistachio praline meringues alternate with a silken lemon and white chocolate buttercream. A final burst of crunch is provided by the crushed pistachio praline topping.

SERVES 12

MERINGUES
1 cup powdered sugar
½ cup pistachio praline powder (see page 54)
5 large egg whites, at room temperature
½ teaspoon cream of tartar
½ cup granulated sugar
½ teaspoon almond extract

LEMON AND WHITE CHOCOLATE BUTTERCREAM
4 ounces white chocolate, Callebaut or Baker's Premium preferred, chopped
⅔ cup plus 2 tablespoons sugar
3 tablespoons water
1 tablespoon light corn syrup
4 large egg whites
¼ teaspoon cream of tartar
½ pound (2 sticks) unsalted butter, softened to about the same temperature as the cooled meringue (72° to 78°F. if tested with an instant-read thermometer)
1 teaspoon vanilla extract
2 tablespoons fresh lemon juice
1 tablespoon plus 1 teaspoon grated lemon zest

1 cup crushed pistachio praline (see page 54)

Good Advice
· Prepare a recipe of pistachio praline. Grind enough praline to make ½ cup of praline powder for the meringues and set aside 1 cup of crushed praline to garnish the top of the cake.

· The buttercream is made with Italian meringue. For more detail on Italian meringue, see page 10.

Doubling the Recipe
Double the ingredients and use a 5-quart bowl to mix the meringue and buttercream mixtures. Use three baking sheets to bake the meringues.

To Freeze the Meringues
Stack the meringues on a plate or cardboard cake circle, placing plastic wrap between each layer. Carefully wrap the stack of meringues with plastic wrap then heavy aluminum

foil. Label with date and contents. Freeze for up to 1 month. Do not stack anything on top of the meringues. Do not defrost the meringues before using them.

To Freeze the Cake

Chill the cake in the freezer until the buttercream is firm, about 30 minutes. Wrap with plastic wrap. Gently press heavy aluminum foil around the cake. Label with date and contents. Freeze up to 1 month.

To Serve

Defrost the wrapped cake in the refrigerator at least 5 hours or overnight. Unwrap the cake and let it sit at room temperature 30 minutes before serving to soften the buttercream. Leftover cake can be covered with plastic wrap and stored in the refrigerator for 1 day.

Prepare the Meringues

1. Position 2 oven racks in the middle and upper third of the oven. Preheat the oven to 225°F. Cut 2 pieces of parchment paper to fit two 17 × 12-inch baking sheets. Mark two 8-inch circles on 1 piece of parchment paper and one 8-inch circle on the other piece of parchment paper. Line the baking sheets with the parchment, marked side down.

2. Mix the powdered sugar and praline powder in a small bowl and set aside. Put the egg whites and cream of tartar in the large bowl of an electric mixer and beat on low speed until the egg whites are foamy. Increase the speed to medium-high and beat until soft peaks form. Reduce the speed to medium and slowly beat in the granulated sugar, 1 tablespoon every 30 seconds. Mix in the almond extract. Remove the bowl from the mixer and use a rubber spatula to fold the powdered sugar mixture into the whites in 2 additions.

3. Use a thin metal spatula to spread the meringue mixture evenly over the 3 marked circles. Smooth the edges of the circles with the metal spatula. The meringues will be about ½ inch thick. Bake about 1½ hours, or until the meringues are crisp and dry. They will not actually harden until they cool. Cool the meringues on the baking sheets.

Prepare the Lemon and White Chocolate Buttercream

4. Preheat the oven to 175°F.

5. Put the white chocolate in a small nonreactive heatproof container and melt it in the oven, about 10 to 12 minutes. Remove the white chocolate from the oven as soon as it is melted and stir until smooth. Set aside to cool.

6. Put the ⅔ cup sugar, the water, and corn syrup in a small saucepan. Cover the saucepan and cook the syrup over low heat until all of the sugar is dissolved, stirring occasionally to help the sugar dissolve. Do not let the syrup boil until the sugar dissolves. Uncover the saucepan, increase the heat to high, and boil the mixture, without stirring, until the syrup measures 240°F. (soft ball stage) on a candy thermometer. Wipe down the sides of the pan with a pastry brush dipped in hot water to dissolve any sugar crystals that form on the side of the pan.

7. Begin beating the egg whites when the sugar syrup begins to boil. Put the egg whites and cream of tartar in a clean large bowl of an electric mixer and beat with clean dry beaters on low speed until the egg whites are foamy and the cream of tartar is dissolved. Increase the speed to medium-high and beat the egg whites to soft peaks. Add the 2 tablespoons of sugar, 1 tablespoon at a time. As soon as the syrup reaches 240°F. (soft ball stage), with the mixer on low speed, slowly pour the hot syrup in a thin stream onto the softly beaten egg whites. If the syrup reaches 240°F. before the egg whites are ready, remove the syrup from the heat for a few seconds and finish beating the egg whites. Pour the syrup in the space between the sides of the bowl and the beaters to prevent as much sugar syrup as possible from splashing onto the sides of the bowl and the beaters. Continue beating the meringue at medium-low speed for 5 minutes. The outside of the bowl will be lukewarm and the meringue will be stiff and have a temperature of 72° to 78°F. if measured with an instant-read thermometer.

8. Beat in the softened butter, 2 tablespoons at a time. Stop the mixer and scrape the bowl once, but do not scrape any sugar syrup that may have splashed onto the side of the bowl and hardened. The meringue will deflate slightly when the butter is added. On low speed, mix in the slightly cooled melted white chocolate, vanilla, lemon juice, and lemon zest. If the buttercream seems too soft to spread, refrigerate it for about 20 minutes to firm slightly, then whisk it for a few seconds until smooth.

9. Place a meringue layer on a serving plate. Spread 1 cup of the buttercream evenly over the meringue. Top with another meringue layer and repeat with 1 cup of buttercream. Top the cake with the remaining meringue layer. Spread the remaining buttercream evenly over the top and sides of the cake. Sprinkle the crushed pistachio praline over the top of the cake.

80TH BIRTHDAY STRAWBERRY AND WHITE CHOCOLATE CAKE

*H*istory has a way of repeating itself. When the Camden Garden Club celebrated its seventy-fifth birthday, I volunteered to bake the birthday cake, and then realized that I would be out of town until the night before the party. That cake became one of my first big bake-and-freeze projects. Recently, the garden club celebrated its eightieth birthday and asked me to bring the birthday cake. After I agreed, I realized we would be on a family vacation until just before the party. This time I didn't even blink an eye, I just baked this white chocolate cake, filled and covered it with strawberry and white chocolate buttercream, and flew off knowing the birthday cake was waiting in my freezer.

SERVES 12

WHITE CHOCOLATE CAKE
1 1/2 cups cake flour
1 teaspoon baking powder
1/4 teaspoon salt
3 ounces white chocolate, Callebaut or Baker's Premium preferred, chopped
1/4 cup water
1/4 pound (1 stick) soft unsalted butter
3/4 cup sugar
2 large eggs
1 teaspoon vanilla extract
1/4 teaspoon almond extract
1/2 cup whole milk, at room temperature or warmed slightly

STRAWBERRY AND WHITE CHOCOLATE BUTTERCREAM
1 pint ripe strawberries, stemmed and cleaned
6 ounces white chocolate, Callebaut or Baker's Premium preferred, chopped
1/2 cup plus 2 tablespoons sugar
3 tablespoons water
1 tablespoon light corn syrup

3 large egg whites

¼ teaspoon cream of tartar

6 ounces (1½ sticks) unsalted butter, softened to about the same temperature as the cooled meringue (72° to 78°F. if tested with an instant-read thermometer)

1 teaspoon vanilla extract

3 cups white chocolate curls (see page 55)

Fresh whole strawberries, for garnish when serving (optional)

Prepare the White Chocolate Cake

1. Position a rack in the middle of the oven and preheat to 350°F. Butter a 9-inch round cake pan with 2-inch-high sides. Line the bottom of the pan with parchment or wax paper and butter the paper.

2. Sift the cake flour, baking powder, and salt together and set aside. Melt the white chocolate and water in a large heatproof container set over, but not touching, a saucepan of barely simmering water, stirring until the chocolate melts and the mixture is smooth. Remove the mixture from over the hot water. Set aside to cool slightly.

3. Put the butter in the large bowl of an electric mixer and beat on medium speed until smooth. Add the sugar slowly, beating until the mixture is fluffy, about 2 minutes. Add the eggs one at a time, beating well after each addition. Beat for 1 more minute. Decrease the speed to low and mix in the white chocolate mixture, the vanilla, and almond extract. Add the flour mixture and the milk alternately, beginning and ending with the flour mixture (3 flour, 2 milk). Stop the mixer and scrape the sides of the bowl before the last addition of flour. Stir any loose flour into the batter. Pour the batter into the prepared pan and spread evenly.

4. Bake about 40 minutes. To test for doneness, gently press your fingers on the middle of the cake. It should feel firm. If it feels firm, insert a toothpick into the center of the cake. When the toothpick comes out clean, the cake is done.

5. Cool the cake in the pan on a wire rack for 10 minutes. Use a small sharp knife to loosen the sides of the cake from the pan. Invert onto the rack and cool thoroughly. Carefully remove the paper from the bottom of the cake.

To Freeze the Unfrosted Cake

Invert the cooled cake onto plastic wrap so the top side is up. Cover the cake tightly with the plastic wrap then heavy aluminum foil. Label with date and contents. Freeze up to 2 months. Defrost the wrapped cake at room temperature, about 1 hour.

To Freeze the Frosted Cake

Chill the frosted cake, uncovered, in the freezer for 1 hour. Cover tightly with plastic wrap. Gently press heavy aluminum foil around the cake. Label with date and contents. Freeze up to 1 month.

To Serve

Defrost the wrapped cake in the refrigerator overnight. Unwrap the cake and allow it to sit at room temperature about 1 hour before serving, or until the buttercream softens. Garnish each serving with a fresh strawberry, if desired. Leftover cake can be covered with plastic wrap and stored in the refrigerator up to 3 days.

Prepare the Strawberry and White Chocolate Buttercream

6. Puree half of the pint of strawberries in a food processor. Strain the strawberries. You should have 1/2 cup of puree. Set it aside. Save any leftover strawberries for another use.

7. Preheat the oven to 175°F.

8. Put the white chocolate in a small nonreactive ovenproof container and melt it in the oven, 8 to 10 minutes. Remove the white chocolate from the oven as soon as it is melted and stir until smooth. Set aside to cool slightly.

9. Put the 1/2 cup sugar, water, and corn syrup in a small saucepan. Cover the saucepan and cook the syrup over low heat until all of the sugar is dissolved, stirring occasionally. Do not let the syrup boil until the sugar dissolves. Uncover the saucepan, increase the heat to high, and boil the mixture without stirring until the syrup measures 240°F. (soft ball stage) on a candy thermometer. Wipe down the sides of the pan with a pastry brush dipped in hot water to dissolve any sugar crystals that form on the side of the pan.

10. Begin beating the egg whites when the sugar syrup begins to boil. Put the egg whites and cream of tartar in a clean large bowl of an electric mixer and beat with clean dry beaters on low speed until the egg whites are foamy and the cream of tartar is dissolved. Increase the speed to medium-high and beat the egg whites to soft peaks. Add the 2 tablespoons of sugar, 1 tablespoon at a time. As soon as the syrup reaches 240°F., with the mixer on low speed, slowly pour the hot syrup in a thin stream onto the softly beaten egg whites. If the syrup reaches 240°F. before the egg whites are ready, remove the syrup from the heat for a few seconds and finish beating the egg whites. Pour the syrup in the space between the sides of the bowl and the beaters to prevent as much sugar syrup as possible from splashing onto the sides of the bowl and the beaters. Continue beating the meringue at medium-low speed for 5 minutes. The outside of the bowl will be lukewarm and the meringue will be stiff and have a temperature of 72° to 78°F. if measured with a food thermometer.

11. Beat in the softened butter, 2 tablespoons at a time. Stop the mixer and scrape the bowl once, but do not scrape any sugar syrup that may have splashed

onto the side of the bowl and hardened. The meringue will deflate slightly when the butter is added. On low speed, mix in the slightly cooled melted white chocolate and the vanilla. Transfer 1½ cups of the buttercream to a small bowl, add the ½ cup strawberry puree, and stir to combine thoroughly. You now have a strawberry buttercream and a white chocolate buttercream. If the buttercreams seem too soft to spread, refrigerate for about 20 minutes to firm slightly, then whisk each buttercream for a few seconds until smooth.

12. Place the cake, top side up, on a serving plate or cardboard cake circle that has the edges lined with overhanging strips of wax paper. With a serrated knife, cut the cake horizontally into 2 even layers. Slide the removable bottom of a tart pan under the top layer and move it to the side. Spread the strawberry buttercream evenly over the bottom layer. Top with the remaining cake layer. Cover the top and sides of cake with the white chocolate buttercream. Spoon white chocolate curls over the top of the cake, then use the spoon to press curls onto the sides of the cake. Carefully remove the wax paper strips from under the cake.

CHOCOLATE CHESTNUT SATIN TORTE

hestnuts have a secret mission when used in this cake. Pureed chest-nuts replace flour and give the cake a remarkable smooth and moist texture while leaving the dominant taste of chocolate. If you run your hands over a piece of satin cloth, you'll have some idea of how luxurious this cake is. The cake batter is mixed in a food processor, proving once again that fancy cakes can still be easy cakes.

SERVES 10

6 ounces semisweet chocolate, chopped
2 ounces unsweetened chocolate, chopped
2 cups peeled unsweetened chestnuts, vacuum packed or canned in water
  and drained (about 10 ounces)
1/4 pound (1 stick) unsalted butter, softened and cut into 8 pieces
1/4 cup powdered sugar
1/3 cup granulated sugar
1 teaspoon vanilla extract
1/4 cup brandy or cognac
5 large eggs
1/2 cup Shiny Chocolate Glaze (page 212), warmed to pouring consistency
10 marrons glacés, for garnish (optional)

I. Position an oven rack in the middle of the oven. Preheat the oven to 175°F. Butter the bottom and sides of a 9-inch round cake pan, 1 3/4 to 2 inches deep. Line the bottom of the pan with parchment or wax paper, butter the paper, and coat the paper lightly with flour.

2. Place the semisweet and unsweetened chocolate in an ovenproof container and melt them in the oven, about 6 to 8 minutes. As soon as the chocolate is melted, remove it from the oven and stir it smooth. Increase the oven temperature to 350°F. Set the chocolate aside to cool slightly.

3. Put the chestnuts in a strainer and rinse under cold water. Pat dry with paper towels. Put the chestnuts in the workbowl of a food processor fitted with the metal blade. Process to puree the chestnuts, about 15 seconds. Add the butter

· I usually bake this cake around the holidays, which is also when my local gourmet food shop stocks canned chestnuts. I buy several cans when they are available so that I have a supply on hand. Williams-Sonoma (see page 295) usually carries vacuum-packed chestnuts during the holiday season.

· The smooth bottom of this cake becomes the top of the cake when it is glazed.

· Marrons glacés, glazed sweetened chestnuts, make a festive garnish for the cake. You can place a single glazed chestnut in the center of the cake or serve a whole glazed chestnut with each slice of cake.

Doubling the Recipe

Double the ingredients and use two pans. Mix the cake in separate batches.

and process until the butter is combined with the chestnuts. Add the powdered sugar and granulated sugar and process 15 seconds. With the motor running, add the vanilla and brandy. The mixture will look smooth. Add the melted chocolate and process until the chocolate is blended into the mixture. With the motor running, add the eggs and process until the eggs are incorporated and the batter is smooth, about 15 seconds. The batter will be thick. Scrape the batter into the prepared pan and smooth the top.

4. Bake 30 minutes, or until a toothpick inserted into the center of the cake comes out clean or with a dry crumb clinging to it. The top of the cake will change from shiny to dull as it bakes.

5. Cool the cake in the baking pan on a wire rack for 10 minutes. Use a small sharp knife to loosen the cake from the sides of the pan. Place the cake rack on top of the cake and invert it. Cool the cake thoroughly, about 1 hour. Carefully remove the paper from the bottom of the cake and discard it. Leave the cake inverted to glaze it.

6. Put a piece of wax paper under the rack to catch and recycle any glaze that drips off the cake. Pour the warm glaze over the cake, spreading the glaze over the sides of the cake with a thin metal spatula. Slide the removable bottom of a tart pan under the cake and transfer it to a serving plate or cardboard cake circle covered with aluminum foil.

To Freeze

Freeze the cake, uncovered, until the chocolate glaze is firm, about 1 hour. Wrap the cake tightly with plastic wrap. Gently press heavy aluminum foil around the cake. Label with date and contents. Freeze up to 1 month.

To Serve

Defrost the wrapped cake in the refrigerator overnight. Let the unwrapped cake soften at room temperature for about 1 hour before serving. Garnish the cake with marrons glacés, if desired. Leftover cake can be covered with plastic wrap and refrigerated up to 5 days.

RAINBOW RIBBON HONEYMOON CAKE

*W*hen Jeff and I were on our honeymoon, we shared a memorable cake in Avallon, France. It consisted of thin, rectangular orange, pistachio, and raspberry cake layers filled with raspberry jam and chocolate. It was the epitome of French sophistication to two young, inexperienced dessert lovers. For years I kept memories of that cake in the back of my mind while I tried to figure out an easy way to bake three differently flavored long cake rectangles. I'm sure the restaurant used sheet pans and prepared three cakes, but that is more cake than one usually needs at home. The solution in the end turned out to be simple. I divided a sponge cake batter into thirds, flavored each portion differently, and baked each flavor separately in a loaf pan. I now had three flavors of long thin layers to spread with raspberry jam and chocolate glaze.

SERVES 8 TO 10

1 recipe batter for 1 Hot Milk Sponge Cake Loaf (page 44)
1/3 cup ground roasted unsalted pistachio nuts
2 tablespoons cake flour
1/2 teaspoon almond extract
1 tablespoon plus 1 teaspoon raspberry puree (see page 162)
1 tablespoon Grand Marnier
1/2 teaspoon grated orange zest
4 tablespoons seedless raspberry fruit spread or jam
1 cup Shiny Chocolate Glaze (page 212), cooled until thickened slightly

I. Position an oven rack in the middle of the oven. Preheat the oven to 350°F. Butter the bottom and sides of 3 loaf pans measuring 9 × 5 inches. Line the bottom of each pan with parchment or wax paper and butter the paper.

2. Have ready 2 medium bowls. Pour 1 1/4 cups of the sponge cake batter into each of the bowls. There will be about 1 1/8 cups of batter left in the original mixing bowl. You will have 3 bowls of batter. In a small bowl, mix the ground pistachio nuts and cake flour together. Use a large rubber spatula to fold the nut mixture and 1/4 teaspoon of the almond extract into the original bowl of batter. Pour into one of the prepared loaf pans. Gently stir the raspberry puree and re-

Good Advice

· If you own three loaf pans, chances are the sizes vary. Instead of purchasing new pans, I bought three 9 × 5-inch disposable aluminum loaf pans. Since they can be washed and used repeatedly, it was an inexpensive solution.

· When cutting the cake into thin layers, it is easier to split the layers evenly if you begin at one narrow end of the cake and cut to the opposite end.

· To fill, use seedless raspberry jam so the filling remains smooth. I use seedless raspberry fruit spread that is sweetened with fruit juice.

Doubling the Recipe

Prepare batter for two sponge loaves, divide it into thirds and flavor it. Double the ingredients for the flavoring. Bake three large loaves, allowing additional baking time, and split each baked loaf into four layers. You will have enough slices to prepare two cakes. Dou-

maining ¼ teaspoon of almond extract into a second bowl of batter and pour into a prepared loaf pan. Gently stir the Grand Marnier and orange zest into the remaining bowl and pour the contents into the remaining loaf pan.

3. Bake until a toothpick inserted in the center of each loaf comes out clean, about 17 minutes.

4. Cool the loaves in the pan on a wire rack for 15 minutes. Use a small sharp knife to loosen the sides of each loaf from the pan. Invert each loaf onto the rack. Carefully remove and discard the paper liner. Turn each loaf right side up and cool thoroughly, about 1 hour. The cake can be filled or the loaves frozen for filling later.

5. Use a large serrated knife to cut each loaf into 2 equal horizontal layers. Begin at a narrow end and cut along the length of the cake. Each layer will be a scant ½ inch thick. Place a pistachio layer, bottom side down, on a long serving platter or piece of cardboard covered with heavy aluminum foil. Place wax paper strips under the bottom of the cake. Spread 1 tablespoon raspberry jam evenly over the cake. Place a raspberry cake layer over the jam. Spread 2 tablespoons of chocolate glaze evenly over the cake. Place an orange cake layer over the glaze. Spread 1 tablespoon raspberry jam evenly over the cake. Add the remaining pistachio layer and glaze with 2 tablespoons chocolate. Add the remaining raspberry layer and glaze with 1 tablespoon jam. Place the remaining orange layer on top of the cake and spread the remaining tablespoon of jam thinly over the ends and sides of the cake. Smooth the sides of the cake with a thin metal spatula. Cover the top, sides, and ends of the cake with the remaining ¾ cup chocolate glaze. Remove the wax paper strips. You will have a 6-layer cake with alternating fillings of raspberry jam and chocolate glaze.

ble the ingredients for the jam and glaze.

To Freeze the Loaves

Wrap each loaf tightly with plastic wrap then wrap the three layers together with heavy aluminum foil. Label with date and contents. Freeze up to 2 months.

To Freeze the Cake

Chill the cake, uncovered, in the freezer for about 1 hour, or until the chocolate glaze is firm. Wrap tightly with plastic wrap. Gently press heavy aluminum foil around the cake. Label with date and contents. Freeze up to 1 month.

To Serve

Defrost the wrapped cake in the refrigerator at least 5 hours or overnight. Unwrap the cake and let it sit at room temperature 30 minutes before serving. Use a large serrated knife and a slight sawing motion to cut the cake. Leftover cake can be covered with plastic wrap and stored in the refrigerator up to 3 days.

MILK CHOCOLATE AND HAZELNUT PRALINE TRUFFLE CAKE

*F*ine European bakeries often sell both chocolates and pastry. *Chocolate candy, cakes, and tarts sit side by side in spotless glass cases. Surrounded by chocolate on a visit to one such shop I thought, "Why not combine the best of both worlds in a cake? Milk chocolate and praline would taste like one, big baked truffle." I did. And it does.*

SERVES 10

12 ounces milk chocolate, Dove Bar or Callebaut preferred, chopped
1 ounce unsweetened chocolate, cut into 2 pieces
1/4 pound (1 stick) unsalted butter, softened and cut into 8 pieces
4 large eggs, separated
1/4 teaspoon cream of tartar
2 tablespoons sugar
1 tablespoon unbleached all-purpose flour
1 teaspoon vanilla extract
6 tablespoons hazelnut praline powder (see page 54)
Powdered sugar, for dusting

1. Position an oven rack in the middle of the oven. Preheat the oven to 375°F. Remove the bottom of an 8-inch springform pan with at least 2³/₄-inch-high sides and wrap the bottom with heavy aluminum foil. Return the foil-wrapped bottom to the springform pan. Butter the pan and aluminum foil.

2. Put the milk chocolate, unsweetened chocolate, and butter in a large heatproof container set over, but not touching, a saucepan of barely simmering water. Stir the mixture until the chocolate and butter are melted and smooth. Remove the chocolate mixture from over the water and pour it into a large mixing bowl.

3. Put the egg whites in a clean large bowl of an electric mixer. Put the egg yolks in a small bowl and set aside. Add the cream of tartar to the egg whites and beat on low speed until the egg whites are foamy and the cream of tartar is dissolved. Increase the speed to medium-high and beat the egg whites to soft peaks. Slowly beat in the sugar, 1 tablespoon at a time. Set aside.

Good Advice

· Wrapping the bottom of the springform pan in aluminum foil ensures that the cake can be easily removed from the springform bottom.

· The center of this cake will fall slightly as it cools. Sift powdered sugar into the center of the cake, leaving a contrasting dark border.

· The cake is rich, so I cut it into ten thin slices.

Doubling the Recipe

Double the ingredients and use two pans. Beat the egg whites in a 5-quart bowl.

4. Whisk the flour into the yolks until the mixture is smooth. Stir the yolk mixture and vanilla into the chocolate mixture. Use the whisk to blend the ingredients together. Reserve 1 tablespoon of praline powder and whisk the remaining 5 tablespoons into the chocolate mixture. Use a large rubber spatula to fold a third of the egg whites into the chocolate mixture. Fold in the remaining egg whites. Pour the batter into the prepared pan. Sprinkle the reserved praline powder over the top.

5. Bake 30 minutes. The center of the cake will be soft.

6. Cool the cake, uncovered, at room temperature for $1\frac{1}{2}$ hours. The center of the cake will sink slightly as it cools. Cover the cake and refrigerate until firm, at least 4 hours or overnight. Use a small sharp knife to loosen the cake from the springform pan. Remove the sides of the pan. Carefully turn the cake over and remove the foil-wrapped springform bottom. Invert the cake onto a serving platter or cardboard cake circle. Sift powdered sugar over the center of the cake.

VARIATION For a quick holiday decoration, place a heart, star, or tree-shape cookie cutter in the center of the powdered sugar topping. Use a small spoon to sprinkle cocoa powder lightly inside the cookie cutter. Carefully lift the cookie cutter off the cake. You will have a dark chocolate heart or other design on the white powdered sugar topping.

To Freeze
Cover the cake tightly with plastic wrap then heavy aluminum foil. Label with date and contents. Freeze up to 3 months.

To Serve
Defrost the wrapped cake in the refrigerator overnight. Unwrap the cake and let it sit at room temperature for about 1 hour before serving. Leftover cake can be covered with plastic wrap and refrigerated up to 5 days.

THE MAGNIFICENT FIVE-LAYER CHOCOLATE BUTTERCREAM CAKE

This cake is for all chocolate buttercream lovers, like me, who can never get enough buttercream with their cake. Five thin layers of sponge cake are filled and covered with five thin layers of chocolate buttercream. Normally, the hardest part about making a multilayered cake is baking all of those thin layers, but I've solved the problem. I bake a Hot Milk Sponge Cake Loaf and split the loaf into five layers. The sponge loaf cuts easily into thin layers and makes a light contrast to the buttercream.

SERVES 12

COFFEE-RUM SYRUP
4 tablespoons hot water
2 teaspoons instant decaffeinated coffee granules
2 tablespoons sugar
2 teaspoons dark rum

CHOCOLATE BUTTERCREAM
6 ounces semisweet chocolate, chopped
1 ounce unsweetened chocolate, chopped
1/2 cup plus 2 tablespoons sugar
3 tablespoons water
1 tablespoon light corn syrup
3 large egg whites
1/4 teaspoon cream of tartar
6 ounces (1 1/2 sticks) unsalted butter, softened to about the same
    temperature as the cooled meringue (72° to 78°F. if tested with an
    instant-read thermometer)
1 teaspoon vanilla extract
1 teaspoon instant decaffeinated coffee dissolved in 1 teaspoon water

1 Hot Milk Sponge Cake (page 44) baked in a 12 × 4 × 2 3/4-inch loaf pan,
    cooled or defrosted just until soft enough to split
2 1/2 cups milk chocolate curls (see page 55)

Good Advice

· Using a long narrow loaf pan to bake the cake gives it a sophisticated look. I use a pan with a 7-cup capacity that measures 12 × 4 × 2 3/4 inches. If the pan is larger than this size, the loaf will not be thick enough to split into five layers. If you have to substitute, use a smaller rather than a larger loaf pan.

· Use a serrated knife and a slight sawing motion to cut the cake into horizontal layers. Measure the height of the cake with a ruler and mark five equal layers to guide you. Begin at a narrow end and cut along the length of the cake. Cutting a loaf that has been frozen and is partially defrosted works better than cutting a freshly baked loaf. For easier cutting of the cake when serving, use the serrated knife and sawing motion again.

· The buttercream is made with Italian meringue. For more detail on Italian meringue, see page 10.

Prepare the Coffee-Rum Syrup

1. Put the water and coffee in a small saucepan and stir to dissolve the coffee. Add the sugar and stir over low heat just until the sugar dissolves. Remove from the heat and mix in the rum. Cool the syrup. The syrup may be covered and stored in the refrigerator for up to 1 week.

Prepare the Chocolate Buttercream

2. Preheat the oven to 175°F. Put the semisweet chocolate and the unsweetened chocolate in an ovenproof container. Melt the chocolate in the oven, 12 to 13 minutes. Remove the chocolate as soon as it is melted and stir it smooth. Set aside to cool slightly.

3. Put the ½ cup sugar, the water, and corn syrup in a small saucepan. Cover and cook over low heat until all of the sugar is dissolved, stirring occasionally to help the sugar dissolve. Do not let the syrup boil until the sugar dissolves. Increase the heat to high and boil, without stirring, until the syrup reaches 240°F. (soft ball stage). Wipe down the sides of the pan with a pastry brush dipped in hot water to dissolve any sugar crystals that form on the side of the pan.

4. Begin beating the egg whites when the sugar syrup begins to boil. Put the egg whites and cream of tartar in a clean large bowl of an electric mixer. With clean dry beaters, beat on low speed for 30 seconds, or until the egg whites are foamy and the cream of tartar is dissolved. Increase the speed to medium-high and beat the egg whites to soft peaks. Add the 2 tablespoons of sugar, 1 tablespoon at a time. As soon as the syrup reaches 240°F., and with the mixer on low speed, slowly pour the hot syrup in a thin stream onto the softly beaten egg whites. If the syrup reaches 240°F. before the egg whites are ready, remove the syrup from the heat for a few seconds and finish beating the egg whites. Try to pour the syrup in the space between the beaters and the sides of the bowl to prevent as much sugar syrup as possible from splashing onto the beaters and the sides of the bowl. Continue beating the meringue at medium-low speed for 5

To Freeze
Chill the cake, uncovered, in the freezer for about 1 hour, or until the buttercream is firm. Wrap tightly with plastic wrap. Gently press heavy aluminum foil around the cake. Label with date and contents. Freeze up to 1 month.

To Serve
Defrost the wrapped cake in the refrigerator at least 5 hours or overnight. Unwrap the cake and let it sit at room temperature 30 minutes before serving. Use a large serrated knife and a slight sawing motion to cut the cake. Leftover cake can be covered with plastic wrap and stored in the refrigerator up to 3 days.

minutes. The outside of the bowl will be lukewarm and the meringue will be stiff and have a temperature of 72° to 78°F. if measured with a food thermometer. Beat in the softened butter, 2 tablespoons at a time. Stop the mixer and scrape the bowl once, but do not scrape any sugar syrup that may have splashed onto the side of the bowl and hardened. The meringue will deflate slightly when the butter is added. Add the slightly cooled melted chocolate, vanilla, and dissolved coffee and mix on low speed until incorporated. If the buttercream seems too soft to spread, refrigerate for about 20 minutes to firm slightly, then whisk for a few seconds until smooth. Makes 3 cups.

5. Place the loaf, top side up, on the counter. Measure the height of the loaf and mark 5 layers. The layers will be about 1/2 inch thick. Use a large serrated knife and a slight sawing motion to cut the loaf into horizontal layers. Begin at a narrow end and cut along the length of the cake. Move each layer to the side and stack the layers in order as you go. Place the bottom cake layer on a long serving platter or piece of cardboard covered with heavy aluminum foil. Brush lightly with coffee-rum syrup. Spread a thin layer of buttercream over the cake, about 1/3 cup. Repeat to fill the remaining layers. Brush the top of the cake lightly with coffee syrup. Spread the remaining buttercream over the top and sides of the cake. Put a 1-inch strip of milk chocolate curls along the center of the cake.

WINTER WHITE YULE LOG

What to have for Christmas dinner dessert is an easy decision at our house. We borrow from the French and have a cake roll shaped like a festive yule log. Different years bring variations of the decorations and fillings, but two things never change—all yule logs must be chocolate, and they must be prepared well in advance and tucked away in the freezer. Christmas is my day for feasting and relaxing, not baking.

My Winter White Yule Log has white chocolate buttercream rolled in a dark Chocolate Soufflé Cake Sheet. When you slice the cake, the white buttercream and dark cake look like the rings of a tree while black-and-white striped chocolate and white chocolate rectangles form striking bark sides along the length of the cake.

SERVES 12 TO 15

CRÈME DE CACAO SYRUP
3 tablespoons water
2 tablespoons sugar
2 tablespoons crème de cacao liqueur

WHITE CHOCOLATE BUTTERCREAM
10 ounces white chocolate, Callebaut or Baker's Premium preferred, chopped
1/2 cup plus 1 tablespoon sugar
3 tablespoons warm water
1 tablespoon light corn syrup
3 large egg whites
1/4 teaspoon cream of tartar
6 ounces (1 1/2 sticks) unsalted butter, softened to about the same temperature as the cooled meringue (72° to 78°F. if tested with an instant-read thermometer)
1 teaspoon vanilla extract
2 tablespoons crème de cacao liqueur

1 Chocolate Soufflé Cake Sheet (page 46), cooled or defrosted
30 pieces black-and-white striped chocolate rectangles (see page 55), measuring 1 × 2 inches

Good Advice
· The buttercream is made with Italian meringue. For more detail on Italian meringue, see page 10.

· Place matching size chocolate pieces opposite each other on the sides of the cake and the cake will cut easily. If you must cut through the chocolate bark, use a large sharp knife dipped in hot water and dried.

Doubling the Recipe
Use two cake rolls and double the remaining ingredients. Use a 5-quart bowl to mix the buttercream.

To Serve

Defrost the wrapped cake overnight in the refrigerator. Unwrap the cake and let it sit at room temperature, loosely covered with plastic wrap, until the buttercream softens, about 1 hour. Cut the cake with a large sharp knife that has been dipped in hot water and dried. It is easiest to cut in between the chocolate rectangles, but the warm knife will cut through the chocolate. Leftover cake can be covered with plastic wrap and refrigerated up to 3 days.

Prepare the Crème De Cacao Syrup

1. Put the water and sugar in a small saucepan and stir over low heat just until the sugar dissolves. Remove from the heat and stir in the crème de cacao. Set the syrup aside to cool. The syrup may be covered and stored in the refrigerator for up to 1 week.

Prepare the White Chocolate Buttercream

2. Preheat the oven to 175°F. Put the white chocolate in a small nonreactive heatproof container and melt it in the oven, about 10 to 12 minutes. Remove the white chocolate as soon as it is melted and stir until smooth. Set aside to cool slightly.

3. Put the 1/2 cup sugar, water, and corn syrup in a small saucepan. Cover the saucepan and cook over low heat until all of the sugar is dissolved, stirring occasionally to help the sugar dissolve. Do not let the syrup boil until the sugar dissolves. Uncover the saucepan, increase the heat to high, and boil the mixture, without stirring, until the syrup measures 240°F. (soft ball stage) on a candy thermometer. Wipe down the sides of the pan with a pastry brush dipped in hot water to dissolve any sugar crystals that form on the side of the pan.

4. Begin beating the egg whites when the sugar syrup begins to boil. Put the egg whites and cream of tartar in a clean large bowl of an electric mixer and beat with clean dry beaters on low speed until the egg whites are foamy and the cream of tartar is dissolved. Increase the speed to medium-high and beat the egg whites to soft peaks. Add the 1 tablespoon sugar. As soon as the syrup reaches 240°F., and with the mixer on low speed, slowly pour the hot syrup in a thin stream onto the softly beaten egg whites. If the syrup reaches 240°F. before the egg whites are ready, remove the syrup from the heat for a few seconds and finish beating the egg whites. Pour the syrup in the space between the sides of the bowl and the beaters to prevent as much sugar syrup as possible from splashing onto the sides of the bowl and the beater. Continue beating the meringue at medium-low speed for 5 minutes. The outside of the bowl will be lukewarm and the meringue will be stiff and have a temperature of 72° to 78°F.

if tested with an instant-read thermometer. Beat in the softened butter, 2 tablespoons at a time. Stop the mixer and scrape the bowl once, but do not scrape any sugar syrup that may have splashed onto the side of the bowl and hardened. The meringue will deflate slightly when the butter is added. On low speed, mix in the slightly cooled melted white chocolate, vanilla, and crème de cacao. If the buttercream seems too soft to spread, refrigerate for about 20 minutes to firm slightly, then whisk for a few seconds until smooth. Makes about 3¾ cups.

5. Unroll the soufflé sheet onto a clean dish towel and remove any paper wrapping. The long side of the cake roll should be parallel to the edge of the counter. Use a pastry brush to lightly brush the top of the cake with the crème de cacao syrup. Use a thin metal spatula to spread 1¾ cups of the white chocolate buttercream evenly over the cake. Roll up the cake like a jelly roll, using the towel to help. The cake should be seam side down. Lightly brush the cake roll with syrup. Cutting at an angle, cut a thin slice from one end of the cake roll. Spread about 2 teaspoons buttercream on top of the roll about 3 inches from either end and place the cake slice on it. This will form a "knot" in the log. Place the cake on a long narrow platter or strip of cardboard covered with heavy aluminum foil. Spread the remaining 2 cups of buttercream over the cake and swirl the buttercream to cover the knot. Wipe off any crumbs that cling to the spatula as you frost the cake roll. Place a line of striped chocolate rectangles against the sides of the log. The short side of the chocolate rectangles should be parallel to the counter and the smooth striped side of the chocolate that was touching the wax paper should be facing out on the log. The chocolate rectangles will stick to the buttercream.

Tube Cakes and Loaf Cakes

Many of these cakes are favorite recipes that friends have shared with me over the years. They are big, proud cakes that are genuine all-occasion desserts. Lisa Ekus triumphed at her first meeting with her in-laws when she brought along her Sour Cream Chocolate Chip Coffee Cake. The Chocolate-glazed Rum Chocolate Chip Cake has helped celebrate a lot of Klivans birthdays. Harriet Bell carries her Walnut and Chocolate Chip Butter Cake to picnics and weekends with friends. Lisa Ward serves her Black Russian Chocolate Chip Cake to company. Closer to home my daughter, Laura, wows her office mates with our family's Ribbon of Fudge Chocolate Cake.

These cakes have another thing in common—every one is simple to mix and can be put together quickly. When these cakes require a topping, it is either baked with the cake or consists of a simple glaze. All of these cakes are good keepers, are easy to wrap and freeze, and can be easily transported. They don't require refrigeration and make a good choice when you volunteer to bring dessert or want to take along a cake on a picnic. The Strawberry and White Chocolate Loaf, the Pear and Chocolate Tea Loaf, or any of the cakes without glaze are easy to mail and make an impressive holiday gift or homemade treat for a child away at school.

Oil and sour cream, two ingredients often included in tube cakes, create a particularly moist texture and fine crumb. Butter produces a thicker batter and slightly denser cake than one prepared with oil. Using oil as the shortening makes it easy to mix the ingredients. Sour cream, an acidic ingredient, requires baking soda to neutralize the acid. The

Mocha Confetti Chiffon Cake has no shortening at all and is low in fat. It gets its moist texture from a batter that contains a small amount of flour in proportion to the liquid ingredients and from the confetti of chocolate chips scattered throughout the cake.

Most of these cakes are at least three inches high and are baked in a tube, bundt, springform, or loaf pan. Tube and bundt pans have a center tube that helps these big cakes bake evenly. Since the sides and bottom of bundt pans are tapered, they have a smaller capacity than a tube pan with the same diameter. Cakes in these smaller tube pans bake for a shorter period of time. A 10-inch diameter tube pan will usually hold fourteen cups and a bundt pan of the same diameter only twelve cups. When a cake of this size bakes in a springform pan, which has no center tube, it requires a longer baking time. A recipe of batter for a large tube pan can be divided between two 8-inch diameter, 8-cup capacity tube pans. These smaller tube cakes are a handy size for holiday gifts. A 9 × 5-inch loaf pan is considered standard, but loaf pans come in so many sizes I include capacity recommendations for loaf pans. I often use a long narrow loaf pan. The loaf looks sophisticated, and the slices make a good serving size.

Buy yourself good quality pans that will bake cakes evenly, release cakes easily, and last for many years. To ensure that cakes release cleanly, I line the smooth bottoms of tube and loaf pans with parchment or wax paper, but it's not possible to line the patterned bottom of a bundt pan. That is why it's crucial to bake with a heavyweight bundt pan that has a smooth finish. It's so frustrating to turn a bundt cake out of the pan and have part of the bottom stick to the pan—believe me, I know. My dark, heavyweight Kaiser La Forme bundt pan has a smooth, shiny baked-on finish; I haven't had one cake stick to it yet.

Many of the tube cakes are served bottom side up. This gives a smooth top and sharp edge when you cover a cake with glaze. A long wide spatula works well for moving these cakes from a cake rack onto a platter. Slide the spatula under the bottom of the cake, place the platter level with the cake and use the spatula to slide the cake onto the platter. I find it safer to do any cake moving after cakes cool thoroughly and before adding a glaze.

LISA WARD'S BLACK RUSSIAN CHOCOLATE CHIP CAKE

Surveys often claim that young people have no interest in cooking or baking. I disagree and offer some proof with this cake from my daughter's friend Lisa Ward, who is a great young cook. The coffee-flavored cake, saturated with a Kahlúa and vodka glaze, reminiscent of a black Russian cocktail, is already a family tradition in Lisa's household.

SERVES 12

CAKE
2³/4 cups cake flour
1 teaspoon baking powder
¹/2 teaspoon salt
4 large eggs
2 cups sugar
1 cup canola or corn oil
1 teaspoon vanilla extract
2 teaspoons instant decaffeinated coffee dissolved in ¹/4 cup warm water
¹/4 cup vodka
1 tablespoon plus 1 teaspoon instant decaffeinated coffee granules
¹/2 teaspoon baking soda
1 cup sour cream
¹/2 cup coarsely chopped walnuts
³/4 cup miniature semisweet chocolate chips (4¹/2 ounces)

KAHLÚA AND VODKA BUTTER GLAZE
¹/4 cup water
¹/4 pound (1 stick) soft unsalted butter
³/4 cup sugar
¹/4 cup Kahlúa
¹/4 cup vodka

Vanilla or coffee ice cream, for serving with the cake (optional)

Prepare the Cake

1. Position an oven rack in the middle of the oven. Preheat the oven to 325°F. Oil the bottom, sides, and center tube of a bundt pan 9¹/2 to 10 inches in diame-

Good Advice
· The amount of glaze will look like too much, but just keep brushing it on the cake. The glaze adds moistness and rich flavor to the cake.

· Bundt pans have a ridged side and bottom so you can't line the bottom with paper. Use a heavyweight pan, oil it well, and coat it with powdered sugar, and you will have no trouble removing the baked cake from the pan.

Doubling the Recipe
Use ³/4 teaspoon salt and double the remaining ingredients. Mix a double recipe of cake in a 5-quart bowl.

ter with sides at least 3¾ inches high. Sprinkle powdered sugar in the pan and tilt the pan to coat the bottom, sides, and center tube lightly with powdered sugar. Tap out any loose powdered sugar.

2. Sift the flour, baking powder, and salt together and set aside. Put the eggs in the large bowl of an electric mixer and mix on medium speed just to combine the yolks and whites. Add the sugar and beat for about 2 minutes, or until the mixture is fluffy, thick, and lightened to a cream color. Decrease the speed to low and slowly mix in the oil, vanilla, dissolved coffee, and vodka. Add the flour mixture and beat on medium speed for 30 seconds. Mix in the coffee granules. Stop the mixer and scrape the sides of the bowl. Rub any lumps out of the baking soda and mix the baking soda into the sour cream. Mix the sour cream into the batter. Stir in the walnuts and chocolate chips. Pour the batter into the prepared pan and spread evenly.

3. Bake 55 to 60 minutes, or until the top of the cake is golden. Gently press your fingers on the top of the cake. If the cake feels firm, insert a toothpick in the center of the cake. When the toothpick comes out clean, the cake is done.

4. Cool the cake in the pan for 15 minutes. Use a small sharp knife to loosen the cake from the top of the sides and center tube of the pan. Invert the cake onto a serving plate. Place wax paper strips under the cake to catch any drips from the glaze.

Prepare the Kahlúa and Vodka Glaze

5. Put the water, butter, and sugar in a small saucepan and stir over medium heat until the sugar dissolves. Increase the heat to medium high and boil for 5 minutes, stirring constantly. Remove the pan from the heat. Slowly mix in the Kahlúa and vodka. The mixture will bubble up. Let cool 5 minutes. Prick the top and sides of the warm cake at 1-inch intervals with a toothpick. Use a pastry brush to brush the glaze over the top, sides, and center hole of the cake. Use all of the glaze. Remove the wax paper strips and discard. Cool the cake thoroughly.

To Freeze

Wrap the cake tightly with plastic wrap. Gently press heavy aluminum foil around the cake. Label with date and contents. Freeze up to 3 months.

To Serve

Defrost the wrapped cake at room temperature about 4 hours. Leave the cake bottom side up for serving. Serve with ice cream, if desired. Leftover cake may be covered with plastic wrap and stored at room temperature up to 3 days.

CHOCOLATE-GLAZED RUM CHOCOLATE CHIP CAKE

ooking through old pictures of family birthday parties reminded me of how often we chose this cake for birthdays. If there is one thing we take seriously at our house, it's choosing birthday cakes, so you can rest assured that this recipe is worth trying.

SERVES 12

CHOCOLATE CHIP CAKE
2¾ cups cake flour
1 teaspoon baking powder
½ teaspoon salt
3 large eggs
2 cups sugar
1 cup canola or corn oil
2 teaspoons vanilla extract
⅛ teaspoon coconut extract
2 tablespoons dark rum
½ teaspoon baking soda
1 cup sour cream
1 cup miniature semisweet chocolate chips (6 ounces)

BUTTER RUM GLAZE
3 tablespoons water
2 ounces (½ stick) soft unsalted butter
¼ cup sugar
2 tablespoons dark rum

SHINY CHOCOLATE GLAZE
⅓ cup whipping cream
4 tablespoons (½ stick) soft unsalted butter
2 tablespoons light corn syrup
6 ounces semisweet chocolate, chopped

Prepare the Chocolate Chip Cake

1. Position an oven rack in the middle of the oven. Preheat the oven to 325°F. Oil the bottom, sides, and center tube of a 9½- or 10-inch tube pan with sides at least 3¾ inches high. Line the bottom with parchment or wax paper and oil the paper.

2. Sift the flour, baking powder, and salt together and set aside. Put the eggs in the large bowl of an electric mixer and mix on medium speed just to combine. Add the sugar and beat for about 2 minutes, or until the mixture is fluffy and thick. De-

· A little coconut extract goes a long way, so measure it carefully.

· The cake will absorb the rum glaze better if you brush warm glaze over a warm cake. Turn the cake upside down before glazing it for a smooth cake.

Doubling the Recipe

Use ¾ teaspoon salt and double the remaining ingredients. Mix a double recipe of cake in a 5-quart bowl.

To Freeze the Glaze

Pour the glaze into a plastic freezer container leaving 1 inch of space at the top of the container. Loosely cover and cool for 1 hour at room temperature. Press a piece of plastic wrap onto the top of the glaze and cover the container tightly. Or, divide each recipe of glaze between two plastic containers. Label with date and contents. Freeze up to 2 months.

crease the speed to low and slowly mix in the oil, vanilla, coconut extract, and rum. Mix in the flour mixture just until it is incorporated. Stop the mixer and scrape the sides of the bowl once during this mixing. Rub any lumps out of the baking soda and mix the baking soda into the sour cream. Mix the sour cream into the batter. Stir in the chocolate chips. Pour the batter into the prepared pan.

3. Bake about 1 hour, or until the top of the cake is golden. Gently press your fingers on the top of the cake. If the cake feels firm, insert a toothpick in the center of the cake. When the toothpick comes out clean, the cake is done.

4. Cool the cake in the pan for 10 minutes. Use a small sharp knife to loosen the cake from the sides and center tube of the pan. Place a piece of wax paper under a wire rack to catch the drips when you glaze the cake. Invert the cake onto the cake rack. Carefully remove and discard the paper lining.

Prepare the Butter Rum Glaze

5. Put the water, butter, and sugar in a small saucepan and stir over medium heat until the sugar dissolves. Increase the heat to medium-high and boil for 1 minute, stirring constantly. Mix in the rum. Remove from the heat and let cool 5 minutes. Prick the top of the warm cake at 1-inch intervals with a toothpick. Use a pastry brush to brush the butter rum glaze over the top, sides, and center hole of the cake. Use all of the glaze. Cool the cake thoroughly.

Prepare the Shiny Chocolate Glaze

6. Put the cream, butter, and corn syrup in a saucepan and stir over medium heat until the mixture is hot. The mixture will form tiny bubbles around the edge of the pan and measure about 175°F. on a food thermometer. Do not let the mixture boil. Remove the pan from the heat and add the chopped chocolate. Let the chocolate melt for about 30 seconds. Gently stir the glaze until all of the chocolate is melted and the glaze is smooth. Let the glaze cool about 30 minutes until it thickens slightly or freeze the glaze for future use. Makes 1 cup.

7. Gently pour about half of the chocolate glaze over the top of the cooled cake. Use a thin metal spatula to spread the glaze inside the hole in the center and over the top of the cake. Spread a layer of glaze over the sides of the cake. Slide the cake onto a cardboard cake circle or serving plate.

To Freeze the Cake

Freeze the cake for 1 hour, or until the chocolate glaze is firm. Wrap tightly with plastic wrap. Gently press heavy aluminum foil around the cake. Label with date and contents. Freeze up to 1 month.

To Serve

Defrost the wrapped cake in the refrigerator overnight. Unwrap the cake and let it sit at room temperature 1 hour before serving. Left-over cake may be covered with plastic wrap and stored in the refrigerator up to 3 days. Bring to room temperature before serving. Defrost the glaze in the covered container overnight in the refrigerator. Warm the glaze in a small saucepan over low heat, stirring frequently, just until it is soft enough to spread.

RIBBON OF FUDGE CHOCOLATE CAKE

If ever there was a pure chocolate cake, this is it. This dark chocolate cake is dense and moist and has a ribbon of truffle sauce running through its center. Slightly Thinner Chocolate Truffle Sauce is the secret to giving the cake its distinctive rich chocolate flavor. When I was writing this book, I baked this cake for my birthday (ahead of time, of course) and served it with ice cream.

SERVES 12

1³/₄ cups unbleached all-purpose flour
¹/₄ cup unsweetened Dutch process cocoa powder, such as Droste or
   Hershey's European Style
1 teaspoon baking powder
¹/₂ teaspoon salt
¹/₂ pound (2 sticks) soft unsalted butter
1¹/₂ cups sugar
5 large eggs
1 teaspoon vanilla extract
2¹/₄ cups Slightly Thinner Chocolate Truffle Sauce (page 50), at room
   temperature
Powdered sugar, for dusting (optional)
Vanilla ice cream, for serving with the cake (optional)

I. Position an oven rack in the middle of the oven. Preheat the oven to 325°F. Butter the bottom, sides, and center tube of a bundt pan 9¹/₂ to 10 inches in diameter with sides at least 3³/₄ inches high. Sprinkle flour in the pan and tilt the pan to coat the bottom, sides, and center tube lightly with flour. Tap out any loose flour.

2. Sift the flour, cocoa powder, baking powder, and salt together and set aside. Put the butter in the large bowl of an electric mixer and mix on low speed for 15 seconds. Add the sugar and beat on medium speed for 2 minutes, or until the mixture is fluffy and lightens in color, about 2 minutes. Add the eggs, one at a time. Beat for 1 minute. Stop the mixer and scrape the bowl once. Mix in the vanilla extract. Decrease the speed to low and add the flour mixture. Stop the

· The truffle sauce must be at room temperature. Warm truffle sauce could alter the batter and baking time and cold truffle sauce is too firm to incorporate easily into the batter. You will need 1¹/₂ recipes of the sauce for the cake.

· To form the truffle sauce ribbon, pour half of the batter into the pan. Carefully make a trench around the center of the batter to hold all of the truffle sauce. This will prevent the truffle sauce from baking onto the side of the pan and possibly causing the cake to stick to the pan.

· Using a good quality heavyweight bundt pan that is buttered and floured carefully also encourages easy removal of the cake from the pan.

Doubling the Recipe

Double the ingredients and use two pans. Mix the batter in a 5-quart bowl.

mixer and scrape the bowl once. Mix just until the flour is incorporated. Reserve ½ cup of the truffle sauce and stir the remaining 1¾ cups truffle sauce into the batter. The batter will be thick.

3. Pour half of the batter into the prepared pan. Use a small spoon to make a 1-inch-deep indentation in the center of the batter. Extend the indentation into a circle completely around the pan. Pour the remaining truffle sauce into the trench. Keep the sauce in the trench and do not let it flow against the sides of the pan. Carefully spoon the remaining batter evenly over the truffle sauce. The batter should completely surround the truffle sauce. Smooth the top of the batter.

4. Bake for 1 hour and 5 minutes. The top of the cake will be firm and slightly cracked. Since the truffle filling remains moist, you cannot test this cake with a toothpick.

5. Cool the cake in the pan 20 minutes. Use a small sharp knife to loosen the cake from the top of the sides and center tube of the pan. Invert the cake onto a wire rack to cool thoroughly. Slide the cooled cake onto a serving platter or cardboard cake circle.

Wrap the cake tightly with plastic wrap. Gently press heavy aluminum foil around the cake. Label with date and contents. Freeze up to 3 months.

To Serve

Defrost the wrapped cake at room temperature about 5 hours. Leave the cake bottom side up for serving. Dust the top of the cake with powdered sugar, if desired. Vanilla ice cream makes a good accompaniment to the cake. Leftover cake may be covered with plastic wrap and stored at room temperature up to 4 days. The flavor of the cake intensifies the second day.

HARRIET'S WALNUT AND CHOCOLATE CHIP BUTTER CAKE

*H*arriet Bell is all I could ask for in an editor. She doesn't stop at editing my books but goes so far as to share treasured family cake recipes with me. When Harriet gave me this recipe, she said that if she had to eat one cake for the rest of her life, this would be it. This large yellow cake is especially light textured. It's from Harriet's midwestern childhood and reminds me of a cake that would win first prize at the county fair.

SERVES 12 TO 16

3 cups unbleached all-purpose flour
1 tablespoon baking powder
1/2 teaspoon salt
4 large eggs
1/2 pound (2 sticks) soft unsalted butter
2 cups sugar
1 1/2 teaspoons vanilla extract
1 cup whole milk
1 1/4 cups coarsely chopped walnuts (about 5 ounces)
1 cup semisweet chocolate chips (6 ounces)

1. Position an oven rack in the middle of the oven. Preheat the oven to 350°F. Butter the bottom and sides of a 9-inch springform pan with sides at least 2³/4 inches high. Sprinkle flour in the pan and tilt the pan to coat the bottom and sides lightly with flour. Tap out any loose flour.

2. Sift the flour, baking powder, and salt together 3 times and set aside. Put the eggs in the large bowl of an electric mixer and beat on high speed until light and foamy, 3 minutes. Set aside.

3. Put the butter in another large bowl of an electric mixer and mix on low speed for 15 seconds. Add the sugar and beat on medium speed for 2 minutes, or until the mixture is fluffy and lightens in color. Stop the mixer and scrape the

- For a light, not-too-dense cake, beat the ingredients extremely well—no skimping on the beating time.

- The cake is baked in a springform pan rather than a tube pan so technically it is not a tube cake, but what I call a tube-type cake.

- The flour must be sifted three times. Cut two pieces of wax paper and sift from one to the other.

- Check the cake carefully at the end of its baking time. A toothpick inserted into the center should come out dry. The large cake usually requires the full baking time.

Doubling the Recipe

The cake is best mixed in separate batches.

sides of the bowl during this mixing. Decrease the speed to low and add the beaten eggs and vanilla. Stop the mixer and scrape the sides of the bowl during this mixing. Return the speed to medium and beat for 2 minutes. The mixture will look curdled, then become smooth. Decrease the speed to low and add the flour mixture and the milk alternately, beginning and ending with the flour mixture (4 flour, 3 milk). Beat about 30 seconds on medium speed after each addition of milk. Stop the mixer and scrape the sides of the bowl after the last addition of flour.

4. Pour one third of the batter into the prepared pan and spread it evenly. Sprinkle one third of the nuts and chocolate chips evenly over the batter. Repeat 2 more times, ending with nuts and chocolate chips.

5. Bake until a toothpick inserted into the center of the cake comes out clean, about 1 hour and 25 minutes.

6. Cool the cake on a wire rack for 10 minutes. Use a small sharp knife to loosen the cake from the sides of the pan. Thoroughly cool the cake in the pan, about 2 hours. Release the sides of the springform pan. Either leave the cake on the springform bottom, or use the small sharp knife to loosen the cake from the bottom of the pan. Slide the removable bottom of a tart pan under the cake and move it to a serving platter or cardboard cake circle.

To Freeze
Wrap the cake tightly with plastic wrap. Press heavy aluminum foil around the cake. Label with date and contents. Freeze up to 3 months.

To Serve
Defrost the wrapped cake at room temperature, about 5 hours. Leftover cake can be covered with plastic wrap and stored at room temperature up to 3 days.

CINNAMON CHOCOLATE MARBLE CAKE

It's easy to produce the two-flavored batter for this cake. Divide the batter and flavor one portion with melted chocolate and the other with cinnamon. A sprinkling of cinnamon and powdered sugar makes an easy and original topping. The cake has an informal homey quality, but you can dress it up by serving it with homemade cinnamon ice cream.

SERVES 12

4 ounces semisweet chocolate, chopped
3 cups cake flour
1½ teaspoons baking powder
½ teaspoon salt
3 large eggs
2 cups sugar
1 cup canola or corn oil
1 teaspoon vanilla extract
1 cup milk, whole or low fat
4 teaspoons ground cinnamon
1 tablespoon powdered sugar mixed with ¼ teaspoon ground cinnamon, for dusting
Cinnamon ice cream (see page 264), for serving (optional)

1. Position an oven rack in the middle of the oven. Preheat the oven to 325°F. Oil the bottom, sides, and center tube of a 9½- or 10-inch tube pan with sides at least 3¾ inches high. Line the bottom with parchment or wax paper and oil the paper.

2. Put the semisweet chocolate in a heatproof container and place it over, but not touching, a saucepan of barely simmering water. Stir the chocolate until it is melted. Remove the saucepan from the heat but leave the chocolate over the water. Set aside.

3. Sift the flour, baking powder, and salt together and set aside. Put the eggs in the large bowl of an electric mixer and mix on medium speed just to combine

Melt the chocolate for this cake over hot water and keep it warm until you combine it with the cake batter. If the melted chocolate cools before you add it to the cake batter, it will thicken the batter considerably. If this happens, spoon the chocolate batter over the cinnamon batter since you will not be able to pour it. The baked cake will be fine.

Doubling the Recipe

Use 2½ teaspoons baking powder and ¾ teaspoon salt and double the remaining ingredients. Mix a double recipe of cake in a 5-quart bowl.

the yolks and whites. Add the sugar and beat for about 2 minutes, or until the mixture is fluffy, thick, and lightened to a cream color. Decrease the speed to low and slowly mix in the oil, vanilla, and milk. Mix in the flour mixture just until it is incorporated. Stop the mixer and scrape the sides of the bowl once during this mixing. Put 1½ cups of batter into a small bowl and stir in the melted chocolate. Stir the cinnamon into the plain batter. Pour half of the cinnamon batter into the prepared pan and spread it evenly. Spread all of the chocolate batter evenly over the cinnamon batter. Spread the remaining cinnamon batter evenly over the chocolate batter. Dip a large rubber spatula in the batter and draw it around the pan and through the center of the batter to marbleize the batter slightly. This will leave large areas of chocolate in the cake.

4. Bake about 1 hour and 20 minutes. Gently press your fingers on the top of the cake. If the cake feels firm, insert a toothpick in the center of the cake. When the toothpick come out clean, the cake is done.

5. Cool the cake in the pan for 10 minutes. Use a small sharp knife to loosen the cake from the sides and the center tube of the pan. Invert the cake onto a wire rack. Carefully remove and discard the paper lining the cake bottom. Place another wire rack on the bottom of the cake and invert the cake so it is right side up. Cool the cake thoroughly. Put the powdered sugar mixture in a small strainer and sift it over the top of the cake. Slide the cake onto a cardboard cake circle or serving plate.

To Freeze

Wrap the cake tightly with plastic wrap, being careful not to disturb the powdered sugar topping. Gently press heavy aluminum foil around the cake. Label with date and contents. Freeze up to 3 months.

To Serve

Defrost the wrapped cake at room temperature, about 5 hours. Serve the cake with cinnamon ice cream, if desired. Leftover cake can be covered with plastic wrap and stored at room temperature up to 3 days.

CHOCOLATE-GLAZED RASPBERRY JAM CAKE

When those first clear, spring days make it hard to wait for the summer berry bonanza, I bake Raspberry Jam Cake. It's a yellow cake swirled with raspberry jam and covered with chocolate.

Good Advice

· For jam, I use a raspberry fruit spread that is sweetened with fruit juice. It has a good, clear fruit flavor without added sugar.

· Have the fruit spread or jam at room temperature and it will incorporate smoothly into the batter. Cold jam forms clumps rather than ripples in the cake.

· I prefer jam with seeds for this cake.

Doubling the Recipe

Use ³/₄ teaspoon salt and double the remaining ingredients. Mix a double recipe of cake in a 5-quart bowl.

SERVES 12

2³/₄ cups cake flour
1 teaspoon baking powder
¹/₂ teaspoon salt
3 large eggs
2 cups sugar
1 cup canola or corn oil
2 teaspoons vanilla extract
³/₄ teaspoon almond extract
¹/₂ teaspoon baking soda
1 cup sour cream
1 cup raspberry fruit spread or jam with seeds, at room temperature
1 cup Shiny Chocolate Glaze (page 212), cooled until thickened slightly

1. Position an oven rack in the middle of the oven. Preheat the oven to 325°F. Oil the bottom, sides, and center tube of a 9¹/₂- or 10-inch tube pan with sides at least 3³/₄ inches high. Line the bottom with parchment or wax paper and oil the paper.

2. Sift the flour, baking powder, and salt together and set aside. Put the eggs in the large bowl of an electric mixer and mix on medium speed just to combine the yolks and whites. Add the sugar and beat for about 2 minutes, or until the mixture is fluffy, thick, and lightened to a cream color. Decrease the speed to low and slowly mix in the oil, vanilla, and almond extract. Mix in the flour mixture just until it is incorporated. Stop the mixer and scrape the sides of the bowl once during this mixing. Rub any lumps out of the baking soda and mix the baking soda into the sour cream. Mix the sour cream into the batter. Put the jam in a small bowl and stir it smooth. Pour the jam over the cake batter. Use a large rubber spatula to gently swirl the jam throughout the batter. Do not incorpo-

rate the jam completely into the batter. Pour the batter into the prepared pan.

3. Bake about 1 hour and 20 minutes. Gently press your fingers on the top of the cake. If the cake feels firm, insert a toothpick in the center of the cake. When the toothpick comes out clean, the cake is done.

4. Cool the cake in the pan for 10 minutes. Use a small sharp knife to loosen the cake from the sides and the center tube of the pan. Invert the cake onto a wire cake rack. Carefully remove and discard the paper lining. Cool the cake thoroughly.

5. Leave the cake bottom side up for glazing. Gently pour about half of the glaze over the top of the cooled cake. Use a thin metal spatula to spread the glaze inside the hole in the center and over the top of the cake. Spread a layer of glaze over the sides of the cake. Spread any remaining glaze on the top of the cake. Slide the cake onto a serving plate or cardboard cake circle.

To Freeze

Freeze the cake for 1 hour, or until the glaze is firm. Wrap tightly with plastic wrap. Gently press heavy aluminum foil around the cake. Label with date and contents. Freeze up to 1 month.

To Serve

Defrost the wrapped cake in the refrigerator overnight. Unwrap the cake and let it sit at room temperature 1 hour before serving. Left-over cake can be covered with plastic wrap and stored in the refrigerator up to 3 days. Bring to room temperature before serving.

CHOCOLATE-COVERED CARAMEL CAKE

I had eaten caramel cakes before but never found one with the intense caramel flavor I wanted until I created this one. Adding a generous amount of caramel sauce—a whole cup—to a yellow cake batter did the trick. When I took this cake to a neighborhood tea party, everyone saw the golden-colored slices and thought it was a pumpkin cake. "It's caramel, covered in chocolate," I said and everyone turned suddenly, making a beeline for the cake.

SERVES 12

CARAMEL CAKE
3 cups cake flour
1½ teaspoons baking powder
½ teaspoon salt
3 large eggs
2½ cups sugar
1 cup canola or corn oil
2 teaspoons vanilla extract
1 cup milk, whole or low fat
1 cup Caramel Sauce (page 52), cooled or defrosted

1 cup Pure Chocolate Glaze (page 112)

Prepare the Caramel Cake

1. Position an oven rack in the middle of the oven. Preheat the oven to 325°F. Oil the bottom, sides, and center tube of a 9½- or 10-inch tube pan with sides at least 3¾ inches high. Line the bottom with parchment or wax paper and oil the paper.

2. Sift the flour, baking powder, and salt together and set aside. Put the eggs in the large bowl of an electric mixer and mix on medium speed just to combine the yolks and whites. Add the sugar and beat for about 2 minutes, or until the mixture is fluffy, thick, and lightened to a cream color. Decrease the speed to

· Cool the caramel sauce thoroughly before adding it to the cake batter. Or defrost frozen caramel sauce in the refrigerator overnight and add the cold caramel sauce to the batter.

· For more detail on preparing the Pure Chocolate Glaze, see page 112.

Doubling the Recipe
Use 2½ teaspoons baking powder and ¾ teaspoon salt and double the remaining ingredients. Mix a double recipe of cake in a 5-quart bowl.

low and slowly mix in the oil, vanilla, and milk. Mix in the flour mixture just until it is incorporated. Stop the mixer and scrape the sides of the bowl once during this mixing. Stir the caramel sauce into the batter. Pour the batter into the prepared pan.

3. Bake about 1 hour and 20 minutes. Gently press your fingers on the top of the cake. If the cake feels firm, insert a toothpick in the center of the cake. When the toothpick comes out clean, the cake is done.

4. Cool the cake in the pan for 10 minutes. Use a small sharp knife to loosen the cake from the sides and the center tube of the pan. Invert the cake onto a wire rack. Carefully remove and discard the paper lining. Cool the cake thoroughly.

5. Leave the cake bottom side up for glazing. Gently pour about half of the glaze over the top of the cooled cake. Use a thin metal spatula to spread the glaze inside the hole in the center and over the top of the cake. Spread a layer of glaze over the sides of the cake. Spread any remaining glaze on the top of the cake. Slide the cake onto a serving plate or cardboard cake circle.

To Freeze

Freeze the cake for 1 hour, or until the glaze is firm. Wrap tightly with plastic wrap. Gently press heavy aluminum foil around the cake. Label with date and contents. Freeze up to 1 month.

To Serve

Defrost the wrapped cake in the refrigerator overnight. Unwrap the cake and let it sit at room temperature 1 hour before serving. Leftover cake can be covered with plastic wrap and stored in the refrigerator up to 3 days. Bring to room temperature before serving.

TRIPLE GINGER AND
DARK CHOCOLATE CAKE

*G*inger is hot, spicy, and fragrant, and so is this cake. Fresh ginger, powdered ginger, and crystallized ginger give this cake its intense ginger taste. A dark chocolate batter marbles the cake and provides a contrast of flavor and color.

SERVES 12

4 ounces semisweet chocolate, chopped
1 ounce unsweetened chocolate, chopped
2¾ cups unbleached all-purpose flour
1 tablespoon plus 1 teaspoon ground ginger
1 teaspoon ground cinnamon
1 teaspoon baking powder
1 teaspoon baking soda
½ teaspoon salt
6 ounces (1½ sticks) soft unsalted butter
2 cups sugar
4 large eggs
1 teaspoon vanilla extract
¼ cup crystallized ginger, cut into ⅛-inch pieces (about 2 ounces)
1¼ cups buttermilk
2 tablespoons finely grated fresh ginger
Powdered sugar, for dusting

I. Position an oven rack in the middle of the oven. Preheat the oven to 175°F. Butter the bottom, sides, and center tube of a 9½- or 10-inch tube pan with sides at least 3¾ inches high. Line the bottom with parchment or wax paper and butter the paper.

2. Place the semisweet and unsweetened chocolate in an ovenproof container and melt the chocolate in the oven, about 8 minutes. As soon as it is melted, remove it from the oven and stir it smooth. Increase the oven temperature to 350°F.

3. Sift the flour, ground ginger, cinnamon, baking powder, baking soda, and salt together and set aside. Put the butter in the large bowl of an electric mixer and mix on low speed for 15 seconds. Add the sugar and beat on medium speed

Good Advice

· Peel the fresh ginger and grate it on the small teardrop-shape holes of a grater. This will puree the fresh ginger.

· Remove two cups of batter for the chocolate batter then add the fresh ginger to the remaining batter. This more intense ginger-flavored batter is a robust contrast to the chocolate batter. The batter is marbleized slightly so there are large sections of chocolate batter throughout the cake.

· Crystallized ginger is available at candy shops, natural food stores, and many supermarkets.

Doubling the Recipe

Use ¾ teaspoon salt and double the remaining ingredients. Mix a double recipe of cake in a 5-quart bowl.

for 2 minutes, or until the mixture is fluffy and lightens from yellow to cream color, about 2 minutes. Add the eggs, one at a time. Beat for 1 minute. Decrease the speed to low and mix in the vanilla and crystallized ginger. Add the flour mixture and the buttermilk alternately, beginning and ending with the flour mixture (3 flour, 2 buttermilk). Stop the mixer and scrape the sides of the bowl after the last addition of flour. Put 2 cups of batter in a small bowl and stir the melted chocolate into this batter. Stir the fresh ginger into the plain batter. Spread half of the ginger batter evenly into the prepared pan. Spread the chocolate batter evenly over the ginger batter. Spread the remaining ginger batter evenly over the chocolate batter. Dip a large rubber spatula in the batter and draw it around the pan and through the center of the batter to marbleize the batter slightly.

4. Bake about 1 hour. To test for doneness, gently press your fingers on the top of the cake. If the cake feels firm, insert a toothpick in the center of the cake. When the toothpick comes out clean, the cake is done.

5. Cool the cake in the pan for 10 minutes. Use a small sharp knife to loosen the cake from the sides and the center tube of the pan. Invert the cake onto a wire rack or cake plate. Carefully remove and discard the paper lining. Place another wire rack on the bottom of the cake and invert the cake. The cake is now right side up. Cool the cake thoroughly. Slide the cooled cake onto a serving platter or cardboard cake circle.

To Freeze
Wrap the cake tightly with plastic wrap. Gently press heavy aluminum foil around the cake. Label with date and contents. Freeze up to 3 months.

To Serve
Defrost the wrapped cake at room temperature about 5 hours. Dust the top of the cake with powdered sugar. Leftover cake may be covered with plastic wrap and stored at room temperature up to 3 days.

SOUR CREAM CHOCOLATE CHIP COFFEE CAKE

L isa Ekus is a renowned cookbook publicist and an excellent cook. She shared this recipe with me and described it as her standard coffee cake for any and all occasions. It has never failed her.

SERVES 12

2 cups unbleached all-purpose flour
1 teaspoon baking powder
1/4 teaspoon salt
1/2 pound (2 sticks) unsalted butter, softened
2 cups sugar
2 large eggs
1 cup sour cream
1/2 teaspoon vanilla extract
1 cup miniature semisweet chocolate chips (6 ounces)
Powdered sugar, for dusting

1. Position an oven rack in the middle of the oven. Preheat the oven to 350°F. Butter the bottom, sides, and center tube of a 12-cup bundt pan, 9½ to 10 inches in diameter with sides at least 3¾ inches high. Sprinkle flour in the pan and tilt the pan to coat the bottom, sides, and center tube. Tap out any loose flour.

2. Sift the flour, baking powder, and salt together and set aside. Put the butter in the large bowl of an electric mixer and mix on low speed for 15 seconds. Add the sugar and beat on medium speed for 2 minutes, or until the mixture is fluffy and lightens from yellow to cream color, about 2 minutes. Add the eggs, one at a time. Beat for 1 minute. Decrease the speed to low and mix in the sour cream and vanilla extract. Add the flour mixture and mix just until incorporated. The batter will be thick. Stir in the chocolate chips. Pour the batter into the prepared pan and spread evenly.

3. Bake about 1 hour, or until the top of the cake is golden and a toothpick inserted into the center of the cake comes out clean. If the toothpick penetrates a chocolate chip, test another spot in the cake.

4. Cool the cake in the pan 15 minutes. Use a small sharp knife to loosen the cake from the top of the sides and the center tube of the pan. Invert the cake onto a wire rack to cool thoroughly. Slide the cake onto a serving platter or cardboard cake circle.

Good Advice

· The cake is baked in a bundt pan. Butter the pan and coat it with flour, and the baked cake will be easily removed from the pan.

· Use miniature chocolate chips. They will not sink to the bottom of the cake but stay evenly distributed throughout the cake.

Doubling the Recipe

Double the ingredients and use two pans. Mix the batter in a 5-quart bowl.

To Freeze

Wrap the cake tightly with plastic wrap. Gently press heavy aluminum foil around the cake. Label with date and contents. Freeze up to 3 months.

To Serve

Defrost the wrapped cake at room temperature about 5 hours. Leave the cake bottom side up for serving. Dust the top of the cake with powdered sugar. Leftover cake can be covered with plastic wrap and stored at room temperature up to 3 days.

MOCHA CONFETTI CHIFFON CAKE

ellow cookbook author Melanie Barnard and I wrote an article together for Eating Well *magazine on low-fat cakes for celebrations and parties. Melanie developed a low fat recipe for a citrus chiffon cake that was moist and rich tasting. I adapted her recipe for the article, using coffee and finely chopped chocolate chips for the flavoring. It's a miraculous cake that has the moistness of a chiffon cake and the lightness of an angel food cake.*

SERVES 12

CHIFFON CAKE
1¹/₃ cups cake flour
1 teaspoon baking powder
1¹/₂ cups sugar
1¹/₂ cups miniature semisweet chocolate chips (9 ounces)
10 large egg whites, at room temperature
³/₄ teaspoon cream of tartar
¹/₄ teaspoon salt
3 large egg yolks
2 tablespoons instant decaffeinated coffee dissolved in ¹/₄ cup warm water
2 teaspoons vanilla extract

COFFEE GLAZE
1 cup powdered sugar
1 teaspoon instant decaffeinated coffee dissolved in 2 tablespoons plus 1
   teaspoon warm water

Prepare the Chiffon Cake

1. Position an oven rack in the middle of the oven. Preheat the oven to 350°F. Line the bottom of a 9¹/₂- or 10-inch tube pan with sides at least 3³/₄ inches high with parchment or wax paper. Do not grease the pan.

2. Sift the flour and baking powder into a medium bowl. Whisk in ³/₄ cup of the sugar. Set aside. Put the chocolate chips in the workbowl of a food processor fitted with the steel blade and process about 30 seconds. Some of the chocolate chips will be finely grated and some will form small crumbs. Set aside.

Good Advice
· Line the bottom of the tube pan with wax paper but do not grease the pan. Cooling the cake upside down in the pan preserves its light texture and the cake could release too soon if the pan were greased. Lining the bottom of the pan with wax paper helps the cake release easily when you are ready to remove it from the pan.

· Process miniature chocolate chips in the food processor to form the chocolate confetti. They process easily into small crumbs of chocolate.

Doubling the Recipe
This large cake must be mixed in separate batches. Double the glaze ingredients for two cakes.

To Freeze

Freeze the cake for 1 hour, or until the glaze is firm. Wrap tightly with plastic wrap. Gently press heavy aluminum foil around the cake. Label with date and contents. Freeze up to 1 month. Do not stack anything on top of the cake.

To Serve

Defrost the wrapped cake at room temperature at least 5 hours or overnight. Use a serrated knife and a sawing motion to cut the cake into wedges. Leftover cake can be covered with plastic wrap and stored at room temperature up to 2 days.

3. Put the egg whites, cream of tartar, and salt in a clean large bowl of an electric mixer and beat with clean dry beaters on low speed until the egg whites are foamy. Increase the speed to medium-high and beat just until soft peaks form. Slowly add the remaining $3/4$ cup sugar, 1 tablespoon at a time. Put the egg yolks in a small bowl. Whisk in the dissolved coffee and the vanilla. Pour the egg yolk mixture over the beaten egg whites and use a large rubber spatula to fold the yolk mixture into the egg whites. Fold in the chocolate chips. Gently fold the flour mixture into the egg mixture, $1/4$ cup at a time, using a $1/4$-cup measuring cup to measure and sprinkle the flour mixture. Pour the batter into the prepared pan and smooth the top with a thin metal spatula.

4. Bake about 1 hour and 5 minutes. Insert a toothpick in the center of the cake. When the toothpick comes out clean, the cake is done.

5. If the tube pan has feet, invert the cake onto them. Or invert the tube pan over the neck of a bottle. Cool thoroughly, about 2 hours. Use a small sharp knife to loosen the cake carefully from the sides and center tube of the pan. Invert the cake onto a cake plate or cardboard cake circle. Carefully remove and discard the paper lining. Turn the cake right side up.

Prepare the Coffee Glaze

6. Put the powdered sugar in a small bowl. Stir the dissolved coffee into the powdered sugar until the mixture is smooth. If the glaze is too thick to pour, add 1 teaspoon of water. Immediately use a small spoon to drizzle the glaze in zigzag lines over the top of the cake. Let some glaze drip down onto the sides of the cake. The glaze will firm as it sits.

STRAWBERRY AND
WHITE CHOCOLATE LOAF

My dad has been packing and shipping strawberries around the country for more than fifty years. Friends know that Dad brings home flats of strawberries so they send their best strawberry recipes to my mom to help her cope with the bounty. Many years ago Sandy Hutchison, a friend of my parents, shared her famous strawberry loaf with us, and it became one of our favorite strawberry recipes. It's a quick tea loaf made exceptionally moist by the addition of sour cream, white chocolate, and crushed strawberries.

MAKES 2 LOAVES

2³/₄ cups unbleached all-purpose flour
1 teaspoon salt
1 teaspoon cream of tartar
¹/₂ teaspoon baking soda
1 cup coarsely chopped strawberries (about 16 large berries)
¹/₂ pound (2 sticks) soft unsalted butter
1¹/₂ cups sugar
1 teaspoon vanilla extract
¹/₂ teaspoon grated lemon zest
4 large eggs
¹/₂ cup sour cream
1 cup walnuts, coarsely chopped
1¹/₃ cups white chocolate chips, Ghirardelli or Guittard preferred (8 ounces)

1. Position an oven rack in the middle of the oven. Preheat the oven to 350°F. Butter 2 loaf pans, preferably long, narrow loaf pans with a 6¹/₂- to 7-cup capacity. Line the bottom of each pan with parchment or wax paper and butter the paper.

2. Sift the flour, salt, cream of tartar, and baking soda together. Set aside. Put the strawberries in a small bowl and crush with a potato masher or whisk. Set aside.

Use 1½ teaspoons salt and double the remaining ingredients. Use four loaf pans.

To Freeze

Wrap the plastic wrap tightly around each loaf. Wrap the heavy aluminum foil around the loaf. Label with date and contents. Freeze up to 3 months.

To Serve

Remove a loaf from the freezer and defrost the wrapped loaf at room temperature at least 5 hours or overnight. Use a large sharp knife to slice the loaf into ½-inch slices and serve at room temperature. Serve with whipped cream cheese, if desired. Leftover loaf can be covered with plastic wrap and stored at room temperature up to 3 days.

3. Put the butter in the large bowl of an electric mixer and mix on low speed for 15 seconds. Slowly add the sugar. Add the vanilla and lemon zest. Increase the speed to medium and beat for 1 minute, or until the mixture lightens from yellow to cream color and looks fluffy. Stop the mixer and scrape the sides of the bowl once. Add the eggs, one at a time, beating each egg completely into the batter before adding another egg. Beat for 1 minute. Stop the mixer and scrape the sides of the bowl during this beating. Stir the sour cream into the crushed strawberries. Decrease the speed to low and add the flour mixture and the strawberry mixture alternately, beginning and ending with the flour mixture (3 flour, 2 strawberry). Stir in the walnuts and 1 cup of the white chocolate chips. Divide the batter evenly between the 2 loaf pans and smooth the tops.

4. Bake 45 to 55 minutes. Gently press your fingers on the top of the loaf. If the loaf feels firm, insert a toothpick in the center. When the toothpick comes out clean, the loaf is done.

5. Cool the loaves thoroughly in the pans on a wire rack. Use a small sharp knife to loosen each loaf from the sides of the pan. Invert each loaf onto a large piece of heavy aluminum foil covered with plastic wrap. Carefully remove and discard the paper liner. Turn each loaf right side up.

6. Preheat the oven to 175°F. Place the remaining ⅓ cup of white chocolate chips in a small nonreactive ovenproof container and melt in the oven, about 5 minutes. Remove the white chocolate chips from the oven as soon as they melt and stir smooth. Use a small spoon to drizzle the melted white chocolate over the top of each loaf. Leave the loaves at room temperature until the white chocolate topping is firm.

PEAR AND CHOCOLATE
TEA LOAF

When the fresh fruit pickings are slim, this tea loaf, made with dried and canned pears, offers a good fruit option. Prepared from a muffinlike batter, the loaf is liberally dosed with chopped chocolate and dried pears. The combination of the chopped dried pears and pureed canned pears produces a moist loaf that keeps well.

MAKES 1 LOAF

1³/₄ cups unbleached all-purpose flour
³/₄ teaspoon baking soda
1¹/₄ teaspoons cream of tartar
¹/₂ teaspoon salt
4 canned pear halves in light syrup, drained
2 large eggs
¹/₄ pound (1 stick) soft unsalted butter, cut into 4 pieces
³/₄ cup sugar
1 teaspoon vanilla extract
¹/₂ teaspoon almond extract
1¹/₂ cups chopped dried pears, in ¹/₄-inch pieces (about 7 ounces)
4 ounces semisweet chocolate, chopped into ¹/₂-inch pieces

1. Position an oven rack in the middle of the oven. Preheat the oven to 350°F. Butter a loaf pan with a 6- to 7-cup capacity.

2. Sift the flour, baking soda, cream of tartar, and salt into a large mixing bowl. Set aside.

3. Put the canned pear halves in the workbowl of a food processor fitted with the steel blade. Process to a puree, about 30 seconds. Add the eggs, butter, sugar, vanilla, and almond extract and process until the mixture is smooth, about 30 seconds. The mixture may look slightly curdled. Stir the egg mixture into the flour mixture, stirring just until the flour is evenly moistened. Reserve 2 tablespoons of the chopped dried pears. Gently stir the remaining dried pears and the chocolate into the batter. Pour the batter into the prepared pan and

Doubling the Recipe

Double the ingredients and use two pans.

To Freeze

Use a small sharp knife to loosen the loaf from the sides of the pan. Invert the loaf onto a large piece of heavy aluminum foil covered with plastic wrap. Turn the loaf right side up. Wrap the plastic wrap tightly around each loaf. Wrap the heavy aluminum foil around the loaf. Label with date and contents. Freeze up to 3 months.

To Serve

Defrost the wrapped loaf at room temperature at least 5 hours or overnight. Use a large sharp knife to slice the loaf into $1/2$-inch slices and serve at room temperature. Leftover tea loaf can be covered with plastic wrap, and stored at room temperature up to 4 days.

smooth the top. Sprinkle the reserved dried pears over the top of the loaf, pressing them gently into the loaf.

4. Bake 50 to 60 minutes, or until a toothpick inserted in the center of the loaf comes out clean. A long, narrow loaf pan requires the shorter baking time. Cool the loaf thoroughly in the pan on a wire rack.

Coffee Cakes and Yeast Cakes

These cakes are the hare and the tortoise of baking. Coffee cakes prepared with a leavening of baking powder or baking soda mix together quickly, while those using yeast as the leavening take some rising time for the yeast to do its work. Coffee and yeast cakes use common ingredients and simple baking techniques and need no frostings or fancy finishes. As soon as the cakes cool, they're ready to eat or freeze. Happily, unlike the hare and the tortoise, both are winners.

Most of these coffee cakes have a crunchy or crumb topping, and many include chocolate chips. Graham cracker crumbs and chocolate chips, almonds and white chocolate chips, or chocolate-flavored crumbs make up the crunchy toppings. Since these are moist cakes, they keep well, usually at least three days at room temperature.

Many of these coffee cakes rise and fill the pan as they bake, so be particular about using the pan size called for in the recipe. If it specifies two-inch-high pan sides, check that your pan has this depth so there won't be a problem of having too much cake batter in the pan.

Yeast doughs are easy. I wish I could write that sentence about ten times because it's so true. Try one of these recipes that use yeast, and you will soon feel comfortable with it.

There are some general guidelines to follow when you use yeast, but don't think of them as rigid rules. I have found yeast to be a forgiving ingredient. If the temperature of added liquids or of the room itself is not exact, yeast adjusts. A dough may take longer to rise if you add cold liquids to it or the dough may rise more quickly than anticipated in a warm kitchen, but these factors will not ruin your cake.

I tested these recipes with envelopes of active dry yeast, which contain about 2 teaspoons of yeast. The envelopes are dated for freshness, and you can usually find them dated at least six months ahead. Dissolve the yeast in the small amount of warm water indicated in the recipe. If the water feels comfortably warm to your hand, it's a good temperature for dissolving the yeast. If measured with a food thermometer, the temperature should read between 95° and 105°F. Milk or melted butter should also be warmed to this temperature before being added to a yeast mixture. A few additional guidelines about working with yeast:

· Yeast likes sugar, so a little sugar is often added to the yeast and water mixture for a growth spurt. About five minutes after the yeast dissolves in the warm water, it will look foamy. This foaming proves that the yeast is still alive and active and assures that the dough will rise.

· A large amount of sugar in sweet doughs, however, reduces the power of yeast to leaven. To compensate for this, some sweet yeast doughs use the sponge mixing method to give the dough an easy start and help it rise. A sponge is a thick batter of dissolved yeast, warm liquid, and some flour. Yeast multiplies quickly in this friendly environment. The increased number of yeast cells in the sponge improves rising.

· Most yeast doughs can have their first rising overnight in the refrigerator while you sleep. Take the dough out of the refrigerator about an hour before you plan to shape it, to bring it back to room temperature.

· An extra rising will not harm the dough. If you're not ready to shape and bake a risen yeast dough, simply punch it down and let it rise again.

· Cover dough with plastic wrap while it rises. This prevents the dough from drying out and keeps it moist and soft. Yeast thrives in warm and humid conditions.

· Kitchen temperatures affect rising times, so rising times will vary. When the dough has approximately doubled in size and risen for about the time given in the recipe, it should be ready. Properly risen dough looks light and fluffy and has a pleasant sweet smell rather than a sour, fermented one.

· Measurements given for flour are usually flexible since humidity and even the specific bag of flour used can affect the amount of flour needed to produce a dough with the correct consistency. When the dough feels soft and smooth but is just dry enough to pull away from the sides of the bowl, it is the right consistency. I once carried a leftover bag of flour from Maine to Florida and prepared two batches of the same yeast dough from the same national brand of flour, but I used the flour from Maine in one and flour purchased in Florida in the other. One batch of dough needed a cup more flour to form a soft dough!

UNCLE HOWIE'S ALL-CHOCOLATE EXTRAORDINARY CHOCOLATE CHIP CAKE

My uncle Howie loves to experiment with his favorite recipes, and I'm often the lucky recipient of his results. One of our all-time favorite recipes is My Mom's Extraordinary Chocolate Chip Cake that appears in Bake and Freeze Desserts. *My uncle decided that an all-chocolate version would give us a new family cake. My mom's cake has never let us down, and it didn't here. This brown sugar chocolate cake, loaded with chocolate chips, takes about ten minutes to put together, tastes even better the day after it is baked, and freezes easily. It will make you famous at the office or at school bake sales (if it gets that far).*

MAKES 12 PIECES

1²/₃ cups unbleached all-purpose flour
¹/₃ cup unsweetened Dutch process cocoa powder, such as Droste or Hershey's European Style, sifted
2 cups (packed) light brown sugar
¹/₄ pound (1 stick) cold unsalted butter, cut into 8 pieces
1 large egg
1 teaspoon vanilla extract
2 tablespoons milk
1 cup sour cream
2 teaspoons baking soda
1¹/₂ cups semisweet chocolate chips (9 ounces)

1. Position the oven rack in the middle of the oven. Preheat the oven to 325°F. Butter an 11 × 7 × 1³/₄-inch ovenproof glass baking dish or baking pan.

2. Put the flour, cocoa, and brown sugar in the large bowl of an electric mixer and mix on low speed for 15 seconds. Add the butter and mix until the butter pieces are the size of peas, about 1 minute. You will still see loose flour. Mix in the egg and vanilla. The mixture will still look dry. Stir the milk into the sour cream. Rub any lumps out of the baking soda and gently mix the baking soda

Good Advice
I bake this cake in an 11 × 7 × 1³/₄-inch ovenproof glass baking pan, which makes a 1¹/₂-inch-high cake. The pan is available at my local grocery store. When I tried baking the cake in the more familiar 13 × 9 × 2-inch pan, the result was more like a brownie in texture and taste. There was nothing wrong with it, but it wasn't the same cake at all.

Doubling the Recipe
Double the ingredients and use two pans.

into the sour cream. Stir the sour cream mixture into the batter. Stir just until the batter is evenly moistened. Stir in the chocolate chips. The batter will be thick. Spread the batter evenly in the prepared baking pan.

3. Bake about 55 minutes. To test for doneness, gently press your fingers on the top of the cake. If it feels firm, insert a toothpick into the center of the cake. When the toothpick comes out clean, the cake is done. If a toothpick penetrates a chocolate chip, test another spot. Cool the cake thoroughly in the pan on a wire rack. The center of the cake will sink slightly.

VARIATION The cake can be dusted with powdered sugar before serving and served with ice cream. Peppermint, coffee, or vanilla ice cream are good flavor choices.

To Freeze
Either cut the cake into 2 or 3 large pieces or 12 individual pieces. Use a narrow spatula to loosen the cake from the sides of the pan. Remove the cake from the pan, using the spatula to loosen the cake from the bottom. Wrap large cake pieces in plastic wrap then heavy aluminum foil. Label with date and contents and freeze. After they are frozen, the large cake pieces can be stacked in the freezer. Wrap small pieces of cake in plastic wrap, place in a metal or plastic freezer container, and cover tightly. Label with date and contents. Freeze up to 3 months.

To Serve
Defrost the wrapped cake at room temperature about 2 hours. Serve within 3 days.

SPICED APPLE CHOCOLATE CRUMB CAKE

y husband, Jeff, gets the credit for this cake. We were sharing a chocolate-covered apple when he had the bright idea for me to include an apple and chocolate dessert in this book. We decided to try a crumb cake and spice it with cinnamon, mace, and orange, flavors appropriate to both chocolate and apples. An interesting thing happened to the chocolate—it merged with the spices and apples so completely that it created a subtly spicy apple-chocolate flavor.

SERVES 8 TO 10

1 1/2 cups grated peeled apples (2 medium apples)
1 tablespoon dark rum
1 3/4 cups unbleached all-purpose flour
1/4 cup unsweetened Dutch process cocoa powder, such as Droste or Hershey's European Style, sifted
1/4 teaspoon salt
3/4 cup (packed) light brown sugar
3/4 cup granulated sugar
1 1/2 teaspoons ground cinnamon
1/2 teaspoon ground mace
1 teaspoon grated orange zest
1/2 cup canola or corn oil
1 cup sour cream
2 large eggs
1 teaspoon vanilla extract
1/2 teaspoon almond extract
1 teaspoon baking powder
1 teaspoon baking soda
Powdered sugar, for dusting

I. Position an oven rack in the middle of the oven. Preheat the oven to 325°F. Oil the bottom and sides of a 9-inch round cake pan 2 inches deep. Line the bottom of the pan with parchment or wax paper and oil the paper.

2. Put the grated apples in a small bowl and stir in the rum. Set aside. Put the flour, cocoa, salt, brown sugar, granulated sugar, cinnamon, mace, and orange

Good Advice

· The ingredient list for this cake may look long, but the ingredients are common ones and the crumb topping and cake are prepared from the same mixture. Since you can mix the cake in less than 5 minutes, it seems like an even trade-off.

· Mace is the membrane covering nutmeg and is similar in taste, but I find it adds a softer spice flavor to cakes than nutmeg. Ground nutmeg is an acceptable substitute.

· The cake is moist, so if you are freezing it on a cardboard cake circle, cover the cardboard with aluminum foil.

Doubling the Recipe

Double the ingredients and use two pans.

zest in the large bowl of an electric mixer. Mix on low speed to blend the ingredients. There will be small lumps of brown sugar in the mixture. Add the oil and mix until the flour is evenly moistened and fine crumbs form. Put 1 cup of the mixture in a small bowl and set aside. Put the sour cream, eggs, vanilla, and almond extract in a small bowl and stir together until the egg is incorporated. Gently stir in the baking powder and baking soda. Add the sour cream mixture to the flour mixture and mix until the batter is evenly moistened. Stir the apple mixture into the batter. Spread the batter evenly in the prepared pan. Sprinkle the reserved crumb mixture evenly over the cake.

3. Bake about 1 hour, or until a toothpick inserted into the center of the cake comes out clean.

4. Cool the cake in the pan on a wire rack for 20 minutes. Use a small sharp knife to loosen the cake from the sides of the pan. Place a flat plate or the bottom of a tart pan or springform pan on top of the cake and invert the cake onto it. Carefully remove and discard the paper liner. Place the wire rack on the bottom of the cake and invert the cake. The cake will be right side up. Replace any of the crumbs that may have fallen off the cake. Cool thoroughly. Sift powdered sugar over the top of the cake.

VARIATION Substitute dried apricots for the apples and omit the rum. Cover ¾ cup dried apricots with boiling water and soak them for 30 minutes. Drain the apricots and pat dry. Cut the apricots into ½-inch pieces and stir them into the batter instead of the apple mixture.

To Freeze
Use a wide metal spatula to slide the cooled cake onto a serving plate or cardboard cake circle covered with aluminum foil. Wrap the cake tightly with plastic wrap then heavy aluminum foil. Label with date and contents. Freeze up to 3 months.

To Serve
Defrost the wrapped cake at room temperature at least 5 hours or overnight. Serve the cake at room temperature. Leftover cake may be covered with plastic wrap and stored at room temperature up to 3 days.

GRAHAM CRACKER CHOCOLATE CHIP CAKE

You have a winner here," Jeff declared the first time he tasted this cake. I agree. Every time I prepare a graham cracker crust with chocolate chips, I bake a small crust for myself to eat. I decided to try baking a cake with graham cracker crumbs and chocolate chips that would duplicate the combination. Here's the winning result.

SERVES 8 TO 10

GRAHAM CRACKER CRUMB TOPPING
½ cup graham cracker crumbs
1 tablespoon unsalted butter, melted
½ cup miniature semisweet chocolate chips (3 ounces)

GRAHAM CRACKER CRUMB CAKE
2 cups graham cracker crumbs
¼ cup unbleached all-purpose flour
1½ teaspoons baking powder
¼ teaspoon salt
¼ pound (1 stick) soft unsalted butter
1 cup sugar
3 large eggs
2 teaspoons vanilla extract
¾ cup whole milk
1 cup pecans, chopped coarsely
1 cup miniature semisweet chocolate chips (6 ounces)

I. Position an oven rack in the middle of the oven and preheat the oven to 325°F. Butter the bottom and sides of a 9-inch round cake pan 2 inches deep. Line the bottom of the pan with parchment or wax paper and butter the paper.

Prepare the Graham Cracker Crumb Topping

2. Put the graham cracker crumbs in a small bowl. Stir in the melted butter. Stir in the chocolate chips. Set aside.

· The batter bubbles up around the edges of the pan as the cake bakes, but it becomes firm when the cake is done.

· Using miniature chocolate chips ensures that there will be lots of chocolate chips in every bite of cake.

Doubling the Recipe
Double the ingredients and use two pans.

Prepare the Graham Cracker Crumb Cake

3. Put the graham cracker crumbs in a medium bowl. Sift the flour, baking powder, and salt into the bowl and stir into the crumbs. Set aside. Put the butter in the large bowl of an electric mixer and beat on medium speed for 15 seconds. Slowly add the sugar and beat for 2 minutes, or until the mixture lightens in color and looks creamy. Add the eggs, one at a time. Beat for 1 minute. Stop the mixer and scrape the bowl once during the beating. Add the vanilla. Decrease the speed to low and add the crumb mixture and the milk alternately, beginning and ending with the crumb mixture (3 crumb mixture, 2 milk). Stop the mixer and scrape the sides of the bowl after the last addition of the crumb mixture. Stir in the pecans and chocolate chips. Spread the batter evenly in the pan. Sprinkle the graham cracker crumb topping evenly over the batter.

4. Bake about 1 hour and 10 minutes. The edges of the batter will bubble up as the cake bakes. To test for doneness, insert a toothpick into the center of the cake. When the toothpick comes out clean, the cake is done.

5. Cool the cake in the pan on a wire rack for 30 minutes. Put the cake in the freezer just until the chocolate chips are firm, about 10 minutes. Use a small sharp knife to loosen the cake from the sides of the pan. Place a flat plate or the bottom of springform pan on top of the cake and invert the cake onto it. Carefully remove and discard the paper liner. Place the wire rack on the bottom of the cake and invert the cake. The cake will be right side up. Replace any of the crumbs that may have fallen off the cake. Cool thoroughly.

To Freeze

Use a large spatula to slide the cooled cake onto a serving plate or cardboard cake circle covered with aluminum foil. Wrap the cake tightly with plastic wrap then heavy aluminum foil. Label with date and contents. Freeze up to 3 months.

To Serve

Defrost the wrapped cake at room temperature at least 5 hours or overnight. Serve the cake at room temperature. Leftover cake may be covered with plastic wrap and stored at room temperature up to 3 days.

MOCHA
CRUMB CAKE

I daydream about founding a "Crumb Lovers Club." At meetings we would feast on desserts loaded with crumbs. This coffee-flavored cake with its soft chocolate and crumb filling and crisp crumb topping could be the club emblem.

SERVES 12

COCOA CRUMB TOPPING
1⅓ cups unbleached all-purpose flour
1½ cups (packed) light brown sugar
2 tablespoons unsweetened Dutch process cocoa powder, such as Droste or Hershey's European Style, sifted
½ teaspoon ground cinnamon
7 tablespoons unsalted butter, melted
2 teaspoons instant decaffeinated coffee dissolved in 2 teaspoons water
6 ounces semisweet chocolate, chopped into ½-inch pieces

MOCHA CAKE
1¾ cups unbleached all-purpose flour
1 teaspoon baking soda
¼ teaspoon salt
1¾ cups sugar
2 large eggs
¾ cup buttermilk
7 ounces (1¾ sticks) unsalted butter, melted
1 teaspoon vanilla extract
1 tablespoon plus 1 teaspoon instant decaffeinated coffee dissolved in 1 tablespoon plus 1 teaspoon water

I. Position an oven rack in the middle of the oven. Preheat the oven to 325°F. Butter a 13×9×2-inch baking pan.

Prepare the Cocoa Crumb Topping

2. Put the flour, brown sugar, cocoa, and cinnamon in a medium bowl and stir together. Press any lumps out of the brown sugar. Add the melted butter

· Use chopped chocolate rather than chocolate chips for this cake. Chocolate chips hold their shape when baked, but chopped chocolate melts and forms an unbroken chocolate layer through the middle of the cake. A clean meat pounder or mallet is a good tool for breaking up the chocolate.

· Melted butter produces crisp crumbs.

Doubling the Recipe
Double the ingredients and use two pans. Mix the cake batter in a 5-quart bowl.

and dissolved coffee and stir until the mixture is evenly moistened and crumbly and fine crumbs up to $\frac{1}{2}$ inch in size are formed. Set aside.

Prepare the Mocha Cake

3. Sift the flour, baking soda, and salt into the large bowl of an electric mixer. Add the sugar and mix on low speed to combine the ingredients. Mix the eggs and buttermilk together and stir into the flour mixture. Add the melted butter, vanilla, and dissolved coffee and mix until the batter is evenly moistened, about 45 seconds. Pour half of the batter into the prepared pan and spread evenly. Sprinkle $1\frac{1}{2}$ cups of the crumb mixture evenly over the batter. Sprinkle the chopped chocolate over the crumbs. Drop spoonfuls of the remaining batter evenly over the chocolate. Use a thin metal spatula to spread the batter evenly over the chocolate. Small bits of chocolate may not be covered by the batter. Sprinkle the remaining crumb mixture evenly over the batter.

4. Bake about 55 minutes. During the first half of the baking time, the batter may bubble up slightly at the edges. To test for doneness, insert a toothpick into the center of the cake. When the toothpick comes out clean, the cake is done. Cool the cake thoroughly in the pan on a wire rack, about 3 hours. Cut the cake into 12 pieces, 3 rows lengthwise and 4 rows across.

To Freeze

Wrap each piece of cake in plastic wrap. Place pieces in a metal or plastic freezer container and cover tightly. Label with date and contents. Freeze up to 3 months.

To Serve

Remove as many cake pieces from the freezer as you need. Defrost the wrapped cake at room temperature about 2 hours. Leftover cake can be covered with plastic wrap and stored at room temperature up to 3 days.

LEMON AND WHITE CHOCOLATE ALMOND CRUNCH CAKE

Lemon and white chocolate complement each other and give this coffee cake a lemon-flavored twist. Lemon zest is a powerhouse flavoring, and I add a hefty measure to this cake. The secret of the extra-crunchy almond topping is to toss the nuts with some egg white and sugar.

SERVES 9

ALMOND CRUNCH TOPPING
1 large egg white
1 cup blanched almonds, coarsely chopped
1 tablespoon plus 1 teaspoon sugar
$\frac{1}{2}$ cup white chocolate chips, Ghirardelli or Guittard preferred (3 ounces)

LEMON AND WHITE CHOCOLATE CAKE
2 cups unbleached all-purpose flour
1 teaspoon baking powder
$\frac{3}{4}$ teaspoon baking soda
$\frac{1}{4}$ teaspoon salt
$\frac{1}{4}$ pound (1 stick) soft unsalted butter
3 tablespoons fresh lemon juice
1 cup sugar
2 large eggs
2 teaspoons grated lemon zest
1 teaspoon vanilla extract
$\frac{1}{2}$ teaspoon almond extract
1 cup sour cream
1 cup white chocolate chips, Ghirardelli or Guittard preferred (6 ounces)

I. Position an oven rack in the middle of the oven and preheat the oven to 325°F. Butter a 9-inch square baking pan 2 inches deep.

Good Advice
· Check to see that cocoa butter is listed as one of the ingredients in the white chocolate chips. Ghirardelli and Guittard brands are good choices.

· Wash and dry lemons before you grate the zest, and grate the lemon zest before you squeeze the juice. Use only the outer yellow zest since the white pith is bitter.

· The cake will rise to the top of the pan, so check to see that it is 2 inches deep.

Doubling the Recipe
Double the ingredients and use two pans.

Mix the Almond Crunch Topping

2. Put the egg white in a medium bowl. Add the almonds and stir until they are evenly coated with egg white. Sprinkle the sugar over the nuts and stir the mixture. Stir in the white chocolate chips. Set aside.

Prepare the Lemon and White Chocolate Cake

3. Sift the flour, baking powder, baking soda, and salt together. Set aside. Put the butter and lemon juice in the large bowl of an electric mixer and beat on medium speed for 15 seconds. Slowly add the sugar and beat for 2 minutes, or until the mixture lightens in color. Add the eggs, one at a time. Beat for 1 minute. Stop the mixer and scrape the bowl once during the beating. Mix in the lemon zest, vanilla, and almond extract. Decrease the speed to low and add the flour mixture and the sour cream alternately, beginning and ending with the flour mixture (3 flour, 2 sour cream). Stop the mixer and scrape the sides of the bowl again after the last addition of flour. Stir in the white chocolate chips. Spread the batter evenly in the pan. Spoon the almond topping evenly over the batter.

4. Bake about 1 hour. The top of the cake will have a light golden color. To test for doneness, insert a toothpick into the center of the cake. When the toothpick comes out clean, the cake is done. Cool the cake in the pan on a wire rack about 2 hours. Use a sharp knife and a sawing motion to cut the cake into 9 square pieces.

VARIATION Bake the cake in a 10-inch round cake pan 2 inches deep. Line the pan with parchment or wax paper. Bake and cool the cake as above. Use a small sharp knife to loosen the cake from the sides of the pan. Invert onto a piece of plastic wrap. Discard the paper liner. Wrap tightly with plastic wrap then with heavy aluminum foil. Label with date and contents. Freeze up to 3 months. Defrost the wrapped cake at room temperature about 4 hours.

To Freeze
Wrap each cake piece in plastic wrap. Put the pieces in a metal or plastic freezer container and cover tightly. Or put the wrapped pieces in a plastic freezer bag and seal. Label with date and contents. Freeze up to 3 months.

To Serve
Remove as many pieces of cake as you want from the freezer and defrost the wrapped cake at room temperature about 2 hours. Leftover cake may be covered with plastic wrap and stored at room temperature up to 3 days.

CHOCOLATE PECAN RUGELACH

Rugelach is a kind of bite-size, crescent-shape filled pastry made with a cream cheese dough that becomes crisp and flaky as it bakes. These pastries always remind me of bakeries in Brooklyn with glass bins holding hundreds of rugelach in assorted flavors. My rugelach have a sweet cinnamon, pecan, and chocolate chip filling that contrasts well with the less sweet cream cheese dough.

MAKES 48 SMALL PASTRIES

CREAM CHEESE DOUGH
2 cups unbleached all-purpose flour
2 tablespoons sugar
1/8 teaspoon salt
10 ounces soft cream cheese, cut into 6 pieces
6 ounces (1 1/2 sticks) cold unsalted butter, cut into 12 pieces
2 tablespoons sour cream
2 teaspoons vanilla extract

CHOCOLATE PECAN FILLING
1/3 cup sugar
2 teaspoons ground cinnamon
3/4 cup pecans, finely chopped
2/3 cup semisweet miniature chocolate chips (4 ounces)

4 tablespoons orange marmalade

Prepare the Cream Cheese Dough

I. Put the flour, sugar, and salt in the large bowl of an electric mixer and mix on low speed just to blend the ingredients. Add the cream cheese and butter and mix until all of the flour is incorporated and crumbs form, about 45 seconds. The largest crumbs will be about 1/2 inch in size. Mix the sour cream and vanilla together. With the mixer running, add the sour cream mixture and mix until a soft dough forms, about 15 seconds. Divide the dough into 4 equal pieces and

Good Advice

· Use miniature chocolate chips and chop the pecans to about 1/8 inch in size, approximately the same size as the chocolate chips.

· After rolling the dough into a circle, spread a thin layer of orange marmalade over it. Use only 1 tablespoon of marmalade for each dough circle; if more marmalade is used, it will leak and burn on the baking sheet.

· Leave the center of the rolled dough circles without pecan-chocolate chip filling, to prevent the filling from leaking out of the rugelach.

Doubling the Recipe

Double the ingredients for the filling and mix the dough in two batches.

form each piece into a round disk. Wrap each disk in plastic wrap and refrigerate until firm, at least 1 hour or overnight.

Prepare the Chocolate Pecan Filling

2. Put the sugar and cinnamon in a small bowl and stir together. Stir in the pecans and chocolate chips.

3. Position 2 oven racks in the middle and upper third of the oven. Preheat the oven to 375°F. Line 2 baking sheets with parchment paper.

4. Remove the dough packages from the refrigerator and unwrap them. If the dough has become cold and hard, let it sit at room temperature for about 5 minutes, or until it is easy to roll. Lightly flour the rolling surface and rolling pin. Roll 1 disk into a $10^{1}/_{2}$-inch diameter circle and trim the edges even. The trimmed circle will be $9^{1}/_{2}$ to 10 inches in diameter. Leaving a $^{3}/_{4}$-inch plain border, use a thin spatula to spread 1 tablespoon of the orange marmalade evenly over the dough. Remove any large pieces of orange rind from the marmalade. Leaving a $^{3}/_{4}$-inch plain border and a $1^{1}/_{2}$-inch plain circle in the center, sprinkle a fourth of the filling (scant $^{1}/_{2}$ cup) evenly over the dough. Press the filling into the dough. Use a large knife to cut the dough into 12 wedges. Roll each wedge up tightly from the wide edge to the point. Place, point side down, 1 inch apart, on the prepared baking sheets. Repeat with the remaining dough to form 48 small rugelach.

5. Bake about 30 minutes, or until the pastry is golden brown. Reverse the baking sheets after 15 minutes, front to back and top to bottom, to ensure even browning.

6. Transfer the rugelach immediately to a wire rack to cool thoroughly.

To Freeze

Place the bottoms of 2 rugelach together and wrap them in plastic wrap. Place in a metal or plastic freezer container and cover tightly. Label with date and contents. Freeze up to 3 months.

To Serve

Remove as many rugelach from the freezer as needed and defrost the wrapped pastries at room temperature about 3 hours. Leftover rugelach may be covered with plastic wrap and stored at room temperature up to 3 days.

· This rich, sweet dough gets a boost from a sponge starter. To make the sponge starter, mix the yeast with some liquid and flour from the cake recipe. The yeast multiples quickly in the soft mixture. This powerful yeast mixture is strong enough to leaven the rich dough.

· I use golden raisins or dried cherries (see page 295) in my kugelhopf. The raisins are traditional, but cherries and chocolate make a good combination. Traditionally citron is added to the dough, but I prefer to glaze orange and lemon zest in a light sugar syrup. Finely grated orange and lemon zest can be substituted for the glazed zest.

· You can mix this dough in a standing electric mixer. Or you can use a handheld mixer to mix the dough up to the point of adding the flour, and then incorporate the flour with a spoon.

· For guidelines on baking with yeast see page 234.

CHOCOLATE KUGELHOPF

Kugelhopf, gugelhupf, or kugelhoff—no matter how you spell it, this light, tender yeast cake filled with fruit, almonds, and chopped chocolate is worth baking. The cake is a specialty of Austria and the Alsatian region of France, but most European countries have their own version. Although you would never guess it from the spectacular finished cake, this yeast batter is simple to prepare and is a good recipe for a first attempt at baking with yeast. The soft kugelhopf batter is beaten rather than kneaded, the dough requires only one rising in the pan, and a bundt pan or tall kugelhopf pan gives the cake its fancy fluted shape.

SERVES 12

GLAZED ORANGE AND LEMON ZEST
1 orange, zest only
1 lemon, zest only
$^2/_3$ cup water
$^1/_2$ cup sugar
1 tablespoon cider vinegar

KUGELHOPF DOUGH
$^1/_2$ cup golden raisins or halved dried cherries
$^1/_4$ cup coarsely chopped blanched almonds
2 tablespoons dark rum
$^1/_4$ cup warm water (95° to 105°F.)
2 teaspoons or 1 package active dry yeast
$^2/_3$ cup plus 1 teaspoon sugar
1 cup warm whole milk (95° to 105°F.)
$3^1/_2$ cups unbleached all-purpose flour
$^1/_4$ pound (1 stick) soft unsalted butter
$^1/_2$ teaspoon salt
4 large eggs, at room temperature
1 tablespoon vanilla extract
1 tablespoon plus 1 teaspoon glazed orange zest, drained and cut into $^1/_4$-inch pieces
1 teaspoon glazed lemon zest, drained and cut into $^1/_4$-inch pieces
6 ounces semisweet chocolate, chopped
Powdered sugar, for dusting

Glaze the Orange and Lemon Zest

I. Using a vegetable peeler and with a slight sawing motion, remove the orange and lemon zest from the fruit in large strips. Trim off any white pith that remains on the zest. Put the orange and lemon strips in a small saucepan and cover with water. Bring to a boil. Drain the strips into a strainer and rinse them with cold water. Put the water, sugar, and vinegar into the small saucepan. Bring to a simmer over medium heat, stirring to dissolve the sugar. As soon as the sugar is dissolved, add the drained orange and lemon zest. Simmer 10 minutes. If using the peel immediately, drain the peel and cool it. Or refrigerate the zest in its syrup for up to 1 week.

Prepare the Kugelhopf

2. Position a rack in the middle of the oven. Generously butter the bottom, sides, and center tube of a bundt or kugelhopf pan with a 12-cup capacity.

3. Put the raisins, almonds, and rum in a small bowl and stir together. Set aside.

4. Put the warm water in a large bowl. Sprinkle the yeast and 1 teaspoon sugar over the water and stir until the yeast dissolves. Let the mixture sit for 5 minutes. The yeast will begin to foam on top. Add the warm milk and 1 cup of the flour and stir to incorporate the flour. The mixture will look like thick pancake batter. Cover the bowl with plastic wrap and let the mixture rest for 1 hour or up to 3 hours. This is the sponge starter.

5. Put the butter, ⅔ cup sugar, and salt in the large bowl of an electric mixer and mix on medium speed until the mixture is blended thoroughly, 1 minute. Add the eggs, one at a time, then beat for 1 minute. Stop the mixer and scrape the bowl during this mixing. The mixture will have small lumps of butter. Decrease the speed to low, stir the sponge starter down, and mix it into the batter until it is incorporated thoroughly, about 2 minutes. Mix in the raisin mixture (including any liquid in the bowl), vanilla, orange zest, lemon zest, and chocolate. Add the remaining flour in 3 additions, mixing until the flour is completely incorporated. Stop the mixer and scrape the dough off the beaters during this

Doubling the Recipe
Double or triple the glazed citrus zest by adding the zest of two oranges and lemons to the syrup. Mix the kugelhopf batter in separate batches and bake the cake in two pans.

To Freeze
Wrap the cake tightly with plastic wrap. Gently press heavy aluminum foil around the cake. Label with date and contents. Freeze up to 3 months.

Defrost the wrapped cake at room temperature about 5 hours. Warm the kugelhopf to return the just-baked taste to it. Preheat the oven to 300°F. Unwrap the cake and rewrap in aluminum foil. Heat for about 20 minutes, until warm. Serve warm or at room temperature. Leave the cake bottom side up for serving. Leftover cake can be covered with plastic wrap and stored at room temperature up to 2 days. After 2 days, butter and toast slices of the cake to freshen it for 2 more days.

mixing. The dough will be soft and sticky. Spread the dough evenly in the prepared pan. Cover with plastic wrap and let rise for 1½ hours. The dough will rise only about 1 inch in the pan.

6. When the kugelhopf dough in the baking pan has 30 minutes of rising time left, preheat the oven to 350°F.

7. Bake 50 minutes, or until the top of the kugelhopf is light brown. Cool the cake in the pan 15 minutes. Use a small sharp knife to loosen the cake from the top of the sides and the center tube of the pan. Invert the cake onto a wire rack to cool thoroughly. Dust with powdered sugar. Slide the cake onto a serving platter or cardboard cake circle.

VARIATION   Substitute 2 teaspoons grated orange zest and 1 teaspoon grated lemon zest for the glazed orange and lemon zest.

CHOCOLATE BABKA

European countries have a rich tradition of yeast-raised coffee cakes. Yeast cakes are rich tasting but use less expensive ingredients such as milk and flour, and require a minimum of costly ingredients like butter and eggs. Babka is a popular example that exists in many versions.

Traditionally, the cake is prepared from a soft yeast dough, swirled with a choice of cinnamon, raisins, sugar, ground nuts, cake crumbs, or chocolate, covered on all sides with crisp crumbs, and baked in a loaf shape. My version of babka is studded with chunks of chocolate and swirled with a chocolate-almond filling.

MAKES 2 LOAVES

BABKA DOUGH
¼ cup warm water (95° to 105°F.)
2 teaspoons or 1 package active dry yeast
¼ cup granulated sugar
¾ cup warm whole milk (95° to 105°F.)
½ teaspoon salt
4 to 4¼ cups unbleached all-purpose flour
2 ounces unsalted butter, cut into 4 pieces
3 large eggs, at room temperature
2 teaspoons vanilla extract
2 teaspoons instant decaffeinated coffee dissolved in 2 teaspoons water

CRISP CRUMBS
⅓ cup granulated sugar
⅓ cup (packed) light brown sugar
1¼ cups unbleached all-purpose flour
½ teaspoon ground cinnamon
⅓ cup unsalted butter, melted

CHOCOLATE-ALMOND-CINNAMON FILLING
¾ cup blanched almonds
½ cup granulated sugar
½ teaspoon ground cinnamon
8 ounces semisweet chocolate, chopped

2 tablespoons unsalted butter, melted, for brushing over dough

Good Advice

· The dough is prepared with a sponge starter, which is described on page 248.

· Make the braided shape of the loaf by rolling the filled dough into a long roll, forming the roll into a figure eight, and twisting it into a braided loaf.

· This recipe has a unique method for covering the sides of the cake with crisp crumbs. Before the cake rises in the pan, you sprinkle it with enough crumbs to cover the top of the cake and fall down the sides of the pan. The cake rises to fill the pan and the crumbs bake onto the sides of the cake.

· Dissolved instant coffee gives the cake a rich light golden brown color but does not add coffee flavor to the cake.

· For guidelines on baking with yeast, see page 234.

Doubling the Recipe
Double all the ingredients. Mix the dough in two batches.

To Serve

Defrost a wrapped loaf at room temperature, about 5 hours. Warm the loaf to return the just-baked taste. Preheat the oven to 300°F. Unwrap the loaf and rewrap in aluminum foil. Heat for about 20 minutes, until warm. Serve warm or at room temperature. Leftover babka can be covered with plastic wrap and stored at room temperature up to 2 days. After 2 days, toast slices of babka to freshen it for 2 more days.

Prepare the Babka Dough

1. Position a rack in the middle of the oven. Generously butter 2 loaf pans with a 6½- to 7-cup capacity.

2. Put the warm water in the large bowl of an electric mixer. Sprinkle the yeast and 1 teaspoon of the sugar over the water and stir until the yeast dissolves. Let the mixture sit for 5 minutes. The yeast will begin to foam on top. Add ½ cup of the warm milk, the remaining sugar, salt, and 1 cup of the flour to the yeast mixture. Stir to incorporate the flour. The mixture will look like thick pancake batter. Cover the bowl with plastic wrap and let the mixture rest for 1 hour. This is the sponge starter.

3. Add the butter to the remaining milk and warm over low heat until the butter is melted and the mixture measures 95° to 105°F. on a food thermometer. Stir the sponge starter down. Add the warm milk mixture, eggs, vanilla, and dissolved coffee to the sponge starter. Use the flat beater to mix on low speed until the mixture is smooth, about 30 seconds. Change to the dough hook and add the remaining flour, 1 cup at a time, on low speed. Add enough flour just to form a smooth, sticky dough that comes away from the sides of the bowl but sticks to the bottom of the bowl. Mix with the dough hook for 3 minutes. Or use a large spoon to mix the dough by hand. As soon as the flour is incorporated into the dough, scrape the dough onto a lightly floured work surface. Knead the dough until it is smooth, about 5 minutes. The dough will be soft but will not stick to the work surface. Knead the dough by pushing down on it, folding it over on itself, and turning the dough as you knead it. Place the dough in a clean buttered bowl and rub the top of the dough with soft butter to coat it. Cover with plastic wrap and let the dough rise for 1 hour, or until about double in size. Or, let the dough rise overnight in the refrigerator.

Prepare the Crisp Crumbs

4. Put the granulated sugar, brown sugar, flour, and cinnamon in a small bowl and stir together. Pour the melted butter over the flour mixture and stir until the mixture is evenly moistened and fine crumbs form. Set aside.

Prepare the Chocolate-Almond-Cinnamon Filling

5. When you are ready to roll the dough, put the almonds, sugar, and cinnamon in the workbowl of a food processor fitted with the steel blade and process until the almonds are so finely ground that no pieces of almond are visible, about 90 seconds.

6. Preheat the oven to 175°F. Place the chocolate in an ovenproof container and melt it in the oven, about 8 minutes. As soon as the chocolate is melted, remove it from the oven and stir it smooth.

7. Punch the air out of the dough. If the dough has been refrigerated and is cold, let it sit at room temperature for 1 hour. Remove half of the dough from the bowl and place it on a lightly floured surface. Roll into a rectangle about 9 inches wide and 1½ times the length of the pan you are using. If the loaf pan is 9 inches long, roll the rectangle 13½ inches long. Leaving a 1-inch border of plain dough, spread half of the melted chocolate evenly over the dough. Sprinkle half of the almond mixture over the chocolate. Roll up lengthwise into a roll. Pinch the seam and the ends together to seal tightly. Place a long piece of wax paper on the counter. Sprinkle ½ cup of the crumb mixture over the wax paper. Brush the roll lightly with melted butter. Roll the filled roll in the crumbs, pressing gently so the crumbs adhere to the dough. Twist the filled roll over itself to form a figure eight. Overlap the ends of the figure eight slightly and pinch to seal. Place in a prepared loaf pan. Pat the dough gently to spread it evenly in the pan. The dough will not touch the sides of the pan in most places. Brush lightly with melted butter. Sprinkle ¾ cup of the crumb mixture over the top of the dough, letting crumbs fall down along the sides of the dough. Cover with plastic wrap and let rise 1 hour. Repeat with the remaining dough, filling, and crumbs to form a second babka and let it rise.

8. When the babka dough in the baking pan has 30 minutes of rising time left, preheat the oven to 350°F.

9. Bake about 1 hour, or until the top is light brown. Cool the loaf in the pan 10 minutes. Use a small sharp knife to loosen the loaf from the sides of the pan. Invert the loaf onto a wire rack, turn right side up, and cool thoroughly.

POTICA

Potica, stacked with an abundance of chocolate-walnut meringue swirls, is central Europe's rococco version of coffee cake. It's a big yeast cake that is noted for the way its many layers are produced. The filling is spread over two long pieces of dough, then each is rolled up into a long roll. The two rolls are stacked on top of each other in a bundt pan and baked into an impressive cake with many swirls when sliced.

MAKES 2 POTICA

SOUR CREAM YEAST DOUGH
1/4 cup warm water (95° to 105°F.)
2 teaspoons or 1 package active dry yeast
1/4 cup plus 1/4 teaspoon granulated sugar
1/4 cup milk, skim, low fat, or whole
1/4 pound (1 stick) soft unsalted butter, cut into 8 pieces
3/4 teaspoon salt
2 large eggs, at room temperature
1 cup sour cream
4 to 4 1/4 cups unbleached all-purpose flour

CHOCOLATE-WALNUT MERINGUE FILLING
8 ounces semisweet chocolate, chopped
2 cups walnuts
1/2 cup (packed) light brown sugar
1/2 teaspoon ground cinnamon
4 large egg whites
1/4 teaspoon cream of tartar
1/3 cup granulated sugar

Powdered sugar, for dusting

Prepare the Sour Cream Yeast Dough

I. Put the warm water in the large bowl of an electric mixer. Sprinkle the yeast and 1/4 teaspoon sugar over the water and stir until the yeast dissolves. Let the mixture sit for 5 minutes. The mixture will look foamy.

2. Put the milk and butter in a small saucepan. Cook over low heat until the butter is melted and the mixture is warm and measures 95° to 105°F. on a food thermometer. Using the flat beater, add the warm milk mixture, remaining 1/4

Good Advice
· This satin-smooth dough is my all-purpose yeast dough for coffee cakes and buns. One recipe is enough for two Potica coffee cakes, two Chocolate-Almond Butterflies, or sixteen Chocolate Cinnamon Twists.

· The dough can rise overnight in the refrigerator, but allow at least 1 hour for the dough to warm to room temperature before rolling and filling it.

· Room temperatures affect yeast dough. In a cool kitchen allow additional rising time. In a warm kitchen the time may be shorter. A 15-minute adjustment is usually sufficient.

· To prepare two Potica coffee cakes requires two bundt pans with a 10- to 12-cup capacity, which few of us have. Most pans with a center tube, preferably fluted, will work. In a pinch, I have substituted a kugelhopf pan with a 7-cup capacity for one of the bundt pans. As the cake bakes, it rises slightly above the rim of the pan, but this is not a prob-

cup sugar, salt, eggs, and sour cream to the yeast mixture and mix on low speed until the mixture is smooth, about 30 seconds. Change to the dough hook and add the flour, 1 cup at a time, on low speed. Add just enough flour to form a smooth, soft dough that comes away from the sides of the bowl. Stop the mixer and scrape loose flour away from the sides of the bowl and into the center of the dough. Mix with the dough hook for 3 minutes. The dough will look smooth. Or use a large spoon to mix the dough by hand. As soon as the flour is incorporated into the dough, scrape the dough onto a lightly floured work surface. Knead the dough until it is smooth, about 5 minutes. The dough will be soft but will not stick to the work surface. Knead the dough by pushing down on it, folding it over on itself, and turning the dough as you knead it. Place the dough in a clean buttered bowl and rub the top of the dough with soft butter to coat it. Cover with plastic wrap and let rise for 1½ hours, or until about double in size. Or, let the dough rise overnight in the refrigerator.

Mix the Chocolate-Walnut Meringue Filling

3. Position an oven rack in the middle of the oven. Preheat the oven to 175°F. Butter the bottom, sides, and center tube of a bundt pan with at least a 10- to 14-cup capacity.

4. Place the chocolate in an ovenproof container and melt it in the oven, about 10 minutes. As soon as the chocolate is melted, remove it from the oven and stir it smooth. Put the walnuts, brown sugar, and cinnamon in the workbowl of a food processor fitted with the steel blade and process until the nuts are finely ground. Transfer the mixture to a medium bowl and stir in the melted chocolate.

5. Put the egg whites and cream of tartar in a clean large bowl of an electric mixer and beat with clean dry beaters on low speed until the egg whites are foamy and the cream of tartar is dissolved. Increase the speed to medium-high and beat the egg whites to soft peaks. Slowly beat in the sugar, 1 tablespoon at a time. Fold a third of the meringue into the nut mixture. Fold the remaining meringue into the nut mixture. Makes about 3¾ cups.

6. Punch the air out of the dough. If the dough has been refrigerated and is cold, let it sit at room temperature for 1 hour. Remove half of the dough from

lem. Other possibilities include a springform pan with a fluted bottom insert or a ring-shaped baking pan with a 10- to 12-cup capacity. A 10-inch diameter tube pan with a wide rather than tapered bottom is rather large for this cake, but an angel food cake pan with a tapered bottom works fine.

· Use a dark colored metal baking pan, if possible; it will give the Potica a beautiful light brown crust.

· Seal all of the dough edges tightly to prevent any filling from leaking out of the cake as it bakes.

· For guidelines on baking with yeast, see page 234.

Doubling the Recipe

Double the ingredients for the filling. Double the ingredients for the dough and use a 5-quart bowl to mix the dough. Bake the cake in four pans or use some of the dough to make butterflies or twists (recipes follow).

To Freeze

Wrap the cake tightly with plastic wrap. Gently press heavy aluminum foil around the cake. Label with date and contents. Freeze up to 3 months.

To Serve

Defrost the wrapped cake at room temperature about 5 hours. Warm the Potica to return the just-baked taste to it. Preheat the oven to 300°F. Unwrap the defrosted cake and rewrap in aluminum foil. Heat for about 20 minutes, or until warm. Leave the cake bottom side up for serving. Leftover Potica may be covered with plastic wrap and stored at room temperature up to 2 days.

the bowl. Divide the dough approximately in half, making one part slightly larger than the other, about $\frac{1}{3}$ cup more dough. Place the smaller portion of dough on a lightly floured surface. Roll into a rectangle about 18 × 7 inches. The dough will be about $\frac{1}{8}$ inch thick. Leaving a 1-inch border of plain dough all around the edges, spread a quarter of the meringue mixture evenly over the dough. Roll up into a roll about 18 inches long. Pinch the seam and the ends together to seal tightly. Place the roll, seam side up, in the prepared pan, overlapping the ends of the roll. Roll the remaining dough into a rectangle about 20 × 8 inches. Leaving a 1-inch border of plain dough, spread a third of the remaining meringue mixture evenly over the dough. Roll up into a roll about 20 inches long. Pinch the seam and the ends together to seal tightly. Place the second roll, seam side down, on top of the roll in the pan, placing the ends on opposite sides of the pan from the ends of the bottom roll so the cake is level. Overlap the ends of the top roll. Cover with plastic wrap and let rise 45 minutes. Repeat to form a second Potica.

7. Position a rack in the middle of the oven. When the Potica dough in the baking pan has 30 minutes of rising time left, preheat the oven to 350°F.

8. Bake about 50 minutes, until the top of the Potica is light brown. Cool the cake in the pan 10 minutes. Use a small sharp knife to loosen the cake from the top of the sides and center tube of the pan. Invert the cake onto a wire rack to cool thoroughly. Dust with powdered sugar. Slide the cooled cake onto a serving platter or cardboard cake circle.

CHOCOLATE-ALMOND BUTTERFLY

*W*hen we lived in Miami, there was a bakery in our neighborhood that specialized in buttery coffee cakes and offered as many as thirty kinds on any given day. Choosing was not easy—except for my daughter Laura. When it was her turn to pick the cake, she never wavered once she found the cake with the chocolate filling and chocolate crumbs— smart cookie, and definitely her mother's daughter.

MAKES 2 CAKES

CRISP CHOCOLATE CRUMB TOPPING
½ cup unbleached all-purpose flour
2 tablespoons unsweetened Dutch process cocoa powder, such as Droste or Hershey's European Style, sifted
⅔ cup sugar
3 tablespoons unsalted butter, melted

CHOCOLATE-ALMOND FILLING
2 cups blanched almonds
1 cup sugar
2 tablespoons unsweetened Dutch process cocoa powder, such as Droste or Hershey's European Style
2 large egg whites
1 teaspoon almond extract

1 recipe Sour Cream Yeast Dough (page 254) that has risen for 1 hour at room temperature or overnight in the refrigerator
3 tablespoons unsalted butter, melted, for brushing the dough
Powdered sugar, for dusting

Mix the Crisp Chocolate Crumb Topping

1. Put the flour, cocoa powder, and sugar in a small bowl. Use a mixing spoon to stir them together. Pour the melted butter over the flour mixture and stir until it is evenly moistened and fine crumbs form. Set aside. Makes about 1¾ cups.

Mix the Chocolate-Almond Filling

2. Put the almonds, sugar, and cocoa powder in the workbowl of a food processor fitted with the steel blade and process until the almonds are finely ground, about 30 seconds. With the motor running, add the egg whites and almond extract. Process until the mixture forms a ball, about 15 seconds.

Good Advice

· This cake can also be formed into a ring. See the variation at the end of the recipe for specific instructions.

· Press the chocolate crumbs firmly onto the dough so they don't fall off when the cake bakes.

· Since the cocoa powder for the filling is processed in a food processor, it is not necessary to sift it. The cocoa powder for the topping should be sifted, however.

· For guidelines on baking with yeast see page 234.

Doubling the Recipe

Double the ingredients for the filling and crumbs. Double the ingredients for the dough and use a 5-quart bowl to mix it. Bake the cakes on four baking sheets.

To Serve

Defrost the wrapped cake at room temperature, about 5 hours. Warm the butterfly to return the just-baked taste to it. Preheat the oven to 300°F. Unwrap the cake and rewrap in aluminum foil. Heat for about 20 minutes, or until warm. Serve warm or at room temperature. Leftover cake can be covered with plastic wrap and stored at room temperature up to 3 days.

3. Position 2 racks in the middle and upper third of the oven. Have ready 2 open-ended baking sheets.

4. Punch the air out of the dough. If the dough has been refrigerated and is cold, let it sit at room temperature for 1 hour. Remove half of the dough from the bowl and place on a lightly floured surface. Roll into a rectangle about 18 × 11 inches. The dough will be thin. Brush the dough lightly with melted butter. Leaving a 1-inch border of plain dough and using half of the filling, drop teaspoons of the filling mixture evenly over the dough. Roll up into a roll about 18 inches long. Pinch the seam and the ends together to seal tightly. With the seam side up, fold the roll in half with the seam on the inside. Pinch the 2 ends together. The roll will now be 2 rolls thick and 9 inches long. Place the roll in the center of a baking sheet. Leaving 2 inches of the center portion of the roll uncut, use a small sharp knife to cut a deep slit, halfway into the roll. Start from each end of the roll and cut toward the center of the roll, cutting the slit along the top center of the roll. The slit at each end will be about 3½ inches long and the center of the roll will not be cut. Lift the cut ends and spread them open and flat to form a butterfly shape. You will see the filling. Brush the top of the roll lightly with melted butter. Press about ¾ cup of the chocolate crumbs onto the top of the butterfly. Cover with plastic wrap and let rise 45 minutes. The dough will look soft and puffed. Repeat with the remaining dough, filling, and crumbs.

5. When the cake has 30 minutes of rising time left, preheat the oven to 350°F.

6. Bake about 40 minutes, or until the sides of the cake are golden. Cool 5 minutes on the baking sheet. Use a large spatula to slide each butterfly onto a wire rack to cool thoroughly. Dust with powdered sugar.

VARIATION To form the cake into a ring, roll half of the dough into a rectangle about 15 × 10 inches. Fill and roll as directed in Step 4 to make a roll about 15 inches. Place the roll on a baking sheet. Form the roll into a circle, pressing the ends together to seal. Use a knife to make 12 slashes about 1 inch apart and about ½ inch deep around the top of the roll. Brush with melted butter and press half of the crumb mixture on the top of the ring. Cover with plastic wrap, let rise about 45 minutes, and bake about 45 minutes, or until golden. Cool as in Step 6.

CHOCOLATE CINNAMON TWISTS

When I was growing up in Lakeland, Florida, we used to go to Maas Brothers department store in Tampa for an occasional shopping spree. The highlight of the day was lunch in the store's restaurant where they served everyone a basket of cinnamon twists. The cinnamon and sugar coating glazed the outside of the buns and seeped down into the crevices of the buns. My version of these cinnamon twists are filled with miniature chocolate chips.

MAKES 16 TWISTS

¾ cup sugar
2 teaspoons ground cinnamon
1 recipe Sour Cream Yeast Dough (page 254) that has risen for 1 hour at room temperature or overnight in the refrigerator
2 tablespoons unsalted butter, melted
⅔ cup miniature semisweet chocolate chips (4 ounces)

Good Advice
· Some chocolate chips and cinnamon sugar will fall out of the buns as you form them. Press the chocolate chips back on the dough and sprinkle the cinnamon sugar over the tops of the twists in the pan.

· For guidelines on baking with yeast see page 234.

Doubling the Recipe
Use a double recipe of sour cream dough. Double the filling ingredients. Bake the twists in two pans.

I. Position an oven rack in the middle of the oven. Butter a 13 × 9 × 2-inch pan.

2. Put the sugar and cinnamon in a small bowl and stir to blend. Punch the air out of the dough and place it on a lightly floured surface. Roll the dough into a rectangle 16 × 14 inches. The long side of the dough should be facing you and parallel to the edge of the counter. Brush the dough lightly with melted butter. Leaving a ½-inch border of plain dough, sprinkle ½ cup of the cinnamon sugar mixture and the chocolate chips evenly over the dough. Press the chocolate chips into the dough. Fold the top third of the dough toward the center. Brush this plain top third of dough lightly with melted butter and sprinkle with the remaining cinnamon sugar. Fold the 2 layers of dough to the bottom edge of dough. Press gently on the dough so the layers adhere to each other. Pinch all of the edges together tightly to seal. You will have a 3-layer strip 16 inches long and about 4½ inches wide.

Wrap the twists tightly in plastic wrap then heavy aluminum foil. Label with date and contents. Freeze up to 3 months. The twists pull apart and you can separate them into portions before freezing them.

To Serve

Remove as many pieces as you need from the freezer. Defrost the wrapped twists at room temperature about 5 hours. Warm the twists to return the just-baked taste to them. Preheat the oven to 300°F. Unwrap the twists and rewrap in aluminum foil. Heat for about 20 minutes, until warm. Serve warm or at room temperature. Leftover twists may be covered with plastic wrap and stored up to 1 day at room temperature.

3. Cut the strip into 16 pieces about 1 inch wide. Pick up a piece by each end and twist the dough tightly in opposite directions. Press any chocolate chips that fall off back into the twist. Place a row of 8 twists along the top half of the prepared pan. Twist the remaining strips and place another row of 8 twists along the bottom half of the pan. Brush the top of the dough lightly with melted butter and sprinkle any cinnamon sugar that fell out of the twists over the top of the dough. Some of the sugar will fall to the bottom of the pan and will form a light glaze on the bottom of the pan. Cover with plastic wrap and let rise for 30 minutes.

4. Preheat the oven to 350°F.

5. Bake about 40 minutes, or until the top is golden. The baked twists will have spread into a large pull-apart cake. Cool the twists in the pan 5 minutes. Use a small sharp knife to loosen the twists from the sides of the pan. Place a wire rack on top of the twists and invert. Place another wire rack on the bottom of the twists and invert again to have the twists right side up. Cool thoroughly.

Ice Cream Sundaes, Sandwiches, and Pies

These desserts remind me most of my childhood. The sundaes at the corner candy shop, the ice cream sandwiches from the ice cream truck, and the special occasion ice cream pies from dairy bars. As I got older, I became a bit more particular. I craved more from a sundae and created my own with homemade cinnamon ice cream and enough rich dark chocolate sauce that would never run out before the ice cream was finished. I put together ice cream sandwiches with crisp homemade cookies, and I made ice cream pies with plenty of crunch and fudge in every bite. These kid-easy desserts will appeal to the most discriminating ice cream lover.

I use a good quality store-bought ice cream for these desserts. Premium ice creams, which have a milkfat content of 14 to 18 percent, are unnecessarily rich. Good quality ice cream, often the local or regional brand in your supermarket, has about 12 percent milkfat. The minimum milkfat content in ice cream allowed by federal government regulations is 10 percent, but a higher milkfat content tastes creamier than economy low fat brands. Since fat keeps ice crystals separated and discourages the formation of large unpleasant tasting ice crystals, a good brand assures that the ice cream will remain creamy when it freezes hard after its slight softening during preparation.

When assembling ice cream sandwiches or ice cream pies, soften the ice cream just until it can be spread but is not melted. On a warm summer day, ice cream can often be spread directly from the freezer. Melted ice cream will make the cookies in ice cream sandwiches soggy and can cause ice crystals to form when the ice cream freezes again. When ice cream melts completely, the air that was churned into the ice cream escapes and even fat cannot prevent the formation of a hard and icy texture. If the cookies for ice cream sandwiches are frozen, assemble the sandwiches with frozen cookies. Soft ice cream is less likely to melt if spread on a cold cookie. Cool any fresh baked cookies thoroughly before using them for ice cream sandwiches. When working with individual desserts such as the ice cream sandwiches and bon bons, put each item in the freezer as soon as it is assembled.

The ice cream pies have cookie crumb crusts, which add a cookies-and-ice-cream quality to the pies. The crusts also taste good when served frozen. I form the ice cream pies in springform pans. These deep pans have room for lots of ice cream, crunchy toppings, and sauces. In addition, the pies unmold easily from springform pans and are easy to cut. To transfer an ice cream pie to a serving platter easily, use a wide spatula to slide the frozen pie from the springform bottom onto the platter.

These ice cream desserts do not lend themselves to long freezer storage. Two weeks is the maximum. If stored in the freezer too long, cookies with ice cream sandwiches soften, peppermint candy on ice cream pies dissolves, and ice cream pies become icy and take on that dreaded freezer taste.

Soften all of these ice cream desserts slightly before serving them, and return any leftover desserts to the freezer after they are served and before they begin to melt. Usually it will take five to ten minutes to soften ice cream, but the time depends on your freezer and kitchen temperature. Ice cream for sundaes should be soft and creamy; ice cream sandwiches should be pleasantly firm, but not rock hard, when you bite into them; and ice cream pies should be easy to cut.

MOCHA BROWNIE SUNDAE WITH WARM COFFEE CARAMEL SAUCE

I did a lot of serious thinking about warm caramel sauce and cold ice cream, sticky sauce and chewy brownies to come up with this live-it-up sundae. It is also a good example of putting together a dessert from components that you've prepared ahead and frozen.

SERVES 12

12 Double Decker Mocha Brownies (page 88), defrosted or at room temperature
1⅓ cups coffee caramel sauce (see page 53), warmed to pouring consistency
3 pints coffee ice cream

Prepare the brownies. Prepare the caramel sauce.

Good Advice
· Since the hot caramel sauce softens the ice cream, it is not necessary to soften the ice cream before serving.

Doubling the Recipe
Double the ingredients.

To Serve
If the brownies are frozen, defrost the wrapped brownies at room temperature for about 3 hours. If the caramel sauce is frozen, defrost it at room temperature for about 5 hours, then warm it in a medium saucepan over low heat to pouring consistency. For each serving, place a brownie in an individual shallow bowl. Top each brownie with ice cream and warm caramel sauce.

CINNAMON ICE CREAM IN CHOCOLATE CUPS WITH DARK CHOCOLATE SAUCE

*W*hen I make homemade ice cream, I prepare flavors that I can't buy like cinnamon ice cream. You can serve the ice cream in glass goblets or sundae dishes, but serving it in Chocolate Cups makes for a very sophisticated dessert.

MAKES 6 SUNDAES

CINNAMON ICE CREAM
1 1/2 cups whole milk
1 1/2 cups whipping cream
2 cinnamon sticks, about 3 inches long
5 large egg yolks
1/2 cup granulated sugar
3 tablespoons (packed) light brown sugar
1 3/4 teaspoons ground cinnamon
2 teaspoons vanilla extract

1 cup Dark Chocolate Sauce (page 49), defrosted and cold
6 Chocolate Cups (page 55)
12 Chocolate Tubes, 3 to 4 inches long (page 55), for garnish (optional)

Prepare the Cinnamon Ice Cream

1. Heat the milk, cream, and cinnamon sticks in a large saucepan just until warm. Turn off the heat and let the mixture sit for 1 hour. Remove and discard the cinnamon sticks. Heat the milk and cream again until a few bubbles form, about 150°F. if measured on a food thermometer. Do not boil the mixture.

2. Put the egg yolks, granulated sugar, brown sugar, and ground cinnamon in the large bowl of an electric mixer and beat at medium speed until the mixture thickens slightly and lightens in color, about 45 seconds. Decrease the speed to low and slowly add the hot milk mixture. Return the mixture to the

Good Advice
· You will need an ice cream machine to churn the ice cream. I use a Simac Il Gelataio SC. This machine has a freezing chamber with a nonstick lining that you chill in the freezer before filling it with the ice cream mixture. It has a small electric motor to churn the ice cream. Any ice cream machine in good working order is satisfactory.

· Long chocolate tubes sticking straight up out of the sundae make a nice edible garnish that resembles cinnamon sticks.

Doubling the Recipe
Double the ingredients.

saucepan and cook the custard, stirring constantly, over medium-low heat until it reaches 170°F. if measured on a food thermometer. Stir the mixture often where the sides and the bottom of the pan meet. The mixture will thicken slightly and leave a path on the back of a spoon when you draw your finger across it. A little steam will just begin to rise from the mixture. Do not boil. Strain the hot mixture into a bowl and stir in the vanilla. Cover and refrigerate until very cold, at least 5 hours or overnight. Stir the mixture several times while it is chilling.

3. Chill a moistureproof carton or plastic freezer container to hold the ice cream. Transfer the custard to an ice cream maker and process according to the manufacturer's directions. Makes about 1 quart.

To Freeze

Transfer the ice cream to the chilled container. Press plastic wrap onto the surface of the ice cream and cover tightly. Label with date and contents. Freeze overnight or up to 10 days.

To Serve

Let the ice cream soften 5 to 10 minutes before serving. Stir the Dark Chocolate Sauce until smooth. Put a scoop of ice cream in each chocolate cup. Top with chocolate sauce and put 2 dark chocolate tubes in the top of each sundae.

MILK CHOCOLATE
ICE CREAM BON BONS

This recipe almost didn't make it into the book. Finding a simple way to cover cold ice cream with warm chocolate wasn't easy. I attempted to dip the ice cream in warm chocolate, but the ice cream melted and dripped into the melted chocolate. I tried pouring melted chocolate over ice cream balls, but the ice cream melted through the chocolate and the chocolate froze in puddle-like edges or drips around the bottom. I coated plastic candy molds with chocolate and filled them with ice cream, but the chocolate stuck to the frozen molds. I oiled the molds, and the chocolate dripped down the sides. I wanted to give up, but I knew that if I persisted these would be worth it. One hot summer afternoon, after I had dripped chocolate all over the inside of my freezer including on most of the wrapped frozen desserts, I gave it one last try. I formed disks of ice cream by packing the ice cream into small paper cups and peeling away the cups when the ice cream was frozen solid. Then I spread melted chocolate over strips of paper and wrapped the chocolate around the ice cream disks. After the chocolate hardened in the freezer, I removed the paper and was left with these open ended bon bons. Take a bite, and you'll know why I kept trying.

MAKES 12 BON BONS AND 6 SERVINGS

1 pint ice cream, softened just until it is easy to scoop
8 ounces milk chocolate, chopped

1. Line a baking sheet with wax paper and put it in the freezer. Put 2 tablespoons ice cream into the bottom of each of twelve 3-ounce paper cups. Use a small spoon to press the ice cream firmly into the cup and smooth the top. Put each cup on the baking sheet in the freezer as you fill it. Freeze the ice cream firm, about 2 hours.

2. Preheat the oven to 175°F. Place the milk chocolate in an ovenproof container and melt it in the oven, 8 to 10 minutes. As soon as the chocolate is melted,

Good Advice

· Use 3-ounce bathroom-size paper cups to shape the ice cream. Pack the ice cream smoothly and firmly into the cups so that there are no air spaces. Let the ice cream freeze thoroughly before proceeding with each step of the recipe, and you will have no trouble, even on a hot summer day.

· Trim the chocolate-lined paper with scissors, and then wash the scissors after trimming the chocolate.

· Since the bon bons have open ends, you can serve an assortment of ice cream flavors and still see what's inside. I like to use a variety of ice cream colors, which is also a good way to use up partial pints of ice cream. Coffee, peppermint, vanilla, and raspberry or strawberry make a good mix of colors.

remove it from the oven and stir it smooth. Cut a large piece of parchment or wax paper to line the kitchen counter. Cut 12 strips of parchment paper 6½ inches long and 2 inches wide. Lay the parchment strips flat on the piece of paper on the kitchen counter. Pour about 1 tablespoon melted chocolate over a parchment strip. Use a thin metal spatula to spread a thin layer of chocolate evenly over the paper, leaving a ½-inch plain edge for easier handling of the parchment strip. Repeat to make 12 chocolate-covered strips. Immediately lift the chocolate-coated paper and move it to a clean section of the paper-lined counter. This forms a smooth chocolate edge on the paper strip. Let the chocolate firm for 3 to 5 minutes, just until it does not drip off the paper when you move it.

3. Remove an ice cream–filled paper cup from the freezer. Peel away the paper cup. You will have a firm disk of ice cream about ¾ inch thick. Place the ice cream disk in the middle of a chocolate-covered strip of paper. Wrap the paper, chocolate side touching the ice cream, around the ice cream. Use clean scissors to trim the edges of the paper so the seam meets evenly. The edges of the paper should not overlap. You will have a band of chocolate wrapped around the ice cream disk. Return the ice cream bon bon to the baking sheet in the freezer until the chocolate is firm, about 15 minutes. Repeat with the remaining ice cream and chocolate strips. When the chocolate is firm, carefully peel the paper from the chocolate.

VARIATION Preheat the oven to 175°F. Place 1 ounce chopped white chocolate in a nonreactive ovenproof container and melt it in the oven, about 8 minutes. As soon as the white chocolate is melted, remove it from the oven and stir it smooth. Fit a small pastry bag with a small writing tip. Put the melted white chocolate in the pastry bag. Turn a finished and frozen ice cream bon bon seam side down and draw zigzag lines of white chocolate in a random pattern over the top of the bon bon. Return to the freezer to firm the white chocolate. Continue with the remaining ice cream bon bons.

Doubling the Recipe
Multiply the ingredients to make as many bon bons as you need.

To Freeze
Wrap each ice cream bon bon in plastic wrap. Place the bon bons in a metal or plastic freezer container and cover tightly. Label with date and contents. Freeze up to 2 weeks.

To Serve
Unwrap the ice cream bon bons and stack them on a platter or place 2 bon bons on each serving plate, seam side down. Serve immediately.

CRISPY PISTACHIO AND ORANGE DREAM FROZEN SANDWICHES

*P*istachio and orange have an affinity for one another. One taste of these pistachio and white chocolate chip cookies filled with orange sherbet and you'll see exactly what I mean. Filling the cookies with sherbet rather than ice cream makes a light, refreshing frozen sandwich.

MAKES 6 FROZEN SANDWICHES

1½ ounces white chocolate, Callebaut or Baker's Premium preferred, chopped
12 Pistachio and White Chocolate Chip Crisps (page 98), frozen
2 pints orange sherbet
Orange slices, for garnish (optional)

I.   Preheat the oven to 175°F. Place the white chocolate in a nonreactive oven-proof container and melt it in the oven, about 8 minutes. As soon as the white chocolate is melted, remove it from the oven and stir it smooth.

2.   Line a baking sheet with wax paper and put it in the freezer. Choose pairs of cookies that are about the same size. Spread the flat bottom of a cookie with about ½ cup sherbet. The sherbet will be about ¾ inch thick. Smooth the edges of the sherbet with a thin metal spatula. Top the sherbet with another cookie, flat side facing down. Put the filled sandwiches on the baking sheet in the freezer. Continue filling and freezing the remaining cookies. Remove the sandwiches from the freezer. Dip a fork in the melted white chocolate and wave it over the top of each sandwich to form thin lines of white chocolate crisscrossing back and forth over each sandwich. Move the fork quickly to create thin lines and work quickly so that the sherbet doesn't melt. Return the sandwiches to the freezer to firm the white chocolate, about 30 minutes.

Good Advice
· The sherbet may not need softening before spreading it on the cookies. If it scoops and spreads easily, do not soften it.

· Spread the sherbet on frozen cookies, to prevent the sherbet from melting.

· Put each sandwich in the freezer as soon as you fill it.

· You will not use all of the second pint of sherbet.

Doubling the Recipe
Prepare as many frozen sandwiches as you need. One recipe of Pistachio and White Chocolate Chip Crisps makes sixteen cookies.

To Freeze
Wrap each frozen sandwich in plastic wrap. Place in a metal or plastic freezer container and cover tightly. Label with date and contents. Freeze up to 1 week.

To Serve
Unwrap the sandwiches and serve frozen. Thin slices of orange make a nice garnish.

CHOCOLATE CHOCOLATE CHIP COOKIE ICE CREAM SANDWICHES WITH HOT FUDGE DIPPING SAUCE

Every time I would put these ice cream sandwiches on the menu at the restaurant, they'd sell out as fast as ice cream melts on a hot summer day. The almost-black cookies are a beautiful contrast to the white vanilla ice cream, and everyone enjoys having his or her own little pitcher of hot fudge sauce. If you have some Chocolate Chocolate Chip Cookies ready in your freezer, this dessert can be assembled in a matter of minutes.

MAKES 6 ICE CREAM SANDWICHES

12 Chocolate Chocolate Chip Cookies (page 62), frozen
2 pints vanilla ice cream, softened
1½ cups Uncle Howie's Hot Fudge Sauce (page 80) or Thick Chocolate Truffle Sauce (page 50), for serving

Choose pairs of cookies that are about the same size. Soften the ice cream about 20 minutes in the refrigerator, just until it is spreadable but not melted. Put a baking sheet in the freezer. Spread the flat bottom of a cookie with about ²/₃ cup ice cream. The ice cream will be about ¾ inch thick. Smooth the edges of the ice cream with a thin metal spatula. Top the ice cream with another cookie, flat side facing down. Put the ice cream sandwich on the baking sheet in the freezer. Continue filling and freezing the remaining cookies.

Good Advice

· Spread the ice cream on frozen cookies, to prevent the softened ice cream from melting.

· Put each ice cream sandwich in the freezer as soon as you fill it.

· You will not use all of the second pint of ice cream.

Doubling the Recipe

Prepare as many ice cream sandwiches as you need. A single recipe of Chocolate Chocolate Chip Cookies makes sixteen cookies.

To Freeze

Wrap each ice cream sandwich in plastic wrap. Place in a metal or plastic freezer container and cover tightly. Label with date and contents. Freeze up to 1 week.

To Serve

Warm the chocolate sauce in a medium saucepan over low heat, stirring frequently. Pour about ¼ cup fudge sauce into each of six small pitchers or small ramekins. Unwrap the ice cream sandwiches and serve each with warm fudge sauce.

OATMEAL TOFFEE CHIP COOKIE ICE CREAM SANDWICHES

Ice cream sandwiches require sturdy cookies, like these crunchy oatmeal toffee cookies, paired with creamy ice cream.

MAKES 8 ICE CREAM SANDWICHES

3 ounces semisweet chocolate, chopped
16 Oatmeal Toffee Chip Cookies (page 94), frozen
2 pints toffee crunch or vanilla ice cream

1. Preheat the oven to 175°F. Place the chocolate in an ovenproof container and melt it in the oven, about 8 minutes. As soon as the chocolate is melted, remove it from the oven and stir it smooth.

2. Choose pairs of cookies that are about the same size. Soften the ice cream about 20 minutes in the refrigerator, until it is spreadable but not melted. Put a baking sheet in the freezer. Spread the flat bottom of a cookie with about $1/2$ cup ice cream. The ice cream will be about $1/2$ inch thick. Smooth the edges of the ice cream with a thin metal spatula. Top the ice cream with another cookie, flat side facing down. Put the ice cream sandwich on the baking sheet in the freezer. Continue filling and freezing the remaining cookies.

3. Remove the sandwiches from the freezer. Dip a fork into the melted chocolate and wave it over the top of each sandwich to form lines of chocolate crisscrossing back and forth over each sandwich. Use all of the chocolate to cover the cookies heavily with chocolate. Work quickly so that the ice cream doesn't melt. Return the sandwiches to the freezer to firm the chocolate, about 30 minutes.

HOT FUDGE SUNDAE CHOCOLATE CHIP PIE

At the height of the summer visitor season, when I had to keep up with the demand at Peter Ott's restaurant and needed a scrumptious dessert that I could put together quickly, Hot Fudge Sundae Chocolate Chip Pie was it. It's a one-step pie that doesn't even require a pie crust. I cut the moist pie into wedges, top it with ice cream, cover it with hot fudge sauce, and can seldom resist testing a piece myself.

SERVES 8

CHOCOLATE CHIP PIE
2 cups unbleached all-purpose flour
1¼ teaspoons baking powder
½ teaspoon salt
1½ cups (packed) light brown sugar
6 tablespoons butter, melted
2 large eggs
1 large egg yolk
1 teaspoon vanilla extract
1 cup semisweet chocolate chips (6 ounces)

2 pints ice cream, for serving with the pie
1 cup Uncle Howie's Hot Fudge Sauce (page 80) or Thick Chocolate
  Truffle Sauce (page 50), warm, for serving with the pie

Prepare the Chocolate Chip Pie

1. Position an oven rack in the middle of the oven. Preheat the oven to 350°F. Butter a 10-inch pie pan.

2. Put the flour, baking powder, salt, and brown sugar in the large bowl of an electric mixer and mix on low speed for 15 seconds. Add the melted butter and mix just to blend the melted butter with the mixture. There will be a lot of loose flour. Add the eggs, egg yolk, and vanilla and mix until a smooth, thick batter forms. Stir in the chocolate chips. Spread the batter in the prepared pie pan.

3. Bake 25 minutes. The center will be a bit soft, and a toothpick inserted into the center will have moist crumbs, but not batter clinging to it. Cool thoroughly.

Good Advice
Serve the pie with a choice of ice cream. Coffee, chocolate, vanilla, cherry vanilla, and raspberry are good flavors with this.

Doubling the Recipe
Use 2 teaspoons baking powder, ¾ teaspoon salt, 5 large eggs, and double the remaining ingredients.

To Freeze
Wrap the cooled pie tightly with plastic wrap, then heavy aluminum foil. Label with date and contents. Freeze up to 2 months.

To Serve
Defrost the wrapped pie at room temperature at least 5 hours or overnight. Top the pie with a scoop of ice cream and spoon warm chocolate sauce over the ice cream. The sauce will drip onto the pie. Leftover pie may be wrapped in plastic wrap and stored at room temperature up to 2 days.

DARK CHOCOLATE AND CHUNKY BANANA ICE CREAM PIE

If you like frozen chocolate-covered bananas then this pie filled with vanilla ice cream and topped with chunks of bananas and dark chocolate truffle sauce is for you. The dark sauce forms an attractive lacy pattern over the bananas.

SERVES 10 TO 12

½ gallon vanilla ice cream, softened until spreadable but not melted
1 Chocolate Wafer Cookie Crumb Crust (page 40) or Oreo Cookie Crumb Crust (page 40) baked in a 9-inch springform pan, cooled or frozen
4 ripe bananas
½ cup Slightly Thinner Chocolate Truffle Sauce (page 50), warmed just until pourable
1 cup Slightly Thinner Chocolate Truffle Sauce (page 50), warm, for serving with the ice cream pie

Use an ice cream spade to spread the softened ice cream in the crumb crust, mounding the ice cream slightly toward center. Cut the bananas at an angle to form ½-inch chunks and place them evenly over the top of the pie. Use a teaspoon to drizzle the ½ cup chocolate sauce in a lacy pattern over the bananas.

· Once the bananas freeze they won't darken as freshly cut bananas do.

Doubling the Recipe

Use two chocolate crumb crusts and double the remaining ingredients.

To Freeze

Freeze the pie 30 minutes to firm the sauce. Wrap the pie tightly with plastic wrap, then cover with heavy aluminum foil, gently pressing the aluminum foil against the pie. Label with date and contents. Freeze overnight or up to 2 weeks. Once the pie is frozen, remove the springform pan. Rewrap with plastic wrap and foil and return to the freezer.

To Serve

Remove the ice cream pie from the freezer and let it soften at room temperature for about 10 minutes. Use a large sharp knife to cut the pie into wedges. Pass the warm chocolate sauce.

CHOCOLATE PEPPERMINT CRUNCH ICE CREAM PIE

Several years ago, I was invited to develop and to demonstrate dessert recipes in New York on behalf of chocolate manufacturers and candy producers. All of the desserts had to feature chocolate or candy as a major ingredient. My kind of assignment. If you can imagine going to the store and buying all the candy and chocolate you can carry, then using it to create desserts, you have some idea of how much fun I had developing the recipes. When it came time to demonstrate a dessert in front of all of those chocolate and candy people, I didn't take any chances and chose this ice cream pie filled with crushed peppermint candy and ripples of chocolate coating.

SERVES 10 TO 12

CHOCOLATE COATING
10 ounces semisweet chocolate, chopped, or semisweet chocolate chips
3 tablespoons vegetable oil

2 pints chocolate ice cream, softened until spreadable but not melted
1 Chocolate Wafer Cookie Crumb Crust (page 40) or Oreo Cookie
   Crumb Crust (page 40) baked in a 9-inch springform pan, cooled or
   frozen
1 cup peppermint candy, coarsely crushed (about $5^{1}/_{2}$ ounces)
2 pints peppermint ice cream, softened until spreadable but not melted
Small candy canes for serving with pie (optional)

Prepare the Chocolate Coating

1. Put the chocolate and vegetable oil in a heatproof container set over, but not touching, a saucepan of barely simmering water. Stir the mixture over the hot water until the chocolate is melted and the mixture is smooth. Remove the saucepan from over the heat. Makes about $1^{1}/_{8}$ cups.

2. Use an ice cream spade to spread the chocolate ice cream over the crumb crust. Sprinkle half of the peppermint candy evenly over the chocolate ice

Good Advice
· Peppermint ice cream is readily available year-round in Maine, but in New York it proved difficult to find. Substitute any mint-flavored ice cream.

· The coating firms quickly after it is removed from the heat, so leave the pan of coating over hot water until you use it.

· At holiday time, garnish each slice of pie with a candy cane.

Doubling the Recipe
Use two chocolate crumb crusts and double the remaining ingredients.

To Freeze
Freeze the pie 15 minutes to firm the coating. Wrap the pie tightly with plastic wrap, then cover with heavy aluminum foil, gently pressing the aluminum foil against the pie. Label with date and contents. Freeze

overnight or up to 2 weeks. Once the pie is frozen, you may remove the springform pan. Dip a dish towel in hot water and wring out the water. Hold the hot towel around the sides of the springform pan for 15 seconds. Release the sides of the pan. Either leave the pie on the springform bottom or slide it onto a serving plate. Rewrap with plastic wrap and foil and return to the freezer.

To Serve

Warm the reserved chocolate coating in the heatproof container over a saucepan of barely simmering water. Remove the ice cream pie from the freezer and let it soften at room temperature for about 10 minutes. Use a large sharp knife to cut the pie into wedges. Place a small candy cane in each slice of pie, if desired. Pour the warm chocolate coating into a small pitcher and pass with the pie.

cream. Use a teaspoon to drizzle 3 tablespoons of the chocolate coating evenly over the peppermint candy. Spread the softened peppermint ice cream evenly over the chocolate coating. Sprinkle the remaining peppermint candy evenly over the peppermint ice cream. Drizzle 2 tablespoons of chocolate coating in thin crisscrossing lines over the peppermint candy. Cover and refrigerate the leftover chocolate coating to serve with the pie. The chocolate coating can be refrigerated up to 2 weeks.

CHOCOLATE CHIP COOKIE DOUGH ICE CREAM PIE

*W*hen you start your own household, you can sometimes fulfill childhood dreams. One of the first things I did when I had my own home was to make a batch of chocolate chip cookie dough and eat it. Other people must have had this same desire because cookie dough is now a popular ingredient for ice cream. This dream-filled ice cream pie has a chocolate chip crumb crust that holds vanilla ice cream and a whole batch of chocolate chip cookie dough topped with some chocolate truffle sauce for good measure.

SERVES 10 TO 12

CHOCOLATE CHIP COOKIE DOUGH
5 tablespoons soft unsalted butter
1/3 cup (packed) light brown sugar
3 tablespoons granulated sugar
Pinch salt
1 teaspoon vanilla extract
1 tablespoon plus 1 teaspoon water
3/4 cup unbleached all-purpose flour
1 cup miniature semisweet chocolate chips (6 ounces)

1/2 gallon vanilla ice cream, softened until spreadable but not melted
1 Graham Cracker Crumb Crust with Chocolate Chips (page 40) baked in a 9-inch springform pan, cooled or frozen
3/4 cup Slightly Thinner Chocolate Truffle Sauce (page 50), warmed just until spreadable

Prepare the Chocolate Chip Cookie Dough

I. Put the butter, brown sugar, granulated sugar, and salt in the large bowl of an electric mixer. Beat on low speed until the mixture is smooth. Mix in the vanilla and water, just until it is incorporated. Mix in the flour, just until it is incorporated. Stir in the chocolate chips. Makes 2 cups cookie dough.

Good Advice

· You could substitute chocolate chip cookie dough ice cream from the supermarket and eliminate preparing the cookie dough. It's good, but there won't be such a generous amount of cookie dough in the pie.

· Since the chocolate chip cookie dough is not baked, the recipe contains no raw egg and requires no leavening ingredients.

Doubling the Recipe

Use two chocolate chip crumb crusts and double the remaining ingredients.

Freeze the pie 15 minutes to firm the sauce. Wrap the pie tightly with plastic wrap, then cover with heavy aluminum foil, gently pressing the aluminum foil against the pie. Label with date and contents. Freeze overnight or up to 2 weeks. Once the pie is frozen, you may remove the springform pan. Dip a dish towel in hot water and wring out the water. Hold the hot towel around the sides of the springform pan for 15 seconds. Release the sides of the pan. Either leave the pie on the springform bottom or slide it onto a serving plate. Rewrap with plastic wrap and foil and return to the freezer.

To Serve

Remove the ice cream pie from the freezer and let it soften at room temperature for about 10 minutes. Use a large sharp knife to cut the pie into wedges.

2. Use an ice cream spade to spread half of the softened ice cream over the crumb crust. Drop about $1\frac{1}{4}$ cups of the cookie dough in teaspoon-size pieces evenly over the ice cream. Drizzle $\frac{1}{4}$ cup of the chocolate sauce over the cookie dough. Spread the remainder of the ice cream over the cookie dough pieces. Drop the remainder of the cookie dough in teaspoon-size pieces evenly over the top of the pie. Drizzle the remaining $\frac{1}{2}$ cup of chocolate sauce over the cookie dough pieces.

Frozen Specialties

What do I serve for dessert when company comes? It's often one of these attractive desserts that don't require any last-minute preparation and can wait in the freezer until I'm ready for them. If a dessert requires unmolding from its pan, I turn it onto a serving platter and return it to the freezer until serving time. Several of the terrines are accompanied by a cold chocolate sauce, but when a dessert calls for a warm sauce, it can be heated up ahead of time and kept warm until needed.

Many of these desserts are mousses that are poured into a loaf pan and frozen. I add a sophisticated look to these terrines by using a long loaf pan that is about twelve inches long rather than the standard nine-inch loaf pan. Lining the bottom of the loaf pan with parchment paper ensures that the desserts release easily from the pan. I tried substituting wax paper, but it tears easily after being moistened by the mousse mixtures. Buttering the bottom of a loaf pan holds the parchment paper liner in place, but the sides of the loaf pan don't need to be buttered. To remove mousse-type desserts from their pan, loosen the sides with a sharp knife, invert them, and pull on the ends of the parchment paper to release the mousse from the pan. Ice cream desserts require the hot towel method for easy removal. Dip a dish towel in hot water and wring out the water. Wrap the hot towel around the sides of an inverted pan for fifteen seconds, pull on the ends of the parchment paper, and the ice cream will release from the pan.

HELEN'S CHOCOLATE AND CARAMEL WALNUT MERINGUE CAKE

I hope you have friends like Helen Hall, who cook so well that you diet for days before going to dinner at their houses. We enjoyed this cake at Helen's home many years ago and when Helen told me how well it freezes, I knew it belonged in this book.

S E R V E S   8   T O   1 0

WALNUT MERINGUES
6 large egg whites
1/2 teaspoon cream of tartar
1 1/4 cups sugar
1 cup toasted walnuts, ground (see page 12)

CHOCOLATE AND COFFEE-CARAMEL FILLINGS
6 ounces semisweet chocolate, chopped
1/3 cup water
1/2 cup sugar
2 tablespoons hot water
3/4 teaspoon instant decaffeinated coffee granules
1/3 cup hot whipping cream
1 1/2 cups cold whipping cream

Prepare the Walnut Meringues

1. Position 2 oven racks in the middle and upper third of the oven. Preheat the oven to 275°F. Cut 2 pieces of parchment paper to fit two 18 × 12-inch baking sheets. Mark two 8-inch circles on each piece of parchment paper. Line the baking sheets with the parchment, marked side down.

2. Put the egg whites and cream of tartar in a clean large bowl of an electric mixer and with clean dry beaters beat on low speed until the egg whites are frothy. Increase the speed to medium-high and beat until soft peaks form. Reduce the speed to medium and slowly beat in 5 tablespoons of the sugar, 1 tablespoon every 30 seconds. Use a large rubber spatula to fold in the remaining sugar and ground walnuts. Use a thin metal spatula to spread the meringue mixture evenly over the 4 marked circles. Smooth the edges of the circles with

· The meringue mixture is mixed differently and more quickly than classic meringues. Most of the sugar is added all at once rather than slowly.

· The meringues bake crisp, but once filled they take on a pleasant but soft, sticky quality if chilled overnight. Since the cake does not become hard when it is frozen, I serve it frozen and never worry about soft meringues.

· Chill the caramel just until it is cool to the touch but not firm. Firm caramel will not combine smoothly with the whipped cream.

Doubling the Recipe
Double all the ingredients. Use a 5-quart bowl to mix the meringue mixture. Use four baking sheets to bake the meringues.

the metal spatula. The meringues will be about $\frac{1}{2}$ inch thick. Bake about $1\frac{1}{2}$ hours, or until the meringues are crisp and dry. Cool the meringues thoroughly on the baking sheets. Peel the parchment paper from the meringues.

Prepare the Chocolate and Coffee-Caramel Fillings

3. Put the chocolate and water in a small saucepan. Stir over low heat until the chocolate melts and the mixture is smooth. Put the chocolate mixture in a medium bowl and cover and refrigerate until the mixture is cool to the touch, but still soft and creamy, about 30 minutes.

4. Put the sugar and hot water in a medium frying pan, about 8 inches diameter. Cook over medium-high heat until the sugar melts, caramelizes, and turns a dark golden color, about 4 minutes. Watch the sugar carefully and stir it with a wooden spoon occasionally to ensure the sugar cooks evenly and all of the sugar caramelizes. Remove from the heat.

5. Stir the instant coffee into the hot cream to dissolve the coffee. Add the coffee mixture to the caramel. The mixture will bubble up, so be careful. Return the pan to low heat to melt any caramel that is not dissolved. Cool 5 minutes. Pour the caramel into a small bowl, cover, and refrigerate until the caramel is cool to the touch, about 20 minutes. Or let the caramel cool at room temperature for 1 hour. The caramel will thicken as it cools. Do not let it get firm.

6. Put the cold cream in the large bowl of an electric mixer. Beat the cream at medium speed until soft peaks form. Put 1 cup of the whipped cream in a medium bowl and whisk in the cool caramel mixture. Set aside. Whisk about $\frac{1}{4}$ cup of whipped cream into the chocolate mixture. Use a large rubber spatula to fold the chocolate into the remaining whipped cream.

7. Place a meringue layer on a serving plate. Spread 1 cup of the chocolate cream evenly over the meringue. Top with another meringue layer and spread the caramel cream over the meringue. Top the cake with another meringue layer and spread 1 cup of the chocolate cream evenly over the meringue. Top the cake with the fourth meringue layer. Fit a pastry bag with a $\frac{1}{4}$-inch plain tip, fill the pastry bag with the remaining chocolate cream, and pipe it in the space between the meringue layers to form a smooth edge.

To Freeze the Meringues

Stack the meringues on a cardboard cake circle or plate, placing plastic wrap between each layer. Carefully wrap the stack of meringues with plastic wrap then heavy aluminum foil. Do not stack anything on top of the meringues. Do not defrost the meringues before using them. The meringues can be frozen for up to 1 month.

To Freeze

Wrap with plastic wrap. Gently press heavy aluminum foil around the cake. Label with date and contents. Freeze up to 1 month.

To Serve

Remove the cake from the freezer 10 minutes before serving time. Dust the top of the cake with powdered sugar. Cut into slices and serve. The meringues and filling do not freeze hard.

CHOCOLATE HAZELNUT PRALINE MARQUISE

Traditionally, a chocolate marquise is a chocolate mousse enriched with butter that has a denser and more silken texture than a classic mousse. The marquise mixture is usually poured into a terrine or loaf pan, unmolded, and served sliced. I often have trouble with it breaking or falling apart when I remove it from the mold, so I decided to try a frozen one. The dessert freezes firm but never hard, unmolds beautifully, and makes a safe marquise.

SERVES 12

$^3/_4$ cup whipping cream
$^1/_4$ pound (1 stick) unsalted butter, cut into 8 pieces
12 ounces semisweet chocolate, chopped
4 large eggs, separated
1 teaspoon vanilla extract
$^1/_4$ teaspoon cream of tartar
$^1/_4$ cup sugar
$^3/_4$ cup ground hazelnut praline (see page 54)
$^1/_2$ cup crushed hazelnut praline (see page 54), for serving

I. Cut a long piece of parchment paper to fit the bottom and overlap the ends of a long narrow loaf pan with a 7- to 8-cup capacity. Use a pan about $12^3/_4 \times 4^1/_4 \times 2^1/_2$ inches. Butter the bottom of the pan and press the parchment paper strip onto the bottom and over the ends of the pan.

2. Put the cream and butter in a medium saucepan and heat over medium-low heat until the cream is hot and the butter is melted. The hot cream mixture will form tiny bubbles around the edge of the pan and measure about 175°F. on a food thermometer. Do not let the mixture boil. Remove the pan from the heat. Add the chopped chocolate, and let it melt in the hot cream mixture for about 30 seconds to soften. Stir the mixture smooth. Put the egg yolks in a small bowl and whisk to break up the yolks. Whisk the yolks into the warm chocolate mixture until they are blended thoroughly. Stir in the vanilla. Return the saucepan to the

Good Advice
· Use a whisk to beat the egg yolks into the warm chocolate mixture and you won't have a problem with the egg yolks curdling as they combine with the warm mixture.

· Use a long loaf pan for the marquise for narrow slices that make a good size for this rich dessert.

· Since the crushed praline topping softens after about 1 week in the freezer, add it when serving the dessert.

Doubling the Recipe
Double all ingredients and use two loaf pans.

heat and cook, stirring constantly, until the temperature measures 160°F. on a food thermometer, about 3 minutes. Pour the mixture into a large bowl and refrigerate until it is cool to the touch, about 30 minutes.

3. Put the egg whites and cream of tartar in a clean large bowl of an electric mixer and with clean dry beaters beat on low speed until the egg whites are foamy. Increase the speed to medium-high and beat just until soft peaks form. Slowly add the sugar, 1 tablespoon at a time. Remove the cooled chocolate mixture from the refrigerator, and whisk about a fourth of the beaten egg whites into the chocolate mixture. Use a rubber spatula to fold in the remaining beaten egg whites. Fold in the ground hazelnut praline. Pour the mixture into the prepared pan.

VARIATION Omit the hazelnut praline for a pure chocolate marquise.

To Freeze

Wrap the marquise tightly with plastic wrap, then heavy aluminum foil. Label with date and contents. Freeze overnight or up to 3 weeks.

To Serve

Remove the marquise from the freezer and unwrap. Use a small sharp knife to loosen the sides of the terrine from the pan. Place a long narrow serving plate on top of the marquise and invert it onto the plate. Release the marquise from the pan by pulling on the ends of the parchment paper and removing the pan. Remove the parchment paper. Sprinkle the crushed hazelnut praline over the top of the marquise. Cut the frozen marquise into slices with a large sharp knife.

SWEET MYSTERY CARAMEL AND CHOCOLATE TERRINE

When you slice into this terrine, the two colors of mousse form a triangular pattern. Guests will be impressed and try to work out how you made such a complicated dessert. As you'll see, it's quite easy, but you're welcome to keep it a sweet mystery.

SERVES 12

1 cup half-and-half
4 large egg yolks
⅓ cup sugar
4 ounces white chocolate, Callebaut or Baker's Premium preferred, finely chopped
¾ cup Caramel Filling (page 52), defrosted or cooled
6 ounces semisweet chocolate, finely chopped
2 cups cold whipping cream
1 teaspoon vanilla extract
1½ cups Dark Chocolate Sauce (page 49), cold, for serving

I. Have ready a baking sheet with 1-inch-high sides or jelly-roll pan. Cut a long piece of parchment paper to fit the bottom and extend over the ends of a long narrow loaf pan with a 7- to 8-cup capacity. Use a pan that measures about 12¾ × 4¼ × 2½ inches. Butter the bottom of the pan and press the parchment paper strip onto the bottom and over the ends of the pan. Rest the bottom of the loaf pan lengthwise along a rim of the baking sheet so that it is tilted at an angle. Put 2 small dishes or bowls on the baking sheet against the bottom of the loaf pan to hold it in place. Weight the dishes with small cans, such as tomato paste cans, to prevent the dishes from sliding. Set aside.

2. Put the half-and-half in a medium saucepan and heat over medium-low heat until hot. The half-and-half will form tiny bubbles around the edge of the pan and measure about 175°F. on a food thermometer. Do not let the half-and-half boil.

Good Advice

· The triangular pattern for the dessert is formed by a tilted loaf pan.

· Since the chocolate mixture is thick enough to hold its shape after it is spread in the pan and firms up faster than the caramel mixture, pour it into the loaf pan first.

· Lightly butter the bottom of the pan to hold the parchment paper secure when the pan is tilted.

Doubling the Recipe

Double the ingredients and use two loaf pans.

3. Put the egg yolks in a medium bowl and use a whisk to mix the sugar into the yolks. Pour the hot half-and-half over the egg yolk mixture while whisking constantly. Pour the mixture back into the saucepan and cook over medium heat, stirring constantly, until the mixture measures 165°F. on a food thermometer. Remove from the heat.

4. Measure ¾ cup of the hot mixture into a large bowl. Mix in the white chocolate and stir until it is melted and smooth. Stir in the caramel filling. Stir the semisweet chocolate into the hot mixture in the saucepan, stirring until the chocolate is melted and smooth. Pour the dark chocolate mixture into a medium bowl. Cover each bowl with plastic wrap and refrigerate just until cool to the touch, about 30 minutes. Stir the mixture occasionally to ensure it cools evenly.

5. Put the cream and vanilla in a clean large bowl of an electric mixer and beat on medium-high speed to soft peaks. Use a rubber spatula to fold half of the cream into the cooled caramel mixture and half of the cream into the cooled chocolate mixture. Cover the caramel mixture with plastic wrap and refrigerate. Pour the chocolate mixture along the lower edge of the prepared loaf pan. Use a thin metal spatula to smooth the angled side of the chocolate mixture. A thin layer of the chocolate mixture should reach to the tilted edge of the pan. You will have a loaf pan half filled with a triangle of chocolate mixture. Carefully put the tilted loaf pan on the baking sheet into the freezer. Freeze until firm, about 1 hour. The chocolate mixture will now hold its angled shape and you can remove the loaf pan from the baking sheet. Pour the cold caramel mixture over the chocolate. Smooth the top.

To Freeze

Freeze the terrine, uncovered, for about 2 hours, until it is cold and firm. Wrap tightly with plastic wrap, then heavy aluminum foil. Label with date and contents. Freeze up to 3 weeks.

To Serve

Remove the terrine from the freezer and unwrap. Use a small sharp knife to loosen the sides of the terrine from the pan. Place a long, narrow serving plate on top of the terrine and invert it. Release the terrine from the pan by pulling on the ends of the parchment paper and removing the pan. Remove the parchment paper. Cut the frozen terrine into slices with a large sharp knife. Spoon chocolate sauce around 1 side of each slice of mousse.

ICED FRESH GINGER MOUSSE WITH DARK CHOCOLATE SAUCE

*S*picy and refreshing, these creamy slices of frozen mousse make a stunning contrast to the almost black chocolate sauce. Steeping fresh ginger in cream and using a garlic press to crush juice from fresh ginger into the mousse lends an assertive ginger flavor to the dessert.

SERVES 12

FRESH GINGER MOUSSE
1/4 cup cold water
1/4 cup coarsely grated peeled fresh ginger
1 3/4 cups cold whipping cream
4 ounces white chocolate, Callebaut or Baker's Premium preferred, chopped
1/3 cup hot water
3/4 cup plus 1 tablespoon sugar
1 tablespoon light corn syrup
4 large egg whites
1/2 teaspoon cream of tartar
1 tablespoon chopped peeled fresh ginger
1 teaspoon vanilla extract

1 1/2 cups Dark Chocolate Sauce (page 49), cold, for serving with the mousse
1/4 cup coarsely chopped crystallized ginger, for serving with the mousse (optional)

Prepare the Fresh Ginger Mousse

1. Cut a long piece of parchment paper to fit the bottom and overlap the ends of a long narrow loaf pan with a 7- to 8-cup capacity. Use a pan that measures about 12 3/4 × 4 1/4 × 2 1/2 inches. Butter the bottom of the pan and press the parchment paper strip onto the bottom and over the ends of the pan.

2. Put the cold water and grated ginger in a small saucepan and cook over medium heat until most of the water evaporates, stirring occasionally, about 3 minutes. Add 1/2 cup of the cream and cook just until small bubbles form around the edge of the saucepan. Do not boil the cream. Put the ginger mixture in a small bowl, cover, and refrigerate for 1 hour or overnight.

Good Advice
· Grate peeled ginger on the large teardrop holes of a grater. Grate from large pieces of ginger to protect your hands from getting scraped.

· The addition of white chocolate to the mousse helps it remain creamy when frozen.

· The mousse is made with Italian meringue. For more detail on preparing Italian meringue, see page 10.

Doubling the Recipe
Double all ingredients. Use a 5-quart mixing bowl for preparing the Italian meringue.

3. Preheat the oven to 175°F. Place the white chocolate in a nonreactive oven-proof container and melt it in the oven, 8 to 10 minutes. As soon as the white chocolate is melted, remove it from the oven and stir it smooth. Set aside.

4. Put the hot water, ¾ cup sugar, and corn syrup in a clean small saucepan. Cover the saucepan and cook the syrup over low heat until all of the sugar is dissolved, stirring occasionally to help the sugar dissolve. Do not let the syrup boil until the sugar dissolves. Increase the heat to high and boil without stirring until the syrup reaches 240°F. (soft ball stage) measured on a candy thermometer. Brush the sides of the pan with a brush dipped in hot water to dissolve any sugar crystals that form on the sides of the pan.

5. When the syrup begins to boil, start beating the egg whites. Put the egg whites and cream of tartar in a clean large bowl of an electric mixer and with clean dry beaters beat on low speed for 30 seconds, just to dissolve the cream of tartar. Increase the speed to medium-high and beat the egg whites to soft peaks. Add the 1 tablespoon sugar. As soon as the syrup reaches 240°F. and with the mixer on low speed, slowly pour the hot syrup in a thin stream onto the egg whites. If the syrup reaches 240°F. before the egg whites are ready, remove the syrup from the heat for a few seconds and finish beating the egg whites. Try to pour the syrup in the space between the sides of the bowl and the beaters to prevent as much sugar syrup as possible from splashing onto the sides of the bowl and the beaters. Increase the speed to medium and beat the meringue for 5 minutes. The outside of the bowl will be lukewarm and the meringue will be stiff and have a temperature of 72° to 78°F. if measured with a food thermometer. Use a large rubber spatula to fold the melted white chocolate into the meringue.

6. Place a strainer over the large bowl of an electric mixer. Pour the chilled ginger mixture into the strainer. Press firmly on the mixture to extract as much cream as possible from the ginger. Remove the strainer and discard the ginger. Put half of the chopped ginger in a clean garlic press, hold the press over the cream in the mixing bowl, and press to extract the ginger juice. Repeat with the remaining chopped ginger. Add the remaining 1¼ cups cream and the vanilla to the bowl and beat on medium speed to soft peaks. Use a large rubber spatula to fold half of the whipped cream into the meringue. Fold the remaining whipped cream into the meringue. Pour the mousse into the prepared pan and smooth the top.

To Freeze

Wrap the mousse tightly with plastic wrap, then heavy aluminum foil. Label with date and contents. Freeze overnight or up to 3 weeks.

To Serve

Remove the mousse from the freezer and unwrap. Use a small sharp knife to loosen the sides of the terrine from the pan. Place a long narrow serving plate on top of the mousse and invert it. Release the mousse from the pan by pulling on the ends of the parchment paper and removing the pan. Remove the parchment paper. Cut the frozen mousse into slices with a large sharp knife. Spoon chocolate sauce around 1 side of each slice of mousse. Scatter several pieces of crystallized ginger on the plate, if desired.

STRIPED WHITE CHOCOLATE AND STRAWBERRY TERRINE

Layers of white chocolate and strawberry mousse form the pink and white stripes in this frozen dessert. Thanks to a generous measure of white chocolate and whipped cream, the frozen terrine has a nice creamy texture.

SERVES 12

1 pint fresh strawberries, washed and hulled
8 ounces white chocolate, Callebaut or Baker's Premium preferred, chopped
1/3 cup hot water
3/4 cup plus 1 tablespoon sugar
1 tablespoon light corn syrup
4 large egg whites
1/2 teaspoon cream of tartar
1 3/4 cups cold whipping cream
1 teaspoon vanilla extract
1 tablespoon Grand Marnier
Fresh strawberries with stems, for garnish

1. Cut a long piece of parchment paper to fit the bottom and overlap the ends of a long narrow loaf pan with a 7- to 8-cup capacity. Use a pan about 12 3/4 × 4 1/4 × 2 1/2 inches. Butter the bottom of the pan and press the parchment paper strip onto the bottom and over the ends of the pan.

2. Puree the strawberries in a food processor until they are smooth. You will have about 1 1/4 cups puree.

3. Preheat the oven to 175°F. Place the white chocolate in a nonreactive oven-proof container and melt it in the oven, 8 to 10 minutes. As soon as the white chocolate is melted, remove it from the oven and stir it smooth.

4. Put the hot water, 3/4 cup sugar, and corn syrup in a clean small saucepan. Cover the saucepan and cook the syrup over low heat until all of the sugar is dissolved, stirring occasionally to help the sugar dissolve. Do not let the syrup boil until the sugar dissolves. Increase the heat to high and boil without stirring until the syrup reaches 240°F. (soft ball stage) on a candy thermometer. Brush the

Good Advice
· Freeze each layer of mousse firm before adding another layer. Check by touching each layer gently with your finger.

· Spread the mousse evenly to the sides of the pan to form even stripes.

· Since the white chocolate is melted without other ingredients, melt it in the oven.

· The mousse is made with Italian meringue. For more detail on preparing Italian meringue, see page 10.

Doubling the Recipe
Double all ingredients. Use a 5-quart mixing bowl for preparing the Italian meringue.

To Freeze
Freeze the terrine, uncovered, for about 1 hour to firm the top. Wrap the terrine tightly with plastic wrap, then heavy aluminum foil. Label with date and contents. Freeze overnight or up to 3 weeks.

sides of the pan with a brush dipped in hot water to dissolve any sugar crystals that form on the sides of the pan.

5. When the syrup begins to boil, start beating the egg whites. Put the egg whites and cream of tartar in a clean large bowl of an electric mixer and with clean dry beaters beat on low speed for 30 seconds, just to dissolve the cream of tartar. Increase the speed to medium-high and beat the egg whites to soft peaks. Add the 1 tablespoon sugar. As soon as the syrup reaches 240°F. and with the mixer on low speed, slowly pour the hot syrup in a thin stream onto the egg whites. If the syrup reaches 240°F. before the egg whites are ready, remove the syrup from the heat for a few seconds and finish beating the egg whites. Try to pour the syrup in the space between the sides of the bowl and the beaters to prevent as much sugar syrup as possible from splashing onto the sides of the bowl and the beaters. Increase the speed to medium and beat the meringue for 5 minutes. The outside of the bowl will be lukewarm and the meringue will be stiff and have a temperature of about 72° to 78°F. if measured with a food thermometer. Use a large rubber spatula to fold the melted white chocolate into the meringue.

6. Put the cream and vanilla in a large bowl of an electric mixer and beat on medium speed to soft peaks. Use a large rubber spatula to fold half of the whipped cream into the meringue, then fold in the remaining whipped cream. There will be about 7 cups of mousse.

7. Put 2 cups of the white chocolate mousse in a medium bowl. Reserve 2 tablespoons of strawberry puree and fold the remaining puree and the Grand Marnier into the 2 cups of mousse. Pour half of the remaining white chocolate mousse, about 2½ cups, into the prepared pan. Spread the mousse into an even layer in the pan. Freeze until firm, about 15 minutes. Test by touching gently with your finger. Refrigerate the remaining white chocolate and strawberry mixtures while the mousse freezes firm. Pour the strawberry mixture into the pan and smooth the top. Freeze until firm, about 15 minutes. Pour the remaining white chocolate mousse into the pan and smooth the top. Drizzle the reserved strawberry puree over the top of the terrine and with the tip of a knife swirl the puree to form a marbleized pattern.

To Serve

Remove the terrine from the freezer and unwrap. Use a small sharp knife to loosen the sides of the terrine from the pan. Place a long narrow serving plate or foil-covered cardboard rectangle on top of the mousse and invert it. Release the mousse from the pan by pulling on the ends of the parchment paper and removing the pan. Remove the parchment paper. Using a long wide spatula to help support the mousse, turn the mousse over so it is marbleized side up. The frozen mousse is sturdy and will not break. Cut the frozen mousse into slices with a large sharp knife. Garnish with whole fresh strawberries or strawberry fans. To make strawberry fans, slice strawberries lengthwise from tip to stem leaving about ½ inch of the stem end intact. Gently spread the sliced portion into a fan shape.

FROZEN MILKY WAY MOUSSE WITH DARK CHOCOLATE SAUCE

*R*emember treating yourself to frozen Milky Way candy bars *when you were a kid? Here's a grown-up frozen mousse version.*

SERVES 12

1½ cups Milky Way candy bars cut into ½-inch pieces (about 6½ ounces)
3 ounces unsweetened chocolate, chopped
6 ounces semisweet chocolate, chopped
2 ounces unsalted butter
3 tablespoons hot water
½ cup plus 1 tablespoon sugar
1 tablespoon light corn syrup
3 large egg whites
¼ teaspoon cream of tartar
1¼ cups cold whipping cream
1 teaspoon vanilla extract
1½ cups Dark Chocolate Sauce (page 49), cold, for serving

1. Cut a long piece of parchment paper to fit the bottom and overlap the ends of a long narrow loaf pan with a 7- to 8-cup capacity. Use a pan about 12¾ × 4¼ × 2½ inches. Butter the bottom of the pan and press the parchment paper strip onto the bottom and over the ends of the pan.

2. Put the Milky Way pieces, unsweetened chocolate, semisweet chocolate, and butter in a heatproof container set over, but not touching, a saucepan of gently simmering water. Stir the mixture constantly until the ingredients are melted and smooth. Pour the chocolate mixture into a large bowl and set aside to cool slightly.

3. Put the hot water, ½ cup sugar, and corn syrup in a clean small saucepan. Cover the saucepan and cook the syrup over low heat until all of the sugar is dissolved, stirring occasionally to help the sugar dissolve. Do not let the syrup boil until the sugar dissolves. Increase the heat to high and boil without stirring un-

Good Advice
· Stir the Milky Way pieces constantly over hot water and they will melt smoothly.

· The mousse is made with Italian meringue. For more detail on preparing Italian meringue, see page 10.

Doubling the Recipe
Double all ingredients. Use a 5-quart mixing bowl for preparing the Italian meringue.

til the syrup reaches 240°F. (soft ball stage) on a candy thermometer. Brush the sides of the pan with a brush dipped in hot water to dissolve any sugar crystals that form on the sides of the pan.

4. When the syrup begins to boil, start beating the egg whites. Put the egg whites and cream of tartar in a clean large bowl of an electric mixer and with clean dry beaters beat on low speed for 30 seconds, just to dissolve the cream of tartar. Increase the speed to medium-high and beat the egg whites to soft peaks. Add the 1 tablespoon sugar. As soon as the syrup reaches 240°F. and with the mixer on low speed, slowly pour the hot syrup in a thin stream onto the egg whites. If the syrup reaches 240°F. before the egg whites are ready, remove the syrup from the heat for a few seconds and finish beating the egg whites. Try to pour the syrup in the space between the sides of the bowl and the beaters to prevent as much sugar syrup as possible from splashing onto the sides of the bowl and the beaters. Increase the speed to medium and beat the meringue for about 4 minutes. The outside of the bowl will be lukewarm and the meringue will be stiff and have a temperature of about 72° to 78°F. if measured with a food thermometer. Use a large rubber spatula to fold half of the meringue mixture into the chocolate mixture, then fold in the remaining meringue.

5. Put the cream and vanilla in a large bowl of an electric mixer and beat on medium speed to soft peaks. Use a large rubber spatula to fold half of the whipped cream into the chocolate mixture, then fold in the remaining whipped cream. Pour the mixture into the prepared pan.

To Freeze
Wrap the mousse tightly with plastic wrap, then heavy aluminum foil. Label with date and contents. Freeze overnight or up to 3 weeks.

To Serve
Remove the mousse from the freezer and unwrap. Use a small sharp knife to loosen the sides of the terrine from the pan. Place a long narrow serving plate on top of the mousse and invert it onto the plate. Release the mousse from the pan by pulling on the ends of the parchment paper and removing the pan. Remove the parchment paper. Slice the mousse into 12 slices, about 1 inch wide. Cut each slice diagonally into 2 triangles. Arrange 2 triangles on each plate. A large offset spatula works well for moving the mousse triangles onto a plate. Spoon cold chocolate sauce around the mousse.

· After the reese roll is covered with the warm chocolate sauce and served, it should not be returned to the freezer.

Doubling the Recipe

Use two chocolate soufflé cake sheets and double the remaining ingredients.

To Freeze

Wrap the cake roll or rolls tightly with plastic wrap. Gently press heavy aluminum foil around each roll. Label with date and contents. Freeze up to 10 days.

To Serve

Unwrap the frozen filled cake roll and put it on a long platter. Spoon 1 cup of warm truffle sauce over the top of the roll. Sprinkle with toasted almonds. Use a large sharp knife to cut the roll into 1/2-inch slices and serve 2 slices for each serving. Overlap the slices on the plate. Pass the remaining warm truffle sauce. To serve an 8-inch roll, pour 1/2 cup sauce over the roll, sprinkle with 1/3 cup almonds, and pass 1/2 cup sauce.

GRANDMA TILLIE'S REESE ROLL

When Uncle Norman Klivans suggested that I put his mother's recipe for reese roll in my book, I sat up and took notice. If he was that interested in a recipe, it must be special since he has no interest in baking. The details of the dessert were a vivid memory. The thin chocolate cake rolled with mint chip ice cream was drenched with a bittersweet chocolate sauce (a thin sauce, not too fudgy or sweet—he was very specific about this) and topped with toasted sliced almonds. Uncle Norman was right: Grandma's reese roll is worth remembering.

MAKES 1 ROLL ABOUT 16 INCHES LONG OR
2 ROLLS ABOUT 8 INCHES LONG

1 baked Chocolate Soufflé Cake Sheet (page 46), cold or defrosted just until soft enough to roll
1/2 cup Slightly Thinner Chocolate Truffle Sauce (page 50), warmed just until spreadable
3 pints mint chocolate chip ice cream, softened just until spreadable but not melted
2 cups Slightly Thinner Chocolate Truffle Sauce (page 50), warm, for serving with 1 full-size roll or two 8-inch rolls
2/3 cup toasted sliced blanched almonds (see page 12), for serving with 1 full-size roll or two 8-inch rolls

Unwrap the cake sheet, and unroll it onto a clean dish towel. Remove any plastic wrap. The long side of the cake roll should be parallel to the edge of the counter. Use a thin metal spatula to spread the 1/2 cup truffle sauce in a thin layer evenly over the cake. Spread about 5 cups of ice cream evenly over the sauce, leaving about a 3/4-inch plain edge at the far end. The ice cream will be about 1/2 inch thick. Using the dish towel to help, roll the cake into a tight roll. Smooth the edges of the ice cream at the ends of the roll. If desired, cut the cake into 2 rolls.

MOCHA AND ALMOND PRALINE MERINGUE BOMBE

Traditionally, a bombe is a dome-shaped dessert with an outer layer of ice cream and a frozen custard center. The frozen custard is similar to unchurned ice cream so I take the easier, and just-as-good route, and make my bombes entirely with store-bought ice cream. By varying ice cream flavors and colors I achieve the desired contrasting layers. Besides ice cream layers, bombes usually include something crunchy or nutty. Here dark chocolate almond praline meringues play a dual role. For chewiness they're sprinkled between the layers of coffee and chocolate ice cream and for crunchiness they're pressed into the outside of the bombe to make a crisp covering.

SERVES 10

CHOCOLATE ALMOND PRALINE MERINGUES

3 tablespoons unsweetened Dutch process cocoa powder, such as Droste or Hershey's European Style
½ cup powdered sugar
3 large egg whites
¼ teaspoon cream of tartar
⅓ cup granulated sugar
1 teaspoon vanilla extract
½ cup ground almond praline (see page 54)

3 pints premium coffee ice cream, softened just until spreadable but not melted
1½ pints premium chocolate ice cream, softened just until spreadable but not melted
1 cup Slightly Thinner Chocolate Truffle Sauce (page 50), warm, for serving

Prepare the Chocolate Almond Praline Meringues

I. Position the oven rack in the middle of the oven. Preheat the oven to 275°F. Cut a piece of parchment paper to fit a baking sheet. Line the baking sheet with the parchment paper.

Good Advice

· This dessert uses pieces of meringue. Simply spread the meringue mixture on a baking sheet, bake it, and break it up. This meringue mixture deflates slightly as it bakes and forms a nice thin, crisp meringue.

· The crushed meringue that is layered with the ice cream softens during freezing but the crushed meringue covering is added at serving time so it remains crisp.

Doubling the Recipe

Double the ingredients and make two bombes.

To Freeze the Meringue

Seal the crushed meringue tightly in a plastic freezer bag and freeze for up to 1 month. It is not necessary to defrost the meringue before using it.

To Freeze the Bombe

Return the remaining crushed meringue (about 2¼ cups) in the sealed bag to the freezer. Cover the bombe tightly with plastic wrap then heavy aluminum foil. Label with date and contents. Freeze overnight or up to 1 week.

Unmold the bombe at least 1 hour or up to 6 hours before serving. Chill the serving plate for about 15 minutes. Remove the bombe from the freezer and unwrap it. Dip a dish towel in hot water and wring out the water. Press the hot towel onto the sides of the bowl for about 25 seconds. Repeat the process with the hot towel. Place the chilled serving plate on top of the bombe and invert the bombe onto the plate. Discard the paper liner. If the bombe does not release easily, repeat the process with the hot towel. Press the reserved crushed meringue firmly over the outside of the bombe. Sprinkle any powdered meringue over the top. Return the bombe to the freezer for 30 minutes to firm the ice cream. Use a large sharp knife to cut the bombe into wedges. Serve with warm chocolate sauce.

2. Sift the cocoa powder and powdered sugar into a small bowl and set aside. Put the egg whites and cream of tartar in a clean large bowl of an electric mixer and with clean dry beaters beat on low speed for about 30 seconds, or until the egg whites are frothy. Increase the speed to medium-high and beat until soft peaks form. Decrease the speed to medium and gradually beat in the granulated sugar, 1 tablespoon at a time. Add the vanilla. Use a rubber spatula to fold the ground almond praline into the meringue mixture. Fold the powdered sugar mixture into the egg whites. Spread the meringue mixture on the prepared baking sheet in a rough rectangle about 13×9 inches and $1/2$ inch thick.

3. Bake about 2 hours, or until the meringue is crisp and dry. Cool the meringue thoroughly on the baking sheet. Peel the parchment paper from the meringue. Crush the meringue with a meat pounder or rolling pin into approximately $1/4$- to $1/2$-inch pieces. Some of the meringue will become powder; use this on the outside of the meringue. You will have about 4 cups of meringue pieces of varying size.

4. Chill a deep round 2-quart bowl or metal mold in the freezer for 15 minutes. Cut a small piece of parchment or wax paper to fit the bottom of the bowl and place it in the bowl. Use an ice cream spade to line the bottom and sides of the chilled bowl with $2^1/2$ pints of the coffee ice cream. The ice cream layer will be about 1 inch thick. Press plastic wrap over the ice cream and freeze until the ice cream is firm, about 1 hour. Remove the bowl from the freezer and discard the plastic wrap. Use the back of a spoon or ice cream spade to smooth the coffee ice cream layer for a smooth-looking edge when the bombe is cut. Pour about $1/4$ cup of the meringue pieces over the bottom of the ice cream. Press about 1 cup of meringue pieces in a thick layer onto the sides of the ice cream. Spread about $1/2$ pint of the chocolate ice cream in the center of the bombe and sprinkle with $1/4$ cup meringue pieces. Repeat the layering of ice cream and meringue and top the meringue pieces with the remaining $1/2$ pint of chocolate ice cream. Spread the remaining coffee ice cream over the chocolate ice cream to form a smooth top.

MACADAMIA
PRALINE
ICE CREAM LOAF

Macadamia nuts are pricey, but a small amount delivers elegance and rich buttery-nutty flavor to a dessert—good value as I see it. Softer than most nuts, macadamias make a hard-crunch praline. Vanilla, raspberry, and chocolate ice cream, separated by the crushed praline and Slightly Thinner Chocolate Truffle Sauce, form the layers of this tricolor loaf. I prefer macadamia nuts as a crushed praline rather than a ground praline since their distinctive, but mild, flavor is lost when ground.

SERVES 10 TO 12

1 pint raspberry ice cream, softened until spreadable but not melted
1 cup crushed macadamia praline (see page 54)
1/2 cup Slightly Thinner Chocolate Truffle Sauce (page 50), warmed just
  until pourable
1 pint vanilla ice cream, softened until spreadable but not melted
1 pint chocolate ice cream, softened until spreadable but not melted
1 cup crushed macadamia praline (see page 54), for serving
1 cup Slightly Thinner Chocolate Truffle Sauce (page 50), warm, for
  serving

Good Advice

· I use a standard loaf pan for this dessert. The long narrow pan that I often use for desserts produces slices that are a bit too small for a satisfying serving. Standard loaf pans actually come in two sizes, $9 \times 5 \times 3$ inches with an 7-cup capacity and $8^{1}/_{2} \times 4^{1}/_{2} \times 2^{1}/_{2}$ inches with a $6^{1}/_{2}$-cup capacity. The larger is preferred here, but either will work.

· Change the ice cream flavors to suit the season; the original raspberry combination for summer; chocolate, coffee, and vanilla for cooler weather; and chocolate, peppermint, and coffee for the holiday season. Choose flavors with an eye to contrasting colors.

· Spread the ice cream carefully to the edges of the loaf pan to produce evenly colored layers when unmolding the loaf.

· To ensure crisp praline, I freeze this dessert for 1 week only and add the praline topping at serving time.

Doubling the Recipe

Double all ingredients. Use two loaf pans.

To Freeze

Wrap the loaf tightly with plastic wrap, then heavy aluminum foil. Label with date and contents. Freeze overnight or up to 1 week.

To Serve

Remove the loaf from the freezer and unwrap. Place a serving plate on top of the loaf and invert it. Dip a dish towel in hot water and wring out the water. Hold the hot towel around the sides of the pan for 15 seconds. Release the ice cream from the pan by pulling on the ends of the parchment paper and removing the pan. Sprinkle 1 cup crushed macadamia praline over the top of the loaf. Cut the loaf into slices with a large sharp knife. Pass the chocolate sauce.

1. Cut a long piece of parchment paper to fit the bottom and overlap the ends of a loaf pan with a 7-cup capacity. Use a pan that measures about $9 \times 5 \times 3$ inches. Butter the bottom of the pan and press the parchment paper strip onto the bottom and over the ends of the pan.

2. Spread the raspberry ice cream in an even layer in the bottom of the pan. Spread the ice cream to the edges of the pan. Sprinkle $1/2$ cup crushed macadamia praline over the ice cream. Drizzle about $1/4$ cup of the chocolate sauce over the praline. Spread the vanilla ice cream evenly in the pan. Sprinkle with another $1/2$ cup praline and $1/4$ cup chocolate sauce. Spread the chocolate ice cream evenly in the pan. Freeze the loaf overnight or up to 1 week.

Mail-Order Sources

American Spoon Foods
1668 Clarion Avenue
P.O. Box 566
Petoskey, MI 49770
(800) 222-5886
Fax: (800) 647-2512
Dried fruits including sweetened
Montmorency cherries and
strawberries.

B and L Specialty Foods
P.O. Box 80068
Seattle, WA 98108-0068
(800) 328-7278
Fax: (800) 366-3746
Callebaut chocolate and Guittard
chocolate chips.

Bridge Kitchenware
214 East 52nd Street
New York, NY 10022
(800) 274-3435
Fax: (212) 758-5387
Large selection of kitchen equipment
and many imported kitchen utensils.

Buchanan Hollow Nut Company
6510 Minturn Road
Le Grand, CA 95333
(800) 532-1500
Fax: (209) 389-4321
Shelled pistachio nuts, walnuts, and
pecans.

Chef's Catalog
3215 Commercial Avenue
Northbrook, IL 60062-1900
(800) 338-3232
Fax: (800) 967-3291
Baking equipment and Kaiser La
Forme bundt pans.

Hadley Fruit Orchards
P.O. Box 495
Cabazon, CA 92230
(800) 854-5655
Fax: (909) 849-8580
Dried fruits and nuts, including dried
pears, unsweetened Bing cherries, and
strawberries.

King Arthur Flour Baker's Catalogue
P.O. Box 876
Norwich, VT 05055-0876
(800) 827-6836
Fax: (800) 343-3002
Equipment and baking ingredients,
including unbleached all-purpose
flour and peeled hazelnuts.

La Cuisine
323 Cameron Street
Alexandria, VA 22314-3219
(800) 521-1176
Fax: (703) 836-8925
Quality baking equipment and
ingredients, including imported
chocolate.

Penzey's Spice House Ltd.
P.O. Box 1440
Waukesha, WI 53187
(414) 574-0277
Fax: (414) 574-0278
Excellent fresh spices and dried herbs.
Source for two high-quality
cinnamons, ground extra fancy China
Tunghing cassia cinnamon and extra
fancy Vietnamese cassia cinnamon.

Previn
2044 Rittenhouse Square
Philadelphia, PA 19103

(215) 985-1996
Fax: (215) 985-0323
Quality baking equipment, including
small tartlet tins.

Sunnyland Farms
P.O. Box 8200
Albany, GA 31706-8200
(800) 999-2488
Fax: (912) 432-1358
Nuts, including unsalted macadamia
nuts, and some dried fruit.

Sweet Celebrations division of Maid of
Scandinavia
P.O. Box 39426
Edina, MN 55439-0426
(800) 328-6722
Fax: (612) 943-1688
Baking equipment, including
cardboard cake circles, pastry bags,
and pastry tips, and Callebaut
chocolate.

Williams-Sonoma
P.O. Box 7456
San Francisco, CA 94120-7456
(800) 541-2233
Fax: (415) 421-5153
Baking equipment and ingredients.

Zingerman's
422 Detroit Street
Ann Arbor, MI 48106-1868
(313) 663-3400
Fax: (313) 769-1235
Callebaut chocolate; ships for 2-day
delivery.

Bibliography

Books

Walter Baker & Co. *Cocoa and Chocolate: a Short History of Their Production and Use.* Dorchester, Massachusetts: Walter Baker & Co., 1899.

Bridge, Fred, and Jean F. Tibbetts. *The Well-Tooled Kitchen.* New York: William Morrow and Company, Inc., 1991.

Gates, June. *Basic Foods.* New York: Holt, Rinehart, and Winston, 1976.

Erdman, Gortner, Frederick Erdman, and Nancy Masterman. *Principles of Food Freezing.* New York: John Wiley and Sons Inc., 1948.

Herbst, Sharon Tyler. *The New Food Lover's Companion.* New York: Barron's, revised 1995.

Hirsch, Sylvia Balser, and Morton Gill Clark. *A Salute to Chocolate.* New York: Gramercy Publishing Company, 1968.

Hoffman, Mable. *Mable Hoffman's Chocolate Cookery.* New York: Dell Publishing Company Inc., 1981.

Kirk, Raymond E., and Donald Othmer. *Encyclopedia of Chemical Technology.* 4th ed., vols. 6 and 3. New York: John Wiley and Sons Inc., 1992.

McGee, Harold. *The Curious Cook.* San Francisco: North Point Press, 1990.

————. *On Food and Cooking.* New York: Macmillan Publishing Company, 1984.

Minifie, Bernard W. *Chocolate, Cocoa and Confectionery: Science and Technology*, 3d ed. New York: Chapman and Hall, 1989.

Morton, Marcia, and Frederic Morton. *Chocolate, An Illustrated History.* New York: Crown Publishers, Inc., 1986.

Rinzler, Carol Ann. *The Book of Chocolate.* New York: St. Martin's Press, 1977.

Sultan, William. *Practical Baking.* 3d ed. Westport, Connecticut: AVI Publishing Company, Inc., 1983.

Wright, Liz. *Chocolate: Food of the Gods.* San Francisco: Chronicle Books, 1993.

Handbooks

The Story of Chocolate, The Chocolate Manufacturers Association of the U.S.A., McLean, Virginia

Sugar's Functional Roles in Cooking and Food Preparation, The Sugar Association, Inc., Washington, D.C.

Index

C

Cadbury (chocolate) Company, 1
Cake, 174–259. *See also* Bundt
    Cakes; Cheesecakes; Coffee
    Cakes; Layer Cakes; Loafs;
    Springform Cakes; Tortes;
    Tube Cakes; Yeast Cakes
  Almond-Chocolate Butterfly, 257
  Babka, Chocolate, 251
  Chiffon, Mocha Confetti, 227
  Chocolate Chestnut Satin Torte,
    196
  Chocolate Chip, All-Chocolate
    Extraordinary, Uncle Howie's,
    236
  Chocolate Chip Birthday, Lisa's,
    184
  Chocolate Chip Black Russian,
    Lisa Ward's, 210
  Chocolate Chip Graham Cracker,
    240
  Chocolate-Covered Caramel, 222
  Chocolate Ganache, 180
  Chocolate-Glazed Raspberry
    Jam, 220
  Chocolate-Glazed Rum
    Chocolate Chip, 212
  Chocolate Pudding-Mousse,
    Gillian's, 135
  Chocolate Soufflé, 46
  Chocolate, with White Chocolate
    and Raspberry Mousse, 176
  Cinnamon Chocolate Marble, 218
  Cinnamon Chocolate Twists, 259
  circles, cardboard, 19
  Dark Chocolate with Fudge
    Frosting, 178
  Devilish Chocolate, 42
  freezing frostings and fillings for,
    28
  freezing meringues for, 28
  Ginger, Triple, and Dark
    Chocolate, 224
  If You Only Live Once
    Chocolate, 174
  Kugelhopf, Chocolate, 248
  Lemon and White Chocolate
    Almond Crunch, 244
  The Magnificent Five-Layer
    Chocolate Buttercream, 202
  Milk Chocolate and Hazelnut
    Praline Truffle, 200
  Mocha Crumb, 242
  pans (Bundt pans, springform
    pans, tube pans), 15. *See also*
    baking pans
  Peach and White Chocolate
    Buttercream, Summertime,
    186
  Pear and Chocolate Tea Loaf, 231
  Rainbow Ribbon Honeymoon,
    198
  Ribbon of Fudge Chocolate, 214
  Spiced Apple Chocolate Crumb,
    238
  Sponge, Hot Milk, 44
  Strawberry and White
    Chocolate, 80th Birthday, 192
  Strawberry and White Chocolate
    Loaf, 229
  Triple Truffle Celebration, 182
  Walnut and Chocolate Chip
    Butter, Harriet's, 216
  Walnut Meringue, Helen's
    Chocolate and Caramel, 278
  Yule Log, Winter White, 205
Candy. *See* Truffles
candy thermometers, 18–19
Cannoli Torte, 72
Caramel
  Chocolate-Covered Cake, 222
  and Chocolate Terrine, Sweet
    Mystery, 282
  and Chocolate Walnut Meringue
    Cake, Helen's, 278
  Filling and Caramel Sauce, 52
  Pecan and Milk Chocolate Tart,
    111
caramelized sugar, 10
cardboard cake circles, 19
Carletti, Antonio, 1
Charlotte, Orange and White
    Chocolate, 130
Cheesecake(s), 150–62
  about, 148–49
  Choco-Colada, 158
  Chocolate-Cherry, 154
  freezing, 28
  Milk Chocolate and Hazelnut
    Praline, Layered, 152
  Mochaccino, 160
  Peanut Butter Cup, 156
  Vanilla and Chocolate Truffle, 150
  White Chocolate and Raspberry
    Ripple, 162
Cherry-Chocolate Cheesecake, 154
Chestnut Chocolate Satin Torte,
    196
Chiffon Cake, Mocha Confetti, 227
Chiffon, Chocolate Pie, My
    Birthday, 104
Choco-Colada Cheesecake, 158
chocolate, 1–7. *See also* Chocolate
    Chip; cocoa; Fudge; Milk
    Chocolate; Mocha; Name of
    Dessert (Cake, Cookies;
    Terrine, Torte, etc.); White
    Chocolate
  Aztecs and, 1
  baking with, 4–5
  bars from cocoa beans,
    processing, 2–3
  as a beverage (early), 1
  blends for unique flavor, 2; nib
    blends, 3
  bloom (fat and sugar), 7
  conching (kneading), 2, 3
  dutching process, 1
  early history of, 1–2